Shakespeare's Dilemmas

American University Studies

Series IV
English Language and Literature

Vol. 61

PETER LANG
New York · Bern · Frankfurt am Main · Paris

Richard Horwich

Shakespeare's Dilemmas

PETER LANG
New York · Bern · Frankfurt am Main · Paris

Library of Congress Cataloging-in-Publication Data

Horwich, Richard.
Shakespeare's dilemmas / Richard Horwich.
p.   cm. — (American university studies. Series IV, English
language and literature ; vol. 61)
Bibliography: p.
1. Shakespeare, William, 1564–1616—Criticism and interpretation.
2. Dilemma in literature. 3. Logic in literature. 4. Psychology in
literature. I. Title. II. Series.
PR3069.D55H67   1988
822.3'3—dc19   87-24216
ISBN 0-8204-0541-8   CIP
ISSN 0741-0700

CIP-Titelaufnahme der Deutschen Bibliothek

Horwich, Richard:
Shakespeare's dilemmas / Richard Horwich. –
New York; Bern; Frankfurt am Main; Paris:
Lang, 1988.
(American University Studies: Ser. 4, English
Language and Literature; Vol. 61)
ISBN 0-8204-0541-8

NE: American University Studies / 04

© Peter Lang Publishing, Inc., New York 1988

Printed by Weihert-Druck GmbH, Darmstadt, West Germany

To my mother and father

Contents

Acknowledgments

Every book is a collaborative endeavor, and this one perhaps more than most; to the many people who gave of their time, their insight, their expertise and their love, I owe much. My colleagues Lawrence Hyman, Robert Viscusi, Ellen Belton, and Julia Hirsch read the manuscript in various stages and made valuable suggestions, and Edward Tayler of Columbia University, in particular, provided a subtle and detailed critique whose perceptions the final version of this work incorporates. Tom Jackson and Wendy Jaffe contributed both the technical advice and the hardware that enabled me to process and revise these many words. And I feel particularly fortunate to have enjoyed the understanding, patience and encouragement of my friends and family, among whom I must mention David Gordon, Harry Wise, Paul Van Hook, Mark Taylor, Rita Wallsh, my daughter Danielle and—more than anyone else— my wife Nancy.

Some previously published materials appear here in revised form, and I am grateful to the editors of *Shakespeare Quarterly* and *Studies in English Literature* for their permission to incorporate them. The research that went into this project was supported (in part) by a grant from The City University of New York PSC-CUNY Research Award Program.

1

Introduction

When John Donne complained in 1611 that "new philosophy calls all in doubt," he provided modern literary scholars and historians with a great convenience: the intellectual posture, the emotional predicament, the world-view of an age encapsulated in a single line of poetry. What we often overlook is the fact that "doubt" is not the invention of that most inventive of poets. It was a recognized literary motif in the ages preceding that of Donne and Shakespeare, and had long since acquired a set of conventions. By the middle of the sixteenth century, sources of instruction in the techniques for representing skepticism, disbelief or uncertainty were available to writers in the form of handbooks such as Thomas Wilson's *The Art of Rhetoric*, which provides, among a list of traditional figures or tropes, Doubt itself: "Dubitatio," or "Doubtfulness," Wilson asserts, is employed "when we make our hearers believe that the weight of the matter causeth us to doubt what we were best to speak . . . [e.g] whether shall I speak or hold my peace? If I speak, you will not hear; if I hold my peace, my conscience condemns my silence" (185).[1]

Wilson's contemporary and colleague George Puttenham employed the more traditional term *dialysis*, but it is clear from his illustration that he had the same figure in mind:

> Were it for grace, or else in hope of gain,
> To say of my deserts, it is but vain:
> For well in mind, in case ye do them bear,
> To tell them oft, it should but irk your ear.
> Be they forgot, as likely should I fail,
> To win with words, where deeds cannot prevail.[2] (232)

1

These definitions and illustrations, like much else contained in the exhaustive and methodical treatises produced by Renaissance rhetoricians, may strike the modern reader as more than a little remote, not only from himself or herself but from Donne and Shakespeare. But there is about *dialysis* a quality, an emanation, that sets it off from the hundreds of tropes that surround it, for the "doubtfulness" at its core is at once rhetorical and psychological. It alone exudes a whiff of human experience—an experience, moreover, in which Donne and Shakespeare exhibited a keen interest. *Dialysis* is a vehicle by which they and other poets and playwrights of the late sixteenth and early seventeenth centuries expressed the sense of helplessness and futility engendered by a certain kind of predicament, whose nature Puttenham clarifies for us when he offers us a more familiar cognate: "Dialysis," he tells us, "is a manner of speech, not so figurative as fit for argument, and worketh not unlike the *dilemma* of the logicians" (230).[3]

For those of us who are not logicians, dilemmas are more than rhetorical strategies or logical curiosities. They are questions that must be asked but that cannot be answered, insoluble problems that nonetheless urgently require solution. The contradiction at their root is both their *sine qua non* and their charm. The donkey who starved to death because he could find no means of deciding which of two identical bales of hay to eat first was done in by a dilemma; less grave but fundamentally similar is the quandary of the freshman philosophy student struggling to work out whether an omnipotent God is capable of creating a rock so heavy that He cannot lift it. Neither are more experienced philosophers immune. A modern logician, Gilbert Ryle, tells us that Immanuel Kant

wholeheartedly believed in Newtonian physics; he also wholeheartedly believed in the autonomy of morals. Yet the Laws of Motion seemed to leave no room for the Moral Law, and the absolute obligation of men to act in certain ways, and therewith the possibility of their doing so seemed to leave no room for the physical necessity of the motions of all, including human, bodies. Neither the truths of science nor the truths of morals could be abandoned, yet each seemed to disqualify the other. (125)

When Ryle and other logicians speak of a dilemma, they employ the term in its (forbiddingly) technical sense: a dilemma is, properly speaking, a syllogism which consists of "a compound hypothetical proposition as the minor, and a simple or disjunctive proposition as the conclusion" (Joseph 363).[4] The result, in layman's language, is that two alternatives simultaneously entail and exclude each other. Perhaps the classic modern example is the dilemma from which Joseph Heller's novel *Catch-22* takes its title. If Yossarian, the pacifist bombardier, wishes not to fly combat missions, he must prove that he is crazy, but anyone who tries to prove that he is crazy in order to be grounded is, by definition, sane. By the same token, anyone who wishes to fly is crazy, and should be grounded—but as soon as he makes this request, he implicitly certifies himself as sane, and must fly. "That's some catch, that Catch-22," remarks Yossarian with admiration (46).

Rigorously defined, dilemmas present not practical but logical difficulties. In popular or non-technical usage, however, the word has come to denote any choice that is difficult to make because the alternatives are of such equal promise or equal disadvantage that one can find no reason for preferring one over the other. Such a predicament is often accompanied by a sense of removal from the rough-and-ready material world in which we normally operate to a plane of abstract calculation, where choices attain a degree of symmetry not often found in nature. A dilemma of this type may consist not of a problem that arises through circumstance but of one created by a mind that tends to impose neat patterns upon the flux of experience, a tendency illustrated by Jake Horner, the protagonist of John Barth's novel *End of the Road*, when he calls our attention to

the fact that when one is faced with . . . a multitude of desirable choices, no one choice seems satisfactory for very long by comparison with the aggregate desirability of the rest, though, compared to any one of the others, it would not be found inferior. (6)

This mode of thought—this tendency to impose upon the flux of experience a sterile and unnatural symmetry, to substitute quantitative values for qualitative ones, to align and balance alternatives so that they bring identical pressures to bear—is vividly described by Barth's Jake Horner when he is asked a question during a personnel interview:

> Instantly a host of arguments against applying for a job at the Wicomico State Teachers College presented themselves for my use, and as instantly a corresponding number of refutations lined up opposite them, one for one, so that the question of my application was held static like the rope marker in a tug-o'-war where the opposing teams are perfectly matched. (8)

Barth's interest in dilemmas, unlike Ryle's, centers on their psychological effects. Because of his predisposition to dilemmas, Jake is in constant danger of paralysis—of will, of thought, even of body. Caught in an eternal oscillation between polar choices, unable to decide which of any pair of alternatives to embrace, he moves only in the direction of psychic entropy. And lest it be supposed that Jake's is an essentially "modern" predicament, explored only be contemporary novelists, consider the dilemma of Achilles in *The Iliad*:

> . . . my mother Thetis the goddess of the silver feet tells me
> I carry two sorts of destiny toward the day of my death. Either,
> if I stay here and fight beside the city of the Trojans,
> my return home is gone, but my glory shall be everlasting;
> but if I return home to the beloved land of my fathers,
> the excellence of my glory is gone, but there will be a long life
> left for me, and my end in death will not come quickly. (9.410–16)

The result of his inability to make this choice is a military career that consists for several years of passive watchfulness. And it is worth noting that when he makes his "decision" at last, it is not a considered one but an impulse upon which he acts when he watches the death and dishonoring of his friend Patroklos.

Achilles's dilemma, though it goes far toward explaining the causes of his behavior, is not a problem peculiar to him in *The*

Iliad; the static balance associated with dilemma-states is a feature of virtually all human affairs in the poem. That is because all human affairs are under the control of the gods, who are themselves locked in a continual state of internecine conflict. It is due to this divine factionalism that the Trojan War has continued for ten years by the time Achilles enters it; mortals are time and again prevented from settling military encounters decisively by the intervention of their immortal seconds. Athena, in particular, takes upon herself the responsibility of maintaining the *status quo*. In one instance, she persuades Lykaon to shoot an arrow at Menelaos,

> But when he had pulled the great weapon till it made a
> circle,
> the bow groaned, and the string sang high, and the arrow,
> sharp-pointed,
> leapt away, furious, to fly through the throng before it.
> Still the blessed gods immortal did not forget you,
> Menelaos, and first among them Zeus' daughter, the spoiler,
> Who standing in front of you fended aside the tearing
> arrow. (4.124–29)

"The spoiler," Zeus's daughter, is of course the same Athena, who embodies in the poem the tendency of equal and opposite forces to neutralize whatever energies are expended—to produce, one might say, dilemmas in physical form.

It is not, of course, the case that all action in the poem is inconclusive; the tendency toward stasis can be and is overcome. But that tendency is always present, and never more so than in the climactic encounter between Achilles and Hector. Achilles slays Hector not because his skill or courage is greater, though this may have been the case. The real cause of his victory is more remote, more abstract than these familiar human virtues:

> But when for the fourth time they had come around to the
> well spring
> then the father balanced his golden scales, and in them

he set two fateful portions of death, which lays men
  prostrate,
one for Achilleus, and one for Hektor, breaker of horses,
and balanced it by the middle; and Hektor's death day was
  heavier
and dragged downward toward death, and Phoibos Apollo
  forsook him. (22.208–13)

We are not meant to understand by all this that the lives of Homeric heroes are fundamentally dissimilar to those of ordinary mortals like ourselves—that Hector and Achilles are in the hands of a mechanistic destiny while the rest of us enjoy freedom of will. On the contrary, what Jean Cocteau called "the infernal machine"—that implacable, irresistible and inexorable fate that patiently overtakes even the greatest of men, and is, in the cases of Hector (as we have seen) and Oedipus (of whom Cocteau was writing) unwilled either by man or god—reveals an important feature of Hellenistic cosmology, making Greek literature extremely receptive to dilemmas, which are, in their balance and symmetry, emblems of that cosmology.

This study is grounded upon the assumption that what was true of the Homeric epic and the age that produced it is equally true of Shakespearean drama and the High Renaissance in England—that the psychology of dilemma figures prominently in several of Shakespeare's works, and that the dilemmas of his characters are often a reflection not only of the worlds in which those characters reside, but beyond them, of the world inhabited by the playwright and his audiences. Before we examine those characters or those various worlds, however, it is necessary to sharpen our conception of what a dilemma is by limiting it, for the temptation to use the term loosely, or as a synonym for other terms that merely resemble or overlap it, is strong. Dilemmas are often confused with riddles, for example, though in most respects riddles and dilemmas are not only different from but opposite to each other. It is worth getting the distinction straight, for in several of Shakespeare's works—notably the so-called "problem comedies"—we encounter both. It is true that riddles and dilemmas alike may function as no more than intellectual entertainments, mere brain-teasers, and it is further true, as Huizinga has pointed out, that some of the "enigmatic questions" associated with primitive religious ritual may be both riddles and dilemmas (110). But riddles are, properly, members of that class of questions which, according to Ryle, "can be solved by calculation," while dilemmas are "problems that perplex" (114), questions that yield to no amount of calculation because the very terms in which they are formulated preclude their being solved. Bernard Knox quite rightly calls the questions that confront the protagonist of Sophocles's *Oedipus the King* "riddles," because they are problems of mathematical calculation (18): What walks on four legs in the morning, two legs in the afternoon, and three legs in the evening? How can one man be the same as many men? There is a single, wholly correct answer to the riddle of the Sphinx, and Oedipus is able to divine, guess, or reason it out: "Man." There is, similarly, a single and wholly correct answer to the other, larger riddle: one man may be the same as many when the many are one who is being described in many ways: the unfortunate destined to kill his father and marry his mother is the same man who rules Thebes, having taken Laius's widow as his wife after an unfortunate encounter with a nameless old man at a place where three roads meet. Nevertheless, Knox is also right to speak of Oedipus as a man caught in a tragic dilemma (32). All the play's riddles are subsumed into a larger question, to which no single or "correct" answer exists. If Oedipus outwits the prophesy and is saved from destruction, the gods are proven fallible and therefore false; if the oracles are true, Oedipus is doomed. The Chorus, asked to ponder these alternatives, refuses to weigh them against each other. Oedipus himself is a man composed of antitheses—first among men and most accursed of men, hunter and prey, prosecutor and criminal—and the very mathematical formulas that are the source of his pride and skill themselves take on the shape of a dilemma in the balance and symmetry of their equations.

Though riddles characteristically assume the form of questions, it is unusual, as Ian Hamnett points out, for their answers to be guessed or reasoned:

> The clues provided in the descriptive element(s) seldom furnish enough evidence for the answer to be definitely gathered from them. . . . Riddles are often 'objectively' susceptible of more than one reasonable and appropriate solution, but in fact only one solution 'counts' as correct. This is no doubt because the author of the riddle perceives the referent first and composes the riddle afterward. (384)

In other words, a riddle is typically a display of wit or ingenuity that happens to take an interrogative form. The answers to riddles fit the questions so perfectly that our pleasure derives largely from the perfection of the fit, and we hardly notice or care that the answer fails to provide us with any useful information. "What is black and white and red (read) all over?" is not a question likely to arise during the course of one's daily routine, and the answer—"A newspaper"—contains no useful fact or worthwhile insight, but merely the explication of a trivial pun.[5] A riddle, in a sense, is thus precisely what a dilemma is not: one is a trivial question to which is fitted a single correct answer, the other a serious question to which there is no answer at all.

Similarly, dilemmas are sometimes viewed as interchangeable with paradoxes, and here we must exercise care in gently separating the two, for there are many points of contact between them. Fortunately for our purposes, Rosalie Colie's *Paradoxia Epidemica* not only defines and illustrates paradox conclusively, but does so in the context of Renaissance literature. Like dilemmas, paradoxes were partly the provenance of logicians and rhetoricians during the sixteenth and seventeenth centuries; the most general meaning of the term, Colie tells us, was "an argument contrary to common opinion or expectation, often contrary to truth," whose function was to display the originality, ingenuity, and brilliance of the arguer—an argument that favored poverty over riches or imprisonment over freedom, for example, or maintained any such unpraiseworthy or indefensible proposition (398).

But the modern conception of paradox as self-contradiction existed during the Renaissance as a sub-category of paradox in general (Colie calls it the "logical" paradox), and it is this quality that links it to dilemma. Her favorite example is the famous paradox known as the "Liar": "Epimenides the Cretan said, 'All Cretans are liars.' If he told the truth, then his statement is a lie, and so he didn't tell the truth; if he lied, then his statement is true, but he did not lie" (6). Her following commentary on this paradox makes it sound much like a dilemma: she calls it "a perfect example of equivocation . . . since its negative and positive meanings are so balanced that one meaning can never outweigh the other" (6). Later, when she amplifies this description, she further emphasizes the dilemmatic aspect of paradox, insisting that its primary function is to be found in its ability to "conjoin disjunctive elements and states of being" (141). How shall we distinguish between paradox and dilemma, then? It is the essence of dilemma, as the term applies to drama and literature, that it should be seen as a plight, a predicament imposed by external circumstance or internal predisposition upon its subject, whom it overwhelms. But the typical paradox, as Colie views it, does not control, is not imposed; rather, its inventor is its master: "Castiglione's *sprezzatura* . . . is the very quality essential to a paradox's life. For a paradox demands of its framers both total control over expression and thought, and the appearance of completely effortless manipulation of expression and thought" (34). Unlike dilemmas, she tells us, "paradoxes do not require—indeed, normally they repel—identification on the part of their audience" (480). It is true that some paradoxes induce a state of psychological ambivalence, such as the internal conflict in Rabelais's Gargantua occasioned by the simultaneous death of his wife and birth of his son, but a dilemma is more than a psychological state; it is a self-thwarting call to action.

If we examine a typical and instructive example of the literary use to which dilemmas were put in the age immediately before Shakespeare's, their relationship to paradox may become clearer. In the first of thirteen "Most Pleasant and Delectable

Questions of Love" found in Boccaccio's *Il Filocolo*, the following problem is posed by a young man named Philocopo: in
order to signify her preference between two suitors, a girl
removes from her head a garland of flowers and places it upon
the head of one of the candidates, simultaneously removing
from the head of the other a garland which she places upon her
own head. Her action is presumed to signify a choice, but
which man has she chosen? Philocopo proclaims at length his
opinion that acceptance is the key to love, and that she has
therefore favored the admirer whose garland she receives.
Fiametta, who moderates the debate, takes the opposite view:
that love is signified by a willingness to give, and that the first
suitor is accordingly the chosen one. What is most significant
here is that the debate is left unresolved. Each argument has its
own merits, and it is presumed sufficient for the underlying
issues—the contraries of giving and receiving, and their importance in love—to have received a hearing. Fiametta at the end
remains unconvinced by Philocopo's argument, but time is
growing short, she says, and besides, "We know very well that
in these our reasonings much might be objected against this
our definition" (32). Such a question as this spans the boundary
between paradox and dilemma; Colie would probably apply to
it the former term, and, though the fact that it is left unresolved
formally inclines it toward the category of dilemma, it never
achieves (or tries to achieve) the affective intensity of which
literary dilemmas are often capable. The "problem" itself does
not compel and absorb our attention like the narratives in *The
Decameron*; it is less a fictive *donné* than a mere hypothesis
introduced, like the perfunctorily-drawn characters themselves, for the sole purpose of raising the question.

   In the second chapter, though, a "question" of a slightly
different sort is raised. A would-be lover is apprehended by his
mistress's brothers and presented with the following ultimatum: he may live with and enjoy the favors of his young and
beautiful mistress for a year, but he must agree to spend
another year with an old and ugly crone. He may determine the
order of these cohabitations, but if he chooses to live with his

lady first, he must promise to bestow upon the old woman the same sexual attentions as he offered his beloved; if he chooses to spend the first year with the hag, he may make love to the girl during the second year only as often as he did to the old woman. With whom should he dwell first?

Here the debate centers upon emotional issues, presented more concretely than the problems of semantic definition encountered in Philocopo's argument, and no more easily resolved. Might the expectation of unpleasantness to come compromise the pleasures of the moment? Might not a distasteful experience in the present taint, or even negate, the possibility of satisfaction in the future? The decision cannot reasonably be made without the results of trial, but trial, according to the brothers' stipulation, is permissible only after the decision has been made. Fiametta suggests choosing to spend the first year with the girl and the second with the hag, on the premise that not to do so would try the patience of Fortune: "Who is certain that after the evil may not follow the worst, as well as the better that is tarried for?" (39) she asks. But it is clear that this principle is brought into play only because no other, more satisfactory basis for choice exists.

Certainly this second "question"—Boccaccio's term is *dubbio*, etymologically related to Wilson's *dubitatio*—shares with paradox its argumentative context and its quality of disjunctiveness. But because the argument is embedded in narrative, however slight and unresolved, it acquires a feature not typical of paradox: it invites the commitment of the reader, shifting the focus of our attention from the skill and ingenuity of the narrator to the helpless suitor's predicament. Thus dilemma may be seen as an offshoot of paradox, as paradox rendered adaptable to the requirements of a narrative or dramatic action. The distinction, admittedly, is not a large or an obvious one, but it is sufficient to account for the fact that, though Colie does treat in some detail the paradoxes found in Shakespeare, her objects of inquiry and her conclusions are different from my own.

Another fairly recent study that shares with this work and

with Colie's an interest in logical self-contradiction is Norman Rabkin's *Shakespeare and the Common Understanding*, in which its author borrows from modern physics the concept of "complementarity" as a means of delineating the "crucially problematic" vision that lies at the center of Shakespeare's art" (2). His description of this vision as it appears in *Hamlet* appears to recapitulate Colie's conception of paradox, and threatens to make my study redundant:

> . . . the play presents an ideal, that of reason, in such a way that we must recognize its absolute claim on our moral allegiance, and then entirely subverts that ideal by demonstrating that its polar opposite is the only possible basis for the action its protagonist is morally committed to perform. . . . The play says to us: choose one or the other, and in doing so you will see how it rules out the other. And yet each makes equally compelling claims on us; at any given moment we feel ourselves drawn irresistibly to one or the other total view of things. (6–7)

Note, however, that Rabkin's concern is with vision, not with action; that he is exploring not Hamlet's choices but those of the audience. In this regard, it might be pointed out that to speak of a dramatic work forcing its audience to "choose" one mode of action or ethical system over another is to use the word in a very flexible sense indeed.[6] To focus on the audience and not on the character is to move away from dilemma and toward paradox; instead of being compelled to choose, a spectator may, after all, simply contemplate the impossibility of choice until he tires of doing so. In a later chapter, I will argue that in the case of Shakespeare's "problem comedies," the response of the spectators is sufficiently empathic with that of the characters as to constitute a dilemma for the audience, but I do not think of *Hamlet* as a play that leaves its audience at a psychic impasse. Nor, perhaps, does Rabkin, for he tells us elsewhere that "we learn to entertain . . . contradictory readings of life" (14); in fact, in his paraphrase of Bohr and Oppenheimer, who coined the term *complementarity*, he admits, "We live easily with complementary answers" (25).[7]

What unites Colie's "epidemic of paradox," Rabkin's "vision of complementarity" and my own interest in dilemmas is our shared conception of Shakespeare's age as preoccupied with "doubleness" of all kinds (or, if one prefers the more narrowly philosophic term, with duality). No one suggests that the Renaissance had a patent on dualism; Wylie Sypher notes that as early as the thirteenth century, Roger Bacon "used the term 'double experience' as if he were already writing about a modern 'dissociation of sensibility'" (*Four Stages* 39), and of course, Platonic "otherworldliness"[8] is nothing if not dualistic in its conception of reality. But it is the age of Shakespeare, Robert Grudin reminds us, for which "the interaction of contrarieties is one of the primary forces of experience" (3).

It is Grudin's thesis that contrariety—the clash of "mighty opposites" from which he takes his title—"can be a positive and regenerative principle" (3). But the divorce of body from mind, of subject from object, of thought from feeling is not usually regarded as an occasion for optimism; Sypher describes the "Mannerist" style of Donne, Milton and Marvell as one of "disproportion, disturbed balance, ambiguity, and clashing impulses" (*Four Stages* 33). The symmetries of medieval rationalism may have pointed toward the haven of religious faith, but the symmetries of the Renaissance pointed instead to the mazes of philosophic Skepticism and the doubt-provoking "new philosophy" of Kepler and Galileo. Dualism expressed itself most naturally in emotional ambivalence, logical disjunction and rhetorical ambiguity; it promoted a mode of thought that was not linear but oscillatory—the mode of thought associated with dilemmas, which were thereby transformed into an important vehicle for the expression of Europe's intellectual predicament from the time of Montaigne until well after the time of Descartes.

The inclination toward dilemmas pervades—indeed, in my view, partially defines—the later Renaissance. One of its interesting features is that it cuts across the conflicts of science, art, religion and philosophy that marked the period; it is not a function of the content of any system of thought, but of the shape, the cast, the style of thinking dictated by the Renaissance *ethos*. Each new intellectual contribution reinforced it; the

Skepticism of Montaigne, the scientific materialism of the astronomers, Bacon's attacks on Scholastic rationalism, the theology of the Reformation and the advent of capitalism all posed new and more excruciating dilemmas, both for their proponents and for the writers who attempted to chronicle their effects. Thus, Richard Popkin's history of Skepticism shows us how the conclusions of Montaigne, which functioned equally well as a defense of Christian doctrine and as a means of undermining it, laid the foundations for Descartes, whose refutation of Skepticism made him, in the view of Gassendi and others, its most effective proponent (55). Thus Hiram Haydn speaks of the "schizophrenic tendency" that marked both the work and the lives of the major English writers at the turn of the seventeenth century, the "extraordinary and epic dichotomy" that "infected" Ralegh, Sidney, Nashe, Bacon and Shakespeare himself (14).

Let us examine a number of threads in that motley fabric, the Renaissance world-view. Perhaps the single most significant contribution of Montaignesque Skepticism is its tendency to shift the focus of attention away from the world of external nature, of "objective reality," and toward the inner world of perception and thought. The "Apology for Raymond Sebond," in which Montaigne's Skeptical doctrine is crystallized, is more than an attack on the rationalism of the Scholastics; it is an indictment of man's pride in his intellect, his knowledge, and his conviction of his superiority to the world of beasts. At the center of Montaigne's thought are two mutually-supportive convictions: first, that reason itself is no more than "the clatter of so many philosophical brains" engaged upon the fool's errand of arranging unverifiable beliefs into arbitrary systems (3: 203), and second, that our knowledge of the world, since it is derived primarily from sense perceptions, is thereby demonstrably unreliable. What reality is, we cannot know, for every person's perception of reality is different:

> That things do not lodge in us in their own form and essence or make
> their entry into us by their own power and authority, we see clearly

enough. Because if that were so, we should receive them in the same way: wine would be the same in the mouth of a sick man as in the mouth of a healthy man; he who has chapped or numb fingers would find the same hardness in the wood or iron handled as another. Thus external objects surrender to our mercy; they dwell in us as we please. (3: 258)

The passage above is prophetic of the self-conscious relativism that marked the age to come. The focus of Montaigne's attention is not on truth or nature but on our understanding of truth and nature—not on the objects of thought but on the subject, the thinker, the thought itself. His concern is essentially epistemological: he is more interested in how we know things and in whether we can know them than he is interested in what we know. The subjectivism implicit in arguments like his is clear enough; in Montaigne's view, the question of what objectively "is," or obtains, is a moot one, pointlessly entertained only by those who live in the hermetically-sealed chamber of deductive rationalism. "Philosophy," he writes, "offers us not what is, or what it believes, but the most plausible and pleasant thing it forges" (3: 228). In Descartes's later reformulation, all one's impressions of external reality are forgeries. For Montaigne's credo (derived from Socrates) 'All I know is that I know nothing,'[9] Descartes substituted a more personal and in some ways a more radical one: 'All I know is that I exist.' Though it was Descartes's intention to discover, in Popkin's words, "fundamental and indubitable truths, the foundations of human knowledge . . . by the very process of doubting" (182–83), the failure of this aim left Descartes mired at the center of a universe that consisted of nothing but mind, unable to bridge the gulf between mind and body, between subject and object.

All of these competing systems of thought were founded upon the premise that the world available to the senses was in some important respects illusory. Accordingly, a number of alternative sites were proposed as the location of "ultimate reality." The distinctive characteristic of the redefinitions and relocations attendant upon this process was a movement away from the apparently rough and unpredictable world of nature as most of us apprehend it, and toward the hushed and abstract realm of disembodied ratiocination. The "new philosophy" itself, for example—the Copernican hypothesis that the plan of the cosmos is heliocentric, with its attendant implications, refined by Kepler and Galileo—entailed a conception of reality that greatly resembled that of Descartes in its later stages. "Galileo," wrote E. A. Burtt, "makes the clear distinction between that in the world which is absolute, objective and immutable, and that which is relative, subjective, fluctuating, and sensible. The former is the realm of knowledge, divine and human; the latter is the realm of opinion and illusion" (84). Certainly Galileo would have rejected most vigorously the Skeptical opinion that objective reality is unknowable. In other ways, however, scientific materialism supported and corroborated the tenets of Skepticism, particularly in its distrust of the senses. For Kepler and Galileo, everything that our senses show us is *necessarily* false; nothing of ultimate reality is available to the senses because that reality consists of nothing more nor less than bodies in motion—bodies too small, and motion too subtle, for the senses to apprehend them. Only geometry could measure and reveal the laws that govern the movement of such bodies, which were given the term "Primary Qualities." What our senses show us are merely "Secondary Qualities," and of them, Galileo wrote,

> I think that these tastes, odours, etc., on the side of the object in which they seem to exist, are nothing else than mere names, but hold their residence solely in the sensitive body; so that if the animal were removed, every such quality would be abolished and annihilated.
>
> (qtd. in Burtt 85)[10]

The effect of this doctrine was to deprive the universe of spirit—to reduce nature, in the words of Alfred North Whitehead, to "a dull affair, soundless, scentless, colourless; merely the hurrying of material, endlessly, meaninglessly . . ." (80). It is upon the proponents of this theory that Shakespeare's La Few heaps contempt when he exclaims, "They say miracles are past, and we have our philosophical persons, to make modern and familiar, things supernatural and causeless" (*All's Well That Ends Well* 2.3.1–3).[11] Nevertheless, these ideas were quickly being accepted by the intellectual community of Europe. Even Sir Francis Bacon, for whom inductive science could not exist without the examination of sense-data, held that sensory experience and the constructions put upon it by the mind were notoriously prone to error: "The mind, when it receives impressions of objects through the sense, cannot be trusted to report them truly, but in forming its notions mixes up its own nature with the nature of things" (*Instauratio Magna* 317).

The scientific revolution, according to Whitehead, "was through and through an anti-intellectualist movement. It was a return to the contemplation of brute fact; and it was based on a recoil from the inflexible rationality of medieval thought" (12). But to read Bacon or Descartes or Galileo is to become aware of the tortuousness of their own mental processes. To advance from deductive to inductive logic is not to abandon logic altogether; to proceed beyond the simple contemplation of "brute fact" to the organizing of such data into a system of hypotheses about the structure of the universe is to mobilize the resources of the reason quite extensively. Norman 0. Brown calls our attention to the contradiction inherent in the fact that

> modern secular humanist intellectuals have in the main followed Plato and Descartes over the abyss into the insane delusion that the true essence of man lies in disembodied mental activity. The philosophers' efforts to overcome the mind-body dualism in theory are betrayed by the philosophers' own practical commitment to the pure life of the mind. The rationalism of the philosophers has only led them further astray. (34)

One need not share Brown's psychoanalytic assumptions to recognize the validity of his point. If "disembodied mental activity" is central to the philosophic tradition that stretches from Plato to Descartes—a tradition that includes Copernicus, Kepler, and Galileo as well[12]—it is central to the conception of man and his relation to the cosmos in the age of Shakespeare.

And one of its most visible products, or symptoms, is the dilemma, in which mental activity shapes "brute fact" into an antithetical puzzle that precludes the rational solution that it demands.

In sum, then, the dilemmas of the late sixteenth and early seventeenth centuries are the problem-children of self-conscious, calculative thought; they are the essence of Renaissance dualism made flesh by being cast in the imperative mood. This assertion, of course, requires testing and illustration, both of which it will receive as we now turn our attention to a number of dilemmas in the literature and drama of the two centuries leading up to Shakespeare. It will be instructive to begin with a writer who lived and wrote in an age when people were presumably less prone to discover or invent dilemmas, and thereafter to trace the changing uses and shapes of dilemmas in successive generations, as the distinctive consciousness of the Renaissance began to appear.

Unlike Boccaccio, for whom dilemmas were little more than quaint puzzles, largely divorced from both the exigencies of human existence and the intricacies of art, Geoffrey Chaucer employed them in *The Canterbury Tales* both as a means of organizing sustained narrative and of illuminating character in some depth. "The Knight's Tale" begins by setting up conditions ideal for the propagation of a dilemma when it introduces us to Palamon and Arcite, two young knights not merely inseparable but almost indistinguishable, "liggynge by and by, / Both in oon armes" (lines 1011–12). The balance is further struck when they both fall in love, at the same moment, with Emilye. Chaucer underlines the static symmetry of the situation by posing a Boccaccian "question" on the occasion of Arcite's being released from prison:

> Yow loveres axe I now this question,
> Who hath the worse, Arcite or Palamon?
> That oon may seen his lady day by day
> But in prison he moot dwelle alway;
> That oother wher hym list may ride or go,
> But seen his lady shal he nevermo. (1347–52)

It is an unanswerable question, a *dubbio*, and Emilye's is a correspondingly impossible choice when Arcite returns from exile, Palamon is freed, and both come a-wooing, for she has no means or grounds for preferring one suitor over the other. Their divine patrons (Diana, Mars and Venus, respectively) further stabilize the impasse by nullifying each other's efforts to decide the ensuing conflict, as does Theseus when he encumbers Palamon and Arcite, already perfectly matched as antagonists, with armies of precisely equal size and force.

The artifice that has produced such monumental symmetry is perfectly consistent with the Knight's promise of a romantic tale. What Chaucer might have supplied at such a juncture is a further piece of conventional artifice to destroy the balance and allow a satisfying solution to emerge. The dilemmas in stories like this one often prove in the end to be riddles, with ingenious, unexpected, and "correct" answers at hand. Such a device in this case would usefully destabilize the situation, providing Emilye and the reader with a set of grounds for making the seemingly impossible choice between identical suitors. But nothing of the sort occurs. The deadlock is broken, but in a manner that has more to do with *realpolitik* than romance. Saturn overrules the lesser deities and decrees for Arcite a bloody death—though it might as easily have been decreed for Palamon. This occurrence produces a resolution that utterly fails to take into account the desires or deserts of any of the characters. Emilye sensibly marries the surviving Palamon, with the implication that she would as readily have married Arcite had *he* survived. Theseus's final statement on the matter is couched in language that makes his proposal sound as statically balanced as the original problem: "I rede that we make of sorwes two / 0 [i.e., *one*] parfit joye, lastynge evermo" (3071–72). But in fact, it is happenstance that disposes of events, not Theseus, and from the characters' point of view, the dilemma must seem to have been resolved by the most fortuitous and unpredictable of means. The realities of chance and change crowd the romantic elements out of the story altogether, along with the romantic sensibilities of the surviving lovers; Chaucer tests throughout the expectations of order and symmetry implicit in the conventions of romance, and finally dispenses with them altogether. The Miller, whose tale follows, may imagine that he is foregrounding the artificiality of the Knight's chivalrous world by contrasting it with the muddy realism of medieval Oxenford, but in fact, his own tale is far more artfully ordered than "The Knight's Tale" has proven to be.

Similarly, in "The Wife of Bath's Tale," a dilemma is the means by which opposing visions of reality are distinguished—visions already implicitly in contrast with each other as the tale begins, with its suggestion of magic and folk-tale following immediately upon the up-to-date realism of the Prologue. At its inception, in keeping with the "land fulfild with fairye" (3) in which he resides, the young knight is presented not with a dilemma but with a riddle: "What thyng is it that wommen moost desiren?" (49). It is a question perplexing to a man accustomed to thinking of women as mere adjuncts to his own desires. A correct answer does exist, one that has the clarity, if not the ingenuity, of most riddle answers: "maistrie." But the knight, unable to reason it out, is forced to trade his own "maistrie" for the answer, raising the further question of whether he is capable of understanding its value and meaning.

The answer to that question is provided by the hag, whom he is obliged by the terms of his agreement to marry . She delivers it by confronting him with a dilemma:

> 'Chees now,' quod she, 'oon of thise thynges tweye;
> To han me foul and old till that I deye,
> And be to yow a trewe, humble wyf,
> And nevere yow displese in al my lyf;
> Or elles ye wol han me yong and fair
> And take youre aventure of the repair
> That shal to youre hous bycause of me. . . . (363–69)

It is almost the same question set by Philocopo, the second interlocutor of Boccaccio's "Thirteen Questions," but a resolution is possible here that was lacking in *Il Filocolo*. The knight is unable to solve the dilemma, as he was unable to solve the riddle, but his reply demonstrates that at last he understands the legitimacy of the claim for female sovereignty: "'I putte me in youre wise governaunce'" (375), he tells his wife. She obliges by introducing a third alternative that destroys the balance between the original two: "'I wol be to yow bothe—/ This is to seyn, bothe fair and good'" (384–85), she promises. Thus the dilemma is not so much resolved as exploded by a joke, an ironic one directed at the knight's cynical and unwarranted assumption that, as Donne was later to put it, "No where / Lives a woman true and fair." The logical contrarieties of the dilemma are shown, by the old woman's magic, not to exclude each other after all, and so choice is unnecessary. It is an irony that cuts several ways—not merely at misogynistic assumptions about wives, but at literary convention and at the Wife of Bath herself, who cannot resolve the paradoxes of love and age as effortlessly as her fictional persona has done.

Like many great artists, Chaucer both reworked the received conventions of his art and abandoned them when it served his purpose to do so. His use of dilemmas as a means of questioning, even of deconstructing, his own narrative structures represents a nice blending of conventionality and innovation. When we search the works of his contemporaries and immediate successors for similar structures or similar devices, however, we find nothing at all comparable. Dilemmas exist, to be sure, in the fiction, poetry and drama of the fifteenth and early sixteenth centuries, but they are supernumerary in character, curious excrescences embedded in narrative that are essentially irrelevant to the meanings or effects of the works containing them.

We might have expected the establishment and increasing popularity of the theater in England to have altered this state of affairs. Jacob Bronowski has argued that of all genres, drama in particular lends itself to the exploration of "the unresolved choice between two directions of action" which is, in his view, implicitly present in every literary work (73). The Morality dramas of the fifteenth century, in particular, would seem to offer a hospitable environment for dilemmas. In them, typical-

ly, a central figure representing *human genus* is wooed, tempted, and simultaneously pulled in opposite directions by alle-
gorized representatives of contrasting ethical imperatives,
personified as vices such as Gluttony or Sloth and virtues such
as Good Deeds or Friendship. So symmetrical is the structure of
this dramatic form that its most curious feature, from our point
of view, may be its failure to embody the characteristic sense of
quandary that we have come to associate with dilemmas.
Though the antitheses are firmly in place, the effect of pressure
neutralized by opposing pressure is absent from such works as
Everyman and *Mankind*. Though in the latter play Mankind
listens patiently to the opposing arguments of Mischief and
Mercy, he is hardly plunged into a dilemma by what he hears.
It is true that he describes himself as a mixture of opposites, a
body and soul "of condition contrary" (J. Q. Adams, lines
189–91), but he never seriously contemplates joining Mischief's
train, and when he is tricked into doing so, he soon abandons
Mischief and repents in good time. The pattern of the Morality
play, as Schell and Schuchter have noted, is that of the
admonitory sermon (viii), and Catholic sermons a century
before the Reformation were hardly designed to raise doubts,
let alone pose knotty problems of doctrine, for their auditors.
The balance of forces in these plays is only apparent; in fact, the
debates occur between figures of vastly unequal persuasive-
ness, which makes their outcomes predictable and easily
achieved.

But when we examine the next surge of theatrical activity in
England, which occurred during the second half of the sixteenth century, we perceive a significant alteration. Not only
has the Copernican revolution, with its attendant dislocations,
begun to permeate English thought and feeling, but a novel
and fashionable rhetoric has appeared along with it, one that
reflects many of the qualities we have come to associate with
dilemmas. The "Euphuistic" style of John Lyly, as Jonas A.
Barish describes it, is marked by the "habit . . . of proceeding
disjunctively, of splitting every idea into its component elements and then symmetrizing the elements so as to sharpen

the sense of division between them" (*Jonson* 23). Barish might be describing dilemmas themselves; in any case, Lyly's style proved an admirable vehicle for displaying them. A convenient example is to be found in Lyly's own play *Endimion*, in which a young man, Eumenides, who has been granted a single wish, debates his alternatives: whether to rescue his friend Endimion, who has been put under a spell, or to possess his beloved Semele:

> Therefore let me ask, What now Eumenides? Whither art thou drawn? Care of Endimion, and the command of Cynthia? Shall he die in a leaden sleep, because thou sleepest in a golden dream? Ay, let him sleep forever, so I slumber but one minute with my Semele. Love knoweth neither friendship nor kindred. Shall I not hazard the loss of a friend, for the obtaining of her for whom I would often lose myself? Fond Eumenides, shall the enticing beauty of a most disdainful lady be of more force than the rare fidelity of a true friend? The love of men to women is a thing common, and of course: the friendship of man to man infinite and immortal. Tush, Semele doth possess my love. Ay, but Endimion hath deserved it. I will help Endimion. I found Endimion unspotted in his truth. Ay, but I shall find Semele constant in her love. I will have Semele. What shall I do? (Thorndike 2: 99)

Having taken the trouble to pose this dilemma, Lyly effortlessly disposes of it by having Eumenides refer the question to his wise old friend Geron, who invokes the familiar conventions regarding the falseness of women's love and the firmness of male friendship. Instantly resolved, Eumenides announces, "Virtue shall subdue affections, wisdom lust, friendship beauty" (2: 99). In the end, he is relieved of all consequences that might have proceeded from his choice, for he is united with both Endimion and Semele. Thus, his self-catechism is merely a device for debating with himself in order to reach a conclusion that the audience might have been expected to find palatable in a romantic comedy (and in most respects rather a slight comedy at that, if we judge by the standards that Shakespeare, Jonson and Middleton were to set in the decades to come). But the language by which Lyly dramatizes Eumenides's state of mind possesses a significance that far surpasses our interest in the character himself or the eventual outcome of his predicament. For if one wished to invent a prose style that perfectly embodied the restless oscillation characteristic of a mind grappling with a dilemma, the result would be rhetoric displaying just the propensity toward balance, repetition and antithesis that Lyly demonstrates here.[13]

The first English dramatist able to make dilemmas serve his dramaturgical requirements to any real extent was Thomas Kyd, whose sole but crucially important play, *The Spanish Tragedy*, anticipated Shakespeare in this and other ways. Kyd's blank verse incorporates the essential hallmarks of Euphuism, but without possessing any measure of Lyly's grace and mellifluousness, and the effect is to make the balances and antitheses all the more starkly apparent. In every aspect—in its overall shape, in its drawing of character, and in the rhetoric of its most important speeches—the play recalls and employs several obvious features of dilemmas. It relentlessly poses unanswerable questions from the first act, in which six accounts of the same battle fail to produce a coherent picture of what transpired during its course, to the fourth (and last), in which Hieronimo, driven mad both by grief for his murdered son and by frustration at his inability to communicate his outrage to the court of Spain, stages a macabre play "in unknown languages" (4.1.173), a grisly spectacle that leaves most of its actors dead at the end, to the utter mystification of the courtly spectators onstage and perhaps Kyd's audience as well.

Not every knotty or unanswered question is a dilemma, of course, and *The Spanish Tragedy* raises questions of many sorts. Some are merely factual: who slew Andrea, and who murdered Horatio, Hieronimo's son? Some are metaphysical: what is the relative weight of responsibility to be borne by men and by gods for the calamities of human existence, and what is the likelihood of divine intervention in human affairs? But the most difficult questions in the play—and the ones that attain the status of true dilemma—are the semantic ones. In Act I, two Spanish youths, Lorenzo and Horatio, hotly debate which of them should receive credit for capturing the Portuguese prince, Balthazar. The facts are not in dispute; it is the criteria for defining *capture* that eludes them:

> *Lorenzo.* This hand first took his courser by the reins.
> *Horatio.* But first my lance did put him from his
>   horse.
> *Lorenzo.* I seized his weapon, and enjoyed it
>   straight.
> *Horatio.* But first I forced him lay his weapon down.
>   (1.2.155–58)

Since they are on opposite sides of the question, these two antagonists can hardly be expected to resolve the dispute. But when Balthazar himself is summoned to break the deadlock, he succeeds only in reinforcing it:

> *King.* Say, worthy prince, to wither didst thou
>   yield?
> *Balthazar.* To him in courtesy, to this perforce:
>   He spake me fair, this other gave me strokes;
>   He promised life, this other threatened death;
>   He won my love, this other conquered me;
>   And truth to say, I yield myself to both.
>   (1.2.160–65)

The speech aptly illustrates Barish's contention that the dominant rhetorical device of the scene (he might have said, of the play as a whole) is antithesis" ("*Spanish*" 68–69). In addition to being undermined by countervailing oppositions, though, the speech is confusing in another way. It is difficult to assign antecedents to Balthazar's pronouns, and the immediate context is of little help in deciding who is meant by "he" or "this." It becomes reasonable to assume that Lorenzo is the courteous, promising, loving captor in view of the close friendship that develops between him and Balthazar, with whom he later conspires to murder Horatio, but these subsequent events cannot shed any light on the speech's referents at the time of its delivery, though in performance it might, of course, be accompanied by an elaborate set of physical gestures to assist the audience's understanding. It hardly matters who is being named at any given point in the speech, however, for by its end, Balthazar has "yielded" himself equally and impartially to both his friend and his enemy. Throughout the play, it is difficult for him to recognize or articulate his feelings for others, even to distinguish between love and hate in the case of Horatio—by whom he claims to have been beaten and insulted, whom he nonetheless professes to admire and love "for chivalry" (1.2.194), and whom he finally murders out of envy. In consenting to conspire with Lorenzo against Horatio, Balthazar displays to us quite clearly the obsessive shuttlings of a mind caught in a dilemma:

> *Lorenzo*. How likes Prince Balthazar this stratagem?
> *Balthazar*. Both well and ill; it makes me glad and sad.
>   Glad, that I know the hinderer of my love,
>   Sad, that I fear she hates me whom I love.
>   Glad, that I know on whom to be revenged,
>   Sad, that she'll fly me if I take revenge. . . .
>   (2.1.110–15)

And so on, for another twenty lines. Dilemmas might almost be called Balthazar's "humour," so great is his propensity to arrange his mental life along their strictly predetermined lines. The inevitable result is to deprive him of all power of self-determination, forcing him always to "yield" himself to those whose decision-making abilities are not paralyzed—even to his "destined plague," Horatio, as we have seen.

Though Balthazar is a character of secondary importance in the play (*The Spanish Tragedy* being Hieronimo's play, almost to the extent that *Hamlet* is Hamlet's), he possesses an undue influence, for it is primarily through his curious psychological predicament that we are introduced to the play's world. It is one in which every question produces several contradictory answers or no answers at all, and in which every course of action is baffled by the presence of some equally feasible alternative. The dilemmas of Balthazar prepare us for those of

Hieronimo, who hangs suspended between action and inaction, between speech and silence, between the expectation of divine justice and the necessity of human revenge, until his bafflement turns to genuine madness and he shrugs off the whole excruciating business of decision-making by wreaking impartial havoc upon the whole court, guilty and innocent alike.

The Spanish Tragedy is not merely a play in which certain characters, in certain scenes, confront dilemmas and attempt to resolve them, in the manner of Lyly's Eumenides. It is, rather, a play to some extent *about* dilemmas. The malaise of Balthazar, whose mind perversely renders all questions unanswerable by the very act of posing them, is to become a familiar affliction in Shakespeare's plays, as we shall see. *The Spanish Tragedy*, written at a time when revolutionary ideas were beginning to shape the world-view of the subsequent generation, is a triumph of theatrical anticipation. When we turn to the works of Kyd's immensely more gifted theatrical successor, we shall find a great debt, one only partially acknowledged by modern scholars. Many more of Shakespeare's plays than *Hamlet* owe something of their structure, language, and sense of character to *The Spanish Tragedy*. It was typical of Shakespeare's genius that he could adapt this inheritance to the larger and more varied purposes of his own art. What had been for Kyd a tragic predicament becomes, for Shakespeare, a human one, independent of the limitations imposed by genre.

Shakespeare's first significant experiment with dilemma, as it happens, occurred in a play classified by some as tragedy and by others as chronicle history. It was not as elaborate as Kyd's use of the device, nor as systematic. In *Richard III* (written about six years after *The Spanish Tragedy* and five years before the earliest of the plays this book will examine in later chapters), neither the play's central character nor the world in which he operates displays the complicated mirroring associated with the dilemmas of Shakespeare's later work. But in a single memorable scene, the moral and emotional predicament in which Richard places Lady Anne when, after having murdered her husband, he woos and overcomes her, vividly and concisely illustrates the process by which a dilemma springs to malignant life, a process which Shakespeare was to dramatize, with significant elaboration, throughout the middle portion of his career.

At the outset of the scene, Anne seems well-armored against dilemma, for her response to her husband's death and to encountering his murderer seems unified and unhesitating. But there is something in her that will accommodate ambivalence, announced to us by her propensity for speaking in Euphuistic antitheses. What is significant is that her desire to balance and to symmetrize verbal constructions is not limited to her own speeches, but extends to Richard's as well. Throughout, she echoes the forms of his speech even as she expresses her hatred and contempt for him, modelling her answers on his suggestions and observations even as she appears to reject them. As their dialogue proceeds, we observe her adjusting her responses so that they more and more closely mirror it:

> *Glou*. Vouchsafe, divine perfection of a woman,
>   Of these supposed crimes, to give me leave
>   By circumstance but to acquit myself.
> *Anne*. Vouchsafe, defus'd infection of a man,
>   Of these known evils, but to give me leave
>   By circumstance t' accuse thy cursed self.
>   (1.2.75–80)

Soon her vilification and his flattery are in perfect synchronization:

> *Glou*. Never came poison from so sweet a place.
> *Anne*. Never hung poison on a fouler toad. (146–47)

It must be admitted that the rhetorical features that operate to lay the foundation for Anne's dilemma in this exchange are found elsewhere throughout the play. Herschel Baker notes that *"Richard III* is very formal in language and its structure. The balance of such a line as 'If you will live, lament; if die, be brief' attests to the relentless artifice that pervades the language of a play where everything is shaped and planned"—to the point where "in the public, choric lamentations the antiphonal exchanges are so stiff and patterned that grief assumes the form of ritual" (Introduction, Riverside 709). But, as Baker also notes, Shakespeare never simply reproduces verbal conventions, but makes them serve his dramaturgic needs. Here, though not in later scenes, the effect of antithesis is to provide a form for the dilemma when it appears, and the effect of antiphony is to foster in the audience a sense that Anne is in some fundamental sense co-operating with her enemy, turning what might have been a struggle to the death into what Richard accurately describes as a "keen encounter of our wits" (115).

Two other rhetorical tendencies work against Anne in this scene, and are instrumental in constructing her dilemma. The first is the fact that her speeches are filled with hyperbole of a not very original or imaginative sort; even before Richard begins his outrageous wooing, her insults and execrations are both immoderate and familiar, as typified by "Avaunt, thou dreadful minister of hell!" (46). The intemperance of such expressions is almost a guarantee that when he invites her to translate her hatred into fatal action, she will recoil, for her words have far outstripped what a gently-reared matron could bring herself to perform. Her hatred is not just given vent through such language, but largely consists of it; further expression in violence is all but out of the question.

The second figure present in her language, the inevitable successor to the first, is anticlimax; when, amazingly, Richard begins to make love to her, there are no new rhetorical heights for her to scale, and her responses begin to slide back down toward the commonplace:

> *Anne.* Ill rest betide the chamber where thou liest!
> *Glou.* So will it, madam, till I lie with you.
> *Anne.* I hope so. (110–12)

"I hope so" seems both curiously muted and, whether unconsciously or not, ambiguous; it weakly affirms the curse she has just delivered, but its position, immediately after he has expressed sexual interest in her, makes it sound almost like an affirmation of that interest—or at least, an expression of generalized assent to the whole complex of his desires.

Anne has a desire of her own: that her eyes "were basilisks, to strike [Richard] dead!" (150). By giving voice to that wish, she provides him with a weapon that he is able to turn against her by offering, several times, to grant it. By the midpoint of the scene, the extent to which her responses are tied to the stimuli he provides is obvious, as he sets up between the contradictory impulses that have begun to war within her a self-neutralizing oscillation:

> *He lays his breast open: she offers at it with his sword.*
> *Glou.* Nay, do not pause: for I did kill King
> 　　Henry—
> But 'twas thy beauty that provoked me.
> Nay, now dispatch: 'twas I that stabb'd young
> 　　Edward—
> But 'twas thy heavenly face that set me on.
> 　　　*She falls the sword.* (179–82)

Assuming that Richard's directions to Anne have a visible effect on her, pushing her forward and back like a horse spurred and reined in quick succession, hers is a predicament that, in its Bergsonian mechanism, might produce on the stage a comic effect—akin to Balthazar's verbal scurryings between "glad" and "sad" early in *The Spanish Tragedy*. Here, Anne's abortive movements would testify to the perfection of Richard's control over her. He has determined, and demonstrated to her, that she is incapable of killing him, even of willing him dead; indeed, at the moment she lets fall the sword, she is incapable of any action whatever. The proper conditions have thus been established for him to deliver his *coup de grace*: "Take up the sword again, or take up me" (183). One critic, at least, has recognized the peculiar significance of that demand: "The moment Anne accepts Richard's definition of a world with only two alternatives . . . she is lost," says Herbert S. Weil, Jr. (43). She may intellectually recognize the existence of a third alternative—"Though I wish thy death, / I will not be thy executioner" (184–85)—but once she has begun to retreat from the possibility of acting upon her fury, the outcome is no longer in doubt.[14]

As is the case with most dilemmas, Anne's is partly the result of a sterile and symmetrical logic imposing itself on the flow of impulse and emotion, aided by a rhetoric that both suitably expresses that logic and (to the extent that the content of thought is determined by the form in which it is expressed) creates it. Richard has formulated a classic dilemma for Anne: a choice between two unthinkable alternatives, killing him and embracing him, in which not choosing either of them paradoxically constitutes choosing the second of them—for another way of putting Richard's ultimatum is, refrain from taking up the sword, and you *have* taken up me.

Anne's refusal either to make the choice or to acknowledge it once it is made may seem to us of no great moment, considering that the result, whatever she does or does not do, will be her taking Richard up. But to Anne herself it remains important that she not assent to that arrangement, or indeed to anything Richard suggests, in a formal or explicit way. Earlier, when he asked her if he wished him to kill himself, she replied, "I have already" (187), and she adopts that strategy again at the end of the scene when she tries to chart a middle course between bidding him farewell and not doing so with "Imagine I have said farewell already" (224). For our purposes, the most interesting example of this non-committal form of assent is the second of the three, a familiar one:

> *Glou.* Vouchsafe to wear this ring.
> *Anne.* To take is not to give.
> *Gloucester slips the ring on her finger.* (201–02)

Shakespeare has adapted Boccaccio's classic *dubbio* of the girl and the garlands (by this time, a "near-cliché," as Weil notes [42]). What we, and Richard, recognize as an unequivocal act of amorous surrender, Anne insists upon presenting as a choice indefinitely deferred. It may be true, as she says, that taking is not so clear an expression of favor as giving, but it may also not be true, as the equally persuasive arguments on both sides in *Il Filocolo* showed. In any case, what it means "to give" is hardly relevant; Anne's choice is not, as she would have it, between taking (Richard's ring) and giving (a ring of her own) but between taking (Richard's sword) and taking (Richard's ring and by extension, himself). The fact that he is still alive to propose that question speaks its answer more eloquently than her words.

Nothing else in the play resembles this scene, and of course Anne herself disappears from the action immediately; thus her struggle and defeat is a kind of set piece, a self-contained demonstration of dilemma. The means by which Anne attempts to cope with it and her defeat by it constitute a rehearsal for the more elaborate dilemmas that are a major element of several of the later plays. In particular, dilemmas are an important feature of the problem comedies *The Merchant of Venice*, *All's Well That Ends Well* and *Measure for Measure* and the romantic tragedies *Othello* and Antony and Cleopatra, as well as the dilemmas of *Hamlet* and *Macbeth*. Since Shakespeare's first sustained employment of dilemmas was in the comedies, it is to them that we now turn.

Notes

¹ In my quotations from this and other rhetorical treatises, I have modernized spelling and punctuation.

² This appears to be an illustration sanctioned by time and tradition; virtually the identical example appears in Richard Sherry's *A Treatise of Schemes and Tropes* (1550):

> What should I speak of mine own good turns toward thee? If thou do remember them, I should not trouble you; if you have forgotten them, when by deeds I have profited nothing, what good can I do in words? (qtd. in Joseph 363)

³ W.S. Howell explains that logic and rhetoric in the sixteenth century were two aspects of what was virtually the same discipline, logic concerning itself with strict and technical proofs, rhetoric with the techniques of persuading other people (presumably less adept or sophisticated) that such proofs were

valid (230). Thomas Blundeville, in his lengthy treatise *The Art of Logic*, mentions *dilemma* only once, dismissing it as "a deceitful argument" (qtd. in Howell 288).

⁴ I have quoted Sr. Miriam Joseph's definition, rather than that of Ryle, Aristotle, or any other logician, out of admiration for its conciseness.

⁵ The pun may not be as trivial as it appears. I am indebted to Stephen Booth for an alternative answer: *"The Daily Worker"*—an answer that "runs backwards, depending on abandonment of the original pun (on 'red' and 'read') for the extra energy acquired by its own pun (on the color red in its literal sense and in its political one)" (*Indefinition* 121).

⁶ Requiring audiences literally to make narrative choices is not unheard of, however. In the Czech pavilion at Montreal's Expo '67, a film was shown that offered its viewers an opportunity to select either of two endings to a story by pressing a red or a green button on the armrests of their seats. More recently, the 1985 adaptation of *The Mystery of Edwin Drood* for the New York musical stage paused to take a vote among the audience as to the desired resolution, and the 1986 film *Clue* (from the popular board game) was made in three separate versions, each with a different ending.

⁷ For an authoritative discussion of the principle of complementarity in modern physics, see Chapter III of Werner Heisenberg's *Physics and Philosophy*. Heisenberg notes a "fundamental paradox" of quantum mechanics: complementarity allows a physicist to maintain alternative views of phenomena simultaneously—to believe, for example, that light consists both of continuous waves and of discrete quanta. To a classical Newtonian physicist, who insists upon physics giving an "objective" account of reality, independent of the physicist himself, this would indeed pose a dilemma, but the quantum physicist resolves the problem by reminding himself that his beliefs concern not contradictory realities but merely differing pictures or models of reality, each of which describes some, but not all, of its features. Thus, says Heisenberg, "what we observe is not nature itself but nature exposed to our method of questioning" (57–58). The principle of complementarity is the means by which the dilemma is resolved; it reconciles the antitheses. We employ the principle in everyday life, Heisenberg tells us, "when we reflect about a decision and the motives for our decision or when we have a choice between enjoying music and analyzing its structure" (179)—a choice that in no way exhibits either the logical or the psychological features of a dilemma.

⁸ I employ, for the sake of brevity, the term used by Arthur O. Lovejoy to denote Plato's distinction between, as Lovejoy puts it, the "world we now and here know—various, mutable, a perpetual flux of states" and the Formal world of "the genuinely 'real' and truly good" (24).

⁹ "The wisest man that ever was, when they asked him what he knew, answered that he knew this much, that he knew nothing" (3: 185).

¹⁰ Burtt's translation is of a passage in Galileo's *Opere Complete* (Florence 1842), 4: 333.

¹¹ Here and throughout this book, all quotations and references to Shakespeare's plays and poems are taken from *The Riverside Shakespeare* (ed. G. Blakemore Evans) unless a note referring the reader to another edition appears.

¹² Thomas S. Kuhn believes that Copernican astronomy is firmly grounded in Renaissance Neoplatonism: "The Neoplatonist leaped at once from the changeable and corrupt world of everyday life to the eternal world of pure spirit, and mathematics showed him how to make that leap. . . . The triangles and circles of plane geometry were the archetypes of all Platonic forms" (127).

¹³ It is Barish's view that the Euphuistic prose style is Shakespeare's prose style, and this is true, as witness Shylock's

> If you prick us, do we not bleed? If you tickle us, do we
> not laugh? If you poison us, do we not die? And if you
> wrong us, shall we not revenge? (3.1.64–67)

I would suggest that the same qualities may be found in much of Shakespeare's blank verse as well, such as Claudius's description of his having

> . . . as 'twere with a defeated joy,
> With an auspicious, and a dropping eye,
> With mirth in funeral, and with dirge in marriage,
> In equal scale weighing delight and dole
> Taken [Gertrude] to wife. (*Hamlet* 1.2.10–14)

¹⁴ It is tempting to invoke here what Gregory Bateson termed the "double bind," for this psychiatric construct has suggestive affinities with Anne's dilemma—both involve contradictory or ambiguous signals that promote not a choice between alternatives but merely indecisive oscillation. A double bind, Bateson says, is "a sequence of experiences such that if [an individual] solves a problem of human relationship at the level at which it is apparently offered, he will find himself in the wrong at some other level" (qtd. in Berger xv). But the double bind is embedded for Bateson (as it is not for Shakespeare) in the etiology of schizophrenia, and I do not wish to discuss Shakespeare's characters in a modern technical vocabulary that might limit or distort our view of them. For that reason, my notion of dilemma throughout this work will rest upon only those logical, rhetorical, psychological and philosophical concepts that were operative in Shakespeare's time.

2

"A Mingled Yarn, Good and Ill Together": From Dilemma to Riddle in the Problem Comedies

1

The Merchant of Venice is a play filled with difficult choices; almost every character, major or minor, is observed at one time or another in the act of deciding between alternatives or lamenting his or her inability to do so. Not every question posed in the play is a dilemma; riddles play an important part, as we shall see. But the play's structure—its alternation of main plots, each set in its own distinctive locale—itself mirrors the structure of a dilemma, and so readily accommodates the choices embedded in it.

A number of the play's critics regard the movement back and forth from Venice to Belmont as itself implying a choice, at least to the extent that the existence of any antithesis does so. The two cities represent, in Sigurd Burckhardt's words, the "realm of law and the realm of love, the public sphere and the private" (211). Venice, the public sphere, is the domain of economic activity, as the title suggests, and we should not be surprised to find in that city what Norman 0. Brown calls the style of thinking that money characteristically promotes: "abstract, impersonal, objective, and quantitative, that is to say, the style of thinking of modern science" (234). Venice is a place where the conduct of business and of life itself typically involves the act of calculation, where debit and credit, profit and loss are precisely weighed; it is to be expected, therefore, that "the impersonal logic, the mechanism, involved in the control of money" (Barber 172) dominates the lives of many of its inhabitants, and finds its most perfect expression in the behavior of Shylock.

Symmetry, if nothing else, seems to require that Belmont represent an alternative, even an antidote, to the impersonality and abstractness of Venice. Venice is a city of marble, where Antonio is confronted with "a stony adversary" (4.1.4.), but Belmont is "a green world" (Sisk 221), where impulse, not logic, reigns. At any rate, current scholarly opinion holds that the lottery of the caskets which takes place there calls more for intuition than for calculation on the part of anyone who would win Portia. Morocco and Aragon, according to this view, fail the test because they approach it as an intellectual puzzle; Bassanio chooses the correct casket "not because he is good at parlor games but because he is, as Nerissa says the winner must be, 'one who shall rightly love'" (Siemon 204).

There is, in truth, much in the play to support and recommend this view. The casket test itself, Nerissa tells Portia, was originally more a matter of its inventor's "good inspirations" (1.2.28) than of rational planning, and even the Prince of Morocco, before making his choice, prays for inspiration, not logic: "Some god direct my judgment!" (2.7.13), he cries. Portia takes both Morocco and Aragon to task for being "deliberate fools" (2.9.80), and thus presumably shares Nerissa's opinion that "Hanging and wiving goes by destiny" (2.9.83).

So it is not surprising that Morocco chooses wrongly when, despairing of inspiration, his judgment directed not by "some god" but by the economic imagery of the inscriptions that accompany the caskets, he attempts to plumb the heart of the mystery through computation: "'Who chooseth me shall get as much as he deserves.' / As much as he deserves! pause there, Morocco, / And weigh thy value with an even hand. . ." (2.7.23–25). As Burckhardt says, both Morocco and Aragon concentrate exclusively upon the riddling mottoes as they attempt to "calculate which of the inscriptions correctly states the relation between their own worth, Portia's worth and the risk of choosing wrongly" (217). It is understandable, then, that we should see Morocco's "weighing" as a vain attempt to quantify and rationalize what he had earlier recognized to be a matter of "blind fortune" (2.1.36)—to impose upon inspiration and impulse the strait-jacket of pragmatic logic, something perhaps native and appropriate to Venice but seemingly out of place in Belmont.

Yet if we look at the scene in which Bassanio makes his choice, it is hard to say unequivocally that he does not calculate as well, that he chooses exclusively at the behest of feeling or inspiration or "the right impulse" (Barnet 27). The scene begins with Portia telling him, "If you do love me, you will find me out" (3.2.41), which may be read as a suggestion that he arrive at his choice through intuition rather than through ratiocination; whether or not the song "Tell me where is fancy bred" (63–72) is a clue designed to aid him,[1] it suggests the same thing. But it is not at all certain that he hears the song. While it is being sung, Bassanio *"comments on the caskets to himself,"* according to the stage direction in Evans's text, and his next speech begins with the word "So" (73), which implies either an extension of, or a conclusion to, some premise—perhaps the song's, that things are seldom what they appear, or one reached during his own musings, whatever they consisted of.

The thirty-four lines that follow sound very much like a "reason" for his choice. They consist of a principle—that "The world is still deceiv'd with ornament" (74)—and several illustrations of it: in religion, in law, in matters of esthetics, "ornament is but the guiled shore / To a most dangerous sea . . ." (97–98). Having articulated and explored that notion at length, Bassanio prefaces his rejection of gold and silver with the words "Therefore then" (101), a phrase that explicitly, even redundantly, indicates a logical process at work. The substance of his thought, as well as its form, resembles that of Aragon, who, like Bassanio, knew that "the fool multitude . . . choose by show" (2. 9.26), but who failed, unfortunately for him, to base his decision upon that principle. Throughout the choosing scene, Bassanio sounds less like a lover guided by intuition than like a man bent on solving a riddle in order to best Portia's dead father at a posthumous contest of wits. The casket scene

is thus of a piece with the rest of the play's world, which seeks
to mislead him with "The seeming truth which cunning times
put on / To entrap the wisest" (3.2.100–01).

The inscriptions that accompany the caskets are, certainly,
riddles in the literal sense of the word—intellectual puzzles,
that is, not exercises in divination. Barber's suggestion that
these mottoes contain "a discontinuity, something hidden so
that the chooser cannot get from here to there by reasoning"
(174) does not disqualify them as riddles; the riddle of the
Sphinx, for instance, which Oedipus solved through a process
of reasoning largely mathematical in nature,[2] also contained
something hidden. It is true, as we have seen in Chapter 1, that
riddles are seldom answered through the exercise of pure logic
alone, and often require an imaginative leap of some sort, but
that is not to say that they do not primarily engage the intellect.
The "discontinuity" that Barber recognizes in the inscriptions is
one of the inevitable features of riddles, which are, according to
one authority, "descriptions of objects in terms intended to
suggest something entirely different" from the reality (Taylor
1)—like a golden casket that proclaims, "Who chooseth me
shall gain what many men desire" and that proves to contain a
death's-head. The principle stated by Bassanio just before his
choice—that appearances are deceiving—is precisely what one
has to assume in order to solve a riddle; it is a comment on the
particular problem set for him by Portia's father, as well as a
generalization about the nature of human society.

Admittedly, Burckhardt is correct when he points out that
Bassanio ultimately ignores the inscriptions and instead "lets
the metals speak to him" (217). Yet speech is typically the
medium of thought, and the misleading implication that riddles invariably contain is clearly present in the physical caskets,
whose composition and outward appearances conceal or even
contradict what is within. It is, in fact, easier to solve the riddle
of the caskets if one ignores what the inscriptions say and
listens only to what the metals say—but only if one listens to
the metals after having adopted the premise, as Bassanio has,
that "The world is still deceived with ornament."

Thus, if we demand to see Bassanio as more spiritually gifted than Morocco and Aragon, and not merely more clever; if we insist that he demonstrate the liberal impulses of a true lover to our satisfaction as well as to that of Portia and her father, the choosing scene will disappoint us, and we must be content with what we have earlier learned of him in Venice, where twice within a short scene we have heard him reaching instantaneous decisions with the aid of his impulsive generosity alone: first he cuts short the laborious prologue to Launcelot Gobbo's plea for employment with "I know thee well, thou hast obtain'd thy suit" (2.2.144), and a few moments later, he gives the same answer to Gratiano's suit before he hears it: "You have obtain'd it" (2.2.177).

But though Bassanio does not so concretely or obviously manifest this quality of unhesitating generosity in Belmont (to be sure, he "gives and hazards all he hath," but only after deliberations as long as Morocco's and Aragon's), he has another opportunity to do so later in the play. It occurs when Portia arranges for a second test of his worthiness by coercing from him, disguised, the trothplight ring with which she bound him to her at the end of the casket scene. To play a trick on him, it would appear, was at least part of her intention in binding him to his pledge, for the last line of the speech with which she accompanies the giving of the ring, immediately after he has chosen the correct casket, marks a change of tone, significantly diminishing the seriousness and romantic intensity of the scene:

> . . . This house, these servants, and this same myself
> Are yours—my lord's!—I give them with this ring,
> Which when you part from, lose, or give away,
> Let it presage the ruin of your love,
> And be my vantage to exclaim on you. (3.2.170–74)

Here we see the ease with which Portia shifts her frames of reference and by so doing, radically changes the scene's emotional tonality, modulating a romantic predicament into a comic ploy. The ring itself, which Portia has presented to

Bassanio as a symbol of her desire to be directed by him, is actually the means by which she directs him, through an elaborate practical joke designed to secure her "vantage" over him. Her description of herself as "an unlesson'd girl, unschool'd, unpractic'd" (159) is as false a representation of her character as is conceivable; her conduct at the trial, and her invention of the ring trick, show us an altogether more experienced, assertive, and sophisticated woman. Bassanio won her because he was able to apply the principle that appearances are deceiving to the riddle of the caskets, but he is utterly taken in by her self-portrait as a guileless and submissive ingenue, as he is later deceived by her masculine attire. It is hard to take seriously the conception of love implied by her earlier statement "If you do love me, you will find me out" when we see how far Bassanio is from discerning her true character at the moment of their betrothal; here, as when he earlier opened the lead casket, it is not Portia but only "Fair Portia's counterfeit" (115) that he discovers. Certainly "you will find me out" is incapable of bearing the weight of meaning attached to it by critics who wish to discern a mystical enlightenment or religious illumination occurring in Bassanio.[3]

The ring trick has been dismissed by many critics who have discussed it as trivial, a needless postscript to a plot already concluded. Barber calls it "a slight business" (186), and James E. Siemon, whose excellent article does much to clarify the play's ending, can account for it only by assuming that Portia perversely wishes to interfere with the smooth course of her own love affair (202). But if it is a practical joke that she plays, we should ask what practical purpose it serves, and how it is related to the action that precedes it. We ought, therefore, to connect it not only with the trial scene, which Siemon does, but with the casket-choosing scene as well—for here, once again, Bassanio is confronted with a difficult choice on whose outcome hangs his future with Portia. It is, however, a different *kind* of choice. When, disguised as the deserving lawyer, she demands the ring in recompense for saving Antonio, she presents her husband not with a riddle but with a dilemma:

two alternatives laden with precisely the same degree of disadvantage. Impulse is of no help to him in deciding which to favor, for by giving free rein to his generous nature he may lose Portia as well as the ring; neither is reason more useful, for Portia has balanced the alternatives so nicely that a reasonable case can be made for either. It is she, in fact, who makes both cases by insisting—first as Balthazar, and later as herself in the role of the injured wife—that sanity and common sense can dictate either course: as Balthazar, she assures Bassanio that Portia will pardon his transgression "if your wife be not a mad woman" (4.1.445); as herself, she demands to know "What man is there so much unreasonable" that he would insist upon possessing an object of such great sentimental and ceremonial value to another (5.1.203–06).

Bassanio's ultimate decision to part with the ring is not so much arrived at as thrust upon him by Antonio; in fact, Bassanio has allowed Balthazar to leave empty-handed, and sends the ring after "him" only when Antonio brings intolerable pressure to bear by pleading, "Let his deservings and my love withal / Be valued 'gainst your wive's commandement" (4.1.450–51). It is just Bassanio's inability to perform this act of calculation that has paralyzed him; so far is he from feeling that the outcome is the result of his own free choice that he later excuses it to Portia by calling it "this enforced wrong" (5.1.240).

Whether his decision is in fact the "right" one or the "wrong" one is impossible to say; it is the nature of dilemmas, as we have seen, that such a question cannot successfully be answered. According to the scale of values that the play has established, love and gratitude are more to be prized than legal compulsion, and much of the action has been a working-out of the principle that it is more blessed to give than to receive. On the other hand, the claims of law cannot simply be set aside; Portia herself has admitted in court that "there is no power in Venice / Can alter a decree established" (4.1.218–19). Notwithstanding our tendency to favor bestowing property over retaining it, which the play has instilled in us to this point, Robert Hapgood makes a case for the view that, in parting with the ring, Bassanio has erred by reaching a decision that "signifies the precedence Bassanio gives his friendship for Antonio over his love for Portia." (26). But is it a given that love for a woman ought to take precedence over love for a friend? This formulation makes Bassanio's dilemma simply a later version of the one that Eumenides faced in Lyly's *Endimion*, when he felt compelled to choose between his best friend and his beloved, and the fact that in each play the ending reveals that love and friendship are not mutually exclusive, and that the choice was an unnecessary one, ought to convince us that for us to decide which alternative should have been chosen is not crucial to our understanding of that ending, and is, indeed, largely a waste of time.

The fact that it is in Venice that Bassanio faces this choice is significant. Where Belmont was full of riddles, Venice is the natural habitat of dilemmas. The first half of the play shows us several instances of Venetians immobilized by indecisiveness, among them Shylock, whose temperament makes him particularly susceptible. By profession a calculator, he is baffled by choices that do not lend themselves to solution by calculation. Antonio's invitation to dinner, for instance, causes him no end of difficulty:

> I am bid forth to supper, Jessica.
> There are my keys. But wherefore should I go?
> I am not bid for love, they flatter me,
> But yet I'll go in hate, to feed upon
> The prodigal Christian. Jessica, my girl,
> Look to my house. I am right loath to go . . .
> (2.5.11–16)

Eventually, he does go, in spite of a strong impulse to stay, as if sheer momentum were carrying him out the door: "By Jacob's staff I swear / I have no mind of feasting forth to-night; / But I will go" (2.5.36–38). And in the very act of leaving, a final qualm causes him to call back, "Perhaps I will return immediately" (2.5.52).

Shylock's servant Launcelot, like his master, also finds it

difficult to make choices. He engages in long and intensive self-examination on the subject of whether or not to leave Shylock's employ. Launcelot is more willing to trust his impulses than Shylock is, if only he can discover what they are: "... well, my conscience says, 'Launcelot, bouge not.' 'Bouge,' says the fiend. 'Bouge not,' says my conscience. 'Conscience,' say I, 'you counsel well.' 'Fiend,' say I, 'you counsel well'" (2.2.19–22). Finally, he budges—"The fiend gives the more friendly counsel," he concludes (30–31). But unlike Launcelot's, Shylock's feelings are characteristically in such a state of turmoil that he can never resolve his emotional dilemmas. Solanio's description of his behavior after Jessica's departure illustrates this maelstrom of feeling:

> I never heard a passion so confus'd,
> So strange, outrageous, and so variable
> As the dog Jew did utter in the streets.
> 'My daughter! 0 my ducats! 0 my daughter! ...'
> (2.8.12–15)

Such states of confusion as Shylock's prepare us for the confusion of Bassanio, who mastered the riddle of the caskets in Belmont but who is now confounded by the dilemma of the ring in Venice. As we have seen, dilemmas, because of their ambiguous nature, are always far more taxing problems than riddles, for riddles have answers that are single and wholly correct, however difficult they may be to arrive at, while dilemmas, by definition, do not. The difference between Belmont and Venice is throughout the play embodied in the difference between riddles and dilemmas—between questions that can be answered neatly and completely and those that can only be resolved imperfectly, by a resigned willingness to choose and then to endure the inevitable dislocations that accompany the choice. "Realistic" problems like those found in Venice hardly ever hold out the prospect of a clear alternative offering unalloyed satisfaction; that is why the happy endings of comedy and romance, which depend on this sense of completeness, are available to us only through dreams, plays, and other forms of wish-fulfillment.

The attraction of Belmont's riddle is that, though one risks losing everything, one may win everything. In Venice, by contrast, the solutions to problems are almost as threatening as the problems themselves. Either Antonio must die, for example, or Shylock must be humiliated and broken, a spectacle that has disturbed audiences for hundreds of years. No third alternative exists to satisfy all the parties, though the Duke wistfully imagines one:

> Shylock, the world thinks, and I think so too,
> That thou but leadest this fashion of thy malice
> To the last hour of act, and then 'tis thought
> Thou'lt show thy mercy and remorse more strange
> Than is thy strange apparent cruelty. . . . (4.1.17–21)

Were Shylock capable of mercy and remorse, and had he the essentially theatrical temperament posited by the Duke, this third alternative might exist. But because such a course of action is a psychological impossibility for Shylock, Portia must neutralize and destroy him, however grim a spectacle it presents to us.

The rigid dualities of Act 4 are apparently softened for some readers in Act 5 by Portia's ring-trick, whose effect, Marilyn Williamson suggests, is to blur the dividing line between the play's two domains, bringing "the sere world of Venice into the green, golden world of Belmont" (593). But that is not literally the case. Bassanio is confronted by his dilemma in Venice, where all problems are dilemmas; when the action returns to Belmont, his dilemma is turned into a riddle, and is therefore soluble—though not by him. A third and heretofore hidden alternative to keeping or giving the ring has existed all along: if he can guess the true identity of the person who asks it, Bassanio will be relieved of his decision. As she was earlier locked in the lead casket, Portia is now hidden in Balthazar;

had Bassanio been able to "find her out" beneath the lawyer's robes, he would have been spared much anxiety as to the consequences of keeping or breaking his oath. But of course he has no reason to regard the lawyer's request for his ring not as literal demand but as a puzzle, and he does not understand that Portia is setting him a riddle when she poses her apparently rhetorical question, "What man is there so much unreasonable, / . . . To urge the thing held as a ceremony?" (5.1.203–06). The answer, of course, is no man, but a woman. All the riddles ask the central questions of the play: where is Portia to be found? underneath her lands, her livings, her friends, her various disguises, who and what is she?

So Bassanio solves the first riddle he confronts, but fails to recognize, and so cannot solve, the second one. For him, the consequences of this failure are relatively trivial; it does not cost him Portia, as failing to answer the riddle of the caskets would have done. But it is of great value to Portia that she has at last her "vantage to exclaim on" him, for it remedies the sole defect of her life in Belmont by restoring to her what from the first she complained of lacking, the power of choice: "0 me, the word choose! I may neither choose who I would, nor refuse who I dislike; so is the will of a living daughter curb'd by the will of a dead father. Is it not hard, Nerissa, that I cannot choose one, nor refuse none?" (1.2.22–26). Nerissa replies that the impulses of dying men are often good ones, and to be sure, the casket test did winnow out the covetous and egotistical suitors, arranging for Portia to marry the worthy Bassanio. But she could have arranged that for herself, without the cumbersome legal machinery of wills and tests. From her perspective, it is beside the point that Bassanio was the man she would have chosen had she been free to choose; by the terms of her father's will, she was compelled to marry him, whether she wished to do so or not. Thus, she invents the ring trick. It is far more than a joke, and hardly an irrelevant appendage. It is, rather, a device by which she exercises her will by accepting Bassanio as her husband through an act of conscious volition—choosing him, as it were, retroactively. According to the terms to which she bound him when she gave him the ring, she has the right to reject him if he parts with it. According to a strict interpretation of the facts, he has given it away, never mind to whom. It is, of course, on one level a game, but her part in it is to baffle and reject him as long as she keeps her identity secret, and when at last she reveals it, choosing to forgive and accept him, she symbolically restores to herself control over her destiny, and responsibility for it. At the same time, she makes Belmont once again a place where wishes, no matter how improbable, can come true; by the end of the play, all problems seem literally to have disappeared. Bassanio has both given the ring and kept his oath; Antonio's ships are safe; Jessica and Lorenzo are secure and rich; the exigencies of life in Venice, where all choices are heavy with dire consequence and all solutions are limited ones, no longer seem to exist. In Belmont, finally, it matters very little which alternatives are chosen, as long as one is free to choose. That is what Bassanio has discovered, through Portia's machinations, and it is what Gratiano emphasizes in the play's final speech, when he confronts Nerissa with its last and least crucial choice. Ironically, it is a dilemma, for there is no clear or correct solution to it, but in practical terms, it hardly makes a difference "Whether till the next night she had rather stay, / Or go to bed now, being two hours to day" (5.1.302–03).

In *The Merchant of Venice*, dilemmas are employed as boundary-markers, a means of indicating, along with the riddles, what sort of milieu the action is set in. Their formal symmetry masks their true nature; they are harbingers of confusion and disorder, and they lead not toward harmony but toward entropy. Their domain, Venice, is in many respects a world like that which the audience left outside the theater, a place of doubt and ambivalence, where an ironic sensibility, not a comic or romantic one, reigns. Unlike Belmont, after all, or the golden worlds of other Shakespearean comedies and romances—the ahistorical Athens of *A Midsummer Night's Dream*, Illyria in *Twelfth Night*, Bohemia in *A Winter's Tale* or *As You Like It*'s Forest of Arden—Venice is a city accessible to Shakespeare's audience through contemporary accounts of travelers, and despite its almost legendary reputation as a center of pleasure and brilliance, Venice was as much a part of sixteenth-century Europe as Shakespeare's London was.

Northrop Frye describes *The Merchant of Venice* as "almost an experiment in coming as close as possible to upsetting the comic balance" before righting it at the end of the play (*Anatomy* 165). It is the function of dilemmas in that experiment to create and define in Venice a world in which truly comic possibilities do not and cannot exist.

2

As Frye's comment about *The Merchant of Venice* suggests, the play makes great difficulties for those who wish to find a generic pigeonhole for it. During the last few decades, scholars have tended to remove it from its chronological position among the earlier and sunnier comedies and to place it in the company of the somewhat later "problem comedies" *All's Well That Ends Well* and *Measure for Measure*, those dark and cynical bedfellows of the great Jacobean tragedies. The resemblance of *The Merchant of Venice* to *All's Well That Ends Well* is particularly striking. Both give us a heroine who has seemed to many readers less sympathetic than they would have her; both give us male lovers who unwittingly bind themselves to contracts which their wives exploit by playing tricks on them; both take as a central theme the issue of one's freedom to choose one's marital partner.[4] *All's Well* has been called Shakespeare's prototypical problem comedy for many reasons: because the happiness of its ending is undercut by the means used to achieve it, leaving us, as Jonas Barish says in his introduction to the Pelican edition of the play, "doubting and uneasy" (16); because the play "is not merry in a deep enough way" (Barber 258); because of its "blending of seemingly jarring worlds" (Price 136) and its concomitant "refusal to fit into the usual generic categories" (Barish 25). But all of these judgments could be made—indeed, have been made—of *The Merchant of Venice*,[5]

and *All's Well That Ends Well* might therefore be considered not
so much an innovation but an amplification, a reworking of
materials originally assembled in the earlier play.

In particular, *All's Well That Ends Well* reworks (with substantial modification) the relationship that exists between riddles
and dilemmas. Where in *The Merchant of Venice* the dilemmas of
Venice and the riddles of Belmont defined the difference in
spirit and quality of life between those two geographical
settings, the two settings of *All's Well That Ends Well*, France
and Italy, cannot be defined in this way. Both are conceived at
least as realistically as Venice was in the earlier work, with the
result that the ensuing riddles seem inappropriate and out of
place in both places—"problems," in effect. *All's Well* exhibits
the same movement from dilemma to riddle and back, but not
as fluidly as *The Merchant of Venice*, at least from the point of
view of audience expectation, though the dilemmas are at last
resolved to the satisfaction of the characters. E. M. W. Tillyard
distinguishes between those "problem plays" that display
problems and those (including this one) that "are problems"
(4); actually, *All's Well* qualifies on both counts, since it makes
problems for its audience by the manner in which it solves
them for its protagonists. What is more, most of the problems
in and out of the play are, as we shall see, dilemmas of one sort
or another.

The most apparent of the several sorts of dilemmas found in
the play are the "series of intellectual dilemmas" referred to by
G. K. Hunter in his introduction to the Arden edition, which
"resemble the *dubii* of the Italian Renaissance" (liv): questions
such as whether disparity in rank is an impediment to marriage, or whether a maiden forfeits her honor if she takes the
initiative in wooing. Hunter is correct in adding that these
occasions for debate, which are not found in the play's source,
are given "metaphysical and emotional implications" (liv); still,
their impact on both characters and audience is less profound
and less central than the complex and obscure dilemma in
whose toils we find the King, a predicament whose implications are social, cultural, and emotional. The King's disease—

diagnosed by his physicians as a "fistula" (1.1.34) or ulcer—
thrusts its victim into a state of emotional ambivalence. Though
to the question of whether he wishes to be cured he responds
with a flat "No" (2.1.69), it is clear from the following passage
that his unwillingness owes more to his sense that death is
fitting and unavoidable than to any real wish to die:

> 1. *Lord.* 'Tis our hope, sir,
>   After well-ent'red soldiers, to return
>   And find your Grace in health.
> *King.* No, no, it cannot be; and yet my heart
>   Will not confess he owes the malady
>   That doth my life besiege. (2.1.5–10)

Earlier, the King had expressed what seemed an unequivocal
desire to be rid of life, when he said of his late friend, Bertram's
father, "Would I were with him!" (1.2.52). But again, it is not so
much a yearning for death that was evident there as a conviction that death is fitting for one worn out by age. The image
through which the King communicates this conviction tells us
a good deal about his conception of the life-process:

> I, after him, do after him wish too,
> Since I nor wax nor honey can bring home,
> I quickly were dissolved from my hive,
> To give some laborers room. (64–67)

His metaphor tells us that he thinks of the world, in both its
natural and social aspects, as a beehive—a utilitarian collective
whose members lead lives of labor, sacrifice and self-abnega-
tion under the control of external compulsions that they are
powerless to change or to ignore. Being old and infirm, he feels
a burden to himself and to others, "the snuff / Of younger
spirits" (1.2.59–60). His intuitive belief that nature "debates"
with sickness, and is thus on the side of life and health, is
contradicted by the judgment of his doctors that his disease is
nature's agent; he answers Helena's offer of a cure by quoting
these physicians to the effect that "laboring art can never
ransom nature / From her inaidible estate" (2.1.118–19). Ter-

ence Hawkes may go too far in suggesting that the King's disease symbolizes "the moral laxity" of his Court, but the malady does seem as much psychogenic as physiological, and Hawkes is certainly correct in identifying it with "an attitude toward life which reveals itself as materialistic, rational, 'explaining' in mode" (85). After the cure has been effected, by means that are "nearer to some variety of occult wisdom, or spirit power, than to anything which we can call medical science" (Knight, *Sovereign* 148), Lafew identifies the King's original state of mind with modern scientific empiricism: "They say miracles are past, and we have our philosophical persons, to make modern and familiar, things supernatural and causeless" (2.3.1–3).

The materialism of the scientific account of life is at the root of the King's despair; until Helena persuades him to adopt a divergent view, he has been himself just such a "philosophical person" as Lafew describes, a man whose vision of nature could not distinguish between human beings and insects, or differentiate between the claims of the species and of its individual members. The King's rationalism at the beginning of the play forces him to conclude that, being old, he is useless, and therefore expendable according to nature's needs and laws; at the same time, his personal inclination, which he imperfectly attempts to suppress, cries audibly for life. "Philosophy" thus forces the King into a quantitative mode of thought that prohibits recognition of the personal, the intangible, or the qualitative. At the same time, however, a strong current of intuition and feeling runs beneath his rationalism, continually subverting it. On the surface, it would appear that his refusal to hear Helena's offer is based on a hard-headed judgment that all remedy is futile, a conviction that imminent death is appropriate to his age and condition, and a need to demonstrate his belief in the efficacy of "philosophy" for the benefit of his subjects, even at the cost of his life:

> I say we must not
> So stain our judgment, or corrupt our hope,

To prostitute our past-cure malady
To empirics, or to dissever so
Our great self and our credit, to esteem
A senseless help when help past sense we deem. (2.1.119–24)

But his talk of "sense" and "judgment" is always shadowed by references to something more personal, which points in the opposite direction. Though he has pronounced his malady "past-cure," some "hope" apparently remains—though, paradoxically, to acknowledge it by seeking a cure elsewhere would "corrupt" it. According to Lafew, he has abandoned his physicians because, by permitting them to minister to him, "he hath persecuted time with hope, and finds no other advantage in the process but only the losing of hope by time" (1.1.14–16). And, though he refuses Helena permission to practice her father's arts on him, the King notes wistfully that were Gerard de Narbon living, he would "try him yet" (1.2.72).

Clearly, some impulse toward life still lives in the King, at war with his belief that he must die; though his vision of the natural and the social order forces him to hold himself expendable, he still believes that in him "Nature and sickness / Debate it at their leisure" (1.2.74–75), a view which, as A. H. Carter remarks, puts nature on the side of his survival (28). Yet he rejects, at first, what Wilson Knight has called the "wonderful posthumous opportunity" (*Sovereign* 150) to consult Gerard de Narbon through the medium of his daughter: "I must not hear thee" (2.1.145), he tells Helena. What he refuses to hear from her, in particular, is the reason that she gives him to hope:

What I can do can do no hurt to try,
Since you set up your rest 'gainst remedy.

. . .

Oft expectation fails, and most oft there
Where most it promises; and oft it hits
Where hope is coldest and despair most fits. (2.1.134–44)

Hunter glosses the phrase "set up your rest" as a gambling term, equivalent to the modern "stake your all' (Arden 2.1.134n); if we read her speech literally, Helena is suggesting that the King's very refusal to seek a cure is his gamble, at long odds, for life. He is indulging in what psychiatrists call magical thinking, and she accurately paraphrases the essence of his thought when she tells him that wishes come true most often "Where hope is coldest. . . ." Her speech sufficiently defines the King's dilemma: the more he hopes for a cure, the more likely he is to be disappointed; if he abandons hope and embraces despair, his expectations of a cure are enhanced—but if he despairs *in order to* enhance his chances, he is, after all, hoping, and is the more likely to be disappointed.

This is superstition packaged as science. From the domain of logical calculation comes the shape of his dilemma, its tauto-logical symmetry and balance; like Lafew, he identifies hope-lessness with the tenets of scientific materialism, which, pur-porting to explain all phenomena according to physical laws, denied to men the solace of irrational or implausible hope. But the proposition that life is governed by an ironic principle through which men achieve only what they do not seek derives not from science but from the conventions of romance, from folk tales in which wishes come true but bring the wisher the opposite of what was wished, or in which the way to achieve a desired end is to learn how not to desire it—as Bassanio learned in *The Merchant of Venice* not to covet the benefits that marrying Portia brought him. Helena is aware that she must employ a system of belief that incorporates the King's magical thinking and can deal with it on its own terms if she is to cure him, and so she neatly embraces the vocabularies of both science and the supernatural when she begs him, "Of heaven, not me, make an experiment" (154). Now his dilemma is further exacerbated; he does not wish to jeopardize his cure by hoping for it, but he understands that he cannot be cured by Helena unless he is willing to undergo such jeopardy.

In the end, hope triumphs. Impressed by the "certainty and confidence" (169) she displays in venturing her life upon her powers, he becomes her "resolv'd patient" (204), able to master his desire to question her more because he has come to believe that "more to know could not be more to trust" (206). And the hope that has become trust is really the secular underpinning of what is soon revealed to be religious faith:

> Methinks in thee some blessed spirit doth speak
> His powerful sound within an organ weak;
> And what impossibility would slay
> In common sense, sense saves another way. (175–78)

When we next encounter the King, he is cured.

The King's dilemma, like the dilemmas of *The Merchant of Venice*, identifies the action of which it forms a part, as well as the character afflicted by it, as belonging to a world that in many respects resembles our own; that is why G. K. Hunter has called the French court "too realistic for the magic that Helena practices there" (xxxiv). The identification of the King's state of mind with the perspective of modern science helps to establish this context, and to set off the magical and romantic vision expounded by Helena, which signals a movement away from realism: the *existence* of a dilemma suggests the world of everyday life, but the *solution* of a dilemma leads away from that world.

The most significant difference between Helena's romantic optimism and the King's ironic pessimism centers upon their contrasting conceptions of time. Temporal movement is to *All's Well That Ends Well* what geographical movement is to *The Merchant of Venice*: its fundamental dynamic. For the King, time is a subversive force that makes the course of life an inexorable passage from youthful vigor to the sickness and impotence of age, and finally to oblivion; nature is for him both the state of health held captive by his disease and the impersonal force which, through the agency of time, destroys all living things. His rationalism has taught him to view all phenomena quantitatively, and to take a quantitative view of the role that time plays in human affairs is to see it as analogous to the role that money plays in *The Merchant of Venice*: time is a precious substance that constantly diminishes by being spent. It flows always in a single direction that takes us from health to sickness, from pleasure to pain, from life to death. The only aspect of time that the King can conceive is what Frank Kermode calls *chronos*—time that merely passes, time that is wasted, "time which is simply 'one damn thing after another'" (47). What Helena offers the King is the conception of time that Kermode terms *kairos*: "a point in time filled with significance, charged with a meaning derived from its relation to the end" (47)[6]—in this case, if not the apocalyptic end to which Kermode alluded, the end to which the play's title refers. In effect, then, Helena will suspend the laws of time as the King has understood them. It is the King's interest in the duration of the cure that calls our attention to its temporal character:

> *King.* Within what space
>   Hop'st thou my cure?
> *Hel.*   The greatest grace lending grace,
>   Ere twice the horses of the sun shall bring
>   Their fiery torcher his diurnal ring,
>   Ere twice in murk and occidental damp
>   Moist Hesperus hath quench'd her sleepy lamp,
>   Or four and twenty times the pilot's glass
>   Hath told the thievish minutes how they pass,
>   What is infirm from your sound parts shall fly,
>   Health shall live free, and sickness freely die.
>   (158–68)

The incantatory rhythms of this speech, so at variance with the language that has preceded it, signify that Helena's are powers of restoration in the literal sense. The two days over which her cure will take place are a mystical interval in which time will appear to run backwards, not only arresting the seemingly inevitable course of the King's passage toward death but rejuvenating him. The paradoxes of the last line tell us that nature's "laws" have been for the moment suspended. Helena's miracle is a refutation of the King's melancholy conviction that time always diminishes life's opportunities as it is itself diminished in store; it is the first application of the principle "all's well that ends well" to the action of the play.

Through her cure, Helena gives the King more time in which to live, but, more important, she alters his understanding of time's effects. With the late and unexpected flowering of physical health and good humor in old age, the King is persuaded of his right to a reposeful period of grace and satisfaction before death. This sense of new and unexpected possibilities brought about by time is elucidated and sharpened for us through Helena's quest for Bertram, which forms the second and central action of *All's Well*. After Helena has imposed, by sheer force of will, her romantic vision of nature upon the mundane world of the play, we discover, as we might have expected, that riddles have replaced dilemmas as the characteristic obstacles that will be encountered. But the riddle Helena herself must solve, which Bertram poses in his letter to her, is, like the King's dilemma, temporal in character: " 'When thou canst get the ring upon my finger, which never shall come off, and show me a child begotten of thy body that I am father to, then call me husband; but in such a "then" I write a never' " (3.2.57–60).

Helena accepts this challenge by taking literally what Bertram meant figuratively. By so doing, she does for Bertram what she did for the King earlier: she turns "never" into "then," revealing possibilities he could not have dreamt of and does not fully comprehend when they are at last revealed to him. This she accomplishes by playing on him the much-maligned "bed-trick," which enables her to answer the riddle implicit in his letter, and then by circulating a false report of her death, which enables her to pose a riddle of her own to Bertram. The two devices, and the two riddles, come together in Diana's paradoxical speech near the end of the play:

> . . . for this lord,
> Who hath abus'd me, as he knows himself,
> Though yet he never harm'd me, here I quit him.
> He knows himself my bed he hath defil'd,
> And at that time he got his wife with child.
> Dead though she be, she feels her young one kick.
> So there's my riddle: one that's dead is quick. . . . (5.3.297–303)

Helena's resurrection is her second temporal miracle, making death a prelude not to oblivion but to marriage and new life. If her deceptions of Bertram need defending (and the history of the play's criticism testifies that they do), the defense must address the morally suspect principle that the end justifies the means, that all is truly well that ends well. But both the means and the ends have been called into question here. Not only does the bed-trick strike G. K. Hunter and others as "irrelevant and tasteless" (xliv), but, in addition, the denouement of the play has been called the least satisfying of Shakespeare's endings; W. W. Lawrence spoke for a multitude of commentators when he wondered whether Shakespeare "meant the final reconciliation of Bertram and Helena to be taken as a prelude to future bliss, or ironically, as a union which must ultimately result in disaster" (32).

It seems unfair to blame Shakespeare alone for creating these discords; it is, after all, Helena, within the boundaries of the play, who is largely responsible for the course and outcome of its action, though of course she is forced to work with considerably less freedom than the playwright himself, since she can originate only solutions to the problems she encounters, not the problems themselves. Absolving her partially of responsibility, however, does not banish the uneasiness she has caused many of the play's critics. The neatness and ingenuity of her solution to Bertram's riddle is impressive, but it leaves the original problem of his distaste for her untouched; it may deprive him of recourse to justice, but not necessarily of our sympathies. How can a piece of deception on Helena's part, after all, no matter how brilliantly conceived, inspire a husband's devotion in a man who goes to war in order to escape "the dark house and the detested wife" (2.3.292)? Leo Salingar touches on this point when he indicts the problem plays as a group for raising "burning moral questions only to solve them in what are still the terms of theatrical ingenuity, instead of by systematic analysis or through discussion pointing to a general conclusion" (312). In the case at hand, the problem is more emotional than moral, and systematic analysis would be no more useful in reaching a conclusion than the means Helena employs, since the problem, as the play presents it, is insoluble: if Bertram is sincere when he says to the King, "I cannot love her" (2.3.145), however misguided or trivial his reasons, Helena's manipulations of him can only increase that sense of "subjection" (1.1.5) of which he never ceases to complain. Helena spends the last four acts constructing and deconstructing riddles, while the audience remains preoccupied with dilemmas of feeling; in generic terms, Helena treats as a comic problem what we take to be a romantic one—though again, it is well to remember that Bertram, not she, dictated both the problem and the terms of its solution.

Thus the shift from dilemma to riddle, accompanied by the physical movement of the action from France to Italy, is in most respects misleading if we expect it to signify here what it signified in *The Merchant of Venice*. Helena's cure of the King seemed to herald, through its sense of limitless new possibilities, a spiritual antidote to his sterile and materialistic conception of a universe in which all forms of life are governed by a single set of mechanical laws operating on men and insects alike. Helena's refutation of this pessimistic vision might have led the King and Bertram into a larger and sunnier world, one in which love could flourish. But when the focus of the play's action moves from the disease of the King to the dislocations of the lovers, we find ourselves still where we began, for Helena, surprisingly, shares many of the King's behavioristic assumptions. She holds (at least in Act 1) an impersonal and quantitative view of love that regards herself and Bertram, if not as insects, as no more than animals, and therefore at the mercy of biological destiny: "The hind that would be mated by the lion / Must die for love" (1.1.91–92), she laments.[7] Soon she determines to transcend these natural obstacles by putting her trust in fortune and guile, but for Bertram the situation remains as Wilson Knight succinctly described it:

> The play's thought depicts a world where the sexual instincts of the male are almost automatic, and the female regularly on the defensive.

> Bertram should have no difficulty in accepting any normally good-look-
> ing woman, provided that the marriage was honorable, and this
> marriage will be made so, as the King clearly asserts. Love in our sense
> would scarcely be essential. (*Sovereign* 113)

This is the view that Helena holds of the man she purports to
love, and what is even more disturbing, events prove her right:
the bed-trick could not have succeeded if Bertram were not
blind or indifferent to any aspect of women beside the physical.
His inability to recognize Helena during their sexual encounter,
which convention protects from scrutiny in the source, must
here be seen as a skeptical comment on Bertram's demand for
the freedom of self-determination in marriage, as a contradiction of his insistence that he can discriminate between Helena
and Diana to the extent of hating one and loving, or at least
lusting after, the other.

Thus both lovers come to seem flawed, and the flaws in both
have to do with our sense of them as driven by external
compulsion to behavior that is unsympathetic when judged by
the traditional standards of romantic love. Though there has of
late been some recognition that these standards are not auto-
matically applicable to all of Shakespeare's comedies,[8] the most
popular view of *All's Well That Ends Well* is still that of Wilson
Knight: Helena is an "overpraised heroine remorselessly track-
ing down an unwilling young man and finally forcing him to
accept her against his will," with the added complication of
Bertram's being "drawn as a dissolute cad" (*Sovereign* 95).

When we come to the play's denouement, we encounter only
more difficulties. Like Portia, Helena creates for her husband
an artificial dilemma that turns out in the end to be a riddle,
permitting the solution of what appeared to be an insoluble
problem. Helena's apparent death reawakens the King's despair and brings to the fore Bertram's perversity: having
despised Helena while she lived, he claims to have fallen in
love with her now that (and possibly for the reason that) she is
dead. The mourning of Bertram and the King for Helena is a
variation on the King's original dilemma: time, once again the

agent of loss, despair, and cruel irony, teaches us the value of what we have by depriving us of it:

> *King.* . . . love that comes too late,
> Like a remorseful pardon slowly carried,
> To the great sender turns a sour offense,
> Crying, "That's good that's gone." (5.3.57–60)

So Bertram, miserable when a husband, is doomed to misery as a widower. But with the appearance of Diana, and the exposition of her "riddle," both men learn again the lesson that Helena teaches throughout the play: that the normal or customary order of life's events is not invariable. One that's dead is "quick" in both senses of the word, and "never" is once again replaced by "then." All of Bertram's apparent alternatives seem to merge and coalesce. He need never, after all, have chosen between Helena, whom he loved only after he lost her, and Diana, whom he ceased to desire as soon as he possessed her; Helena has arranged for him to experience the illicit excitement of lust without jeopardizing the moral security of a chaste marriage. He is given—twice, at that—the sensation or illusion of free choice, though in fact he is protected in the first case from the sin of loving a woman who is not his wife and in the second from the folly of loving a woman who is dead. Like Parolles, instead of being "crush'd with a plot" (4.3.325), he is in the end advantaged by being duped. His fellows in the Shakespearean canon are not romantic lovers like Orlando, Sebastian and Ferdinand but the *alazons*, Shylock, Malvolio and Caliban, who, lacking the human talent for freely choosing, are better off having their choices made for them by others of superior intelligence or judgment. Certainly Bertram betrays no dismay at having been tricked by his wife; on the contrary, he is delighted by her sleight-of-hand, like a child at a magic show: "If she, my liege, can make me know this clearly, / I'll love her dearly, ever, ever dearly" (5.3.315–16), he exclaims.[9] It is the ephemeral quality of his enthusiasm in this speech that causes many critics to doubt his sincerity; this, his last condition for accepting Helena, seems as frivolous and arbitrary as his earlier ones, though more easily satisfied. In the source, by contrast, the Count Beltramo (who corresponds to Bertram) gives many and substantial reasons for accepting Giletta as his wife: he listens carefully to her explanation, "and perceiving her constant mind and good wit, and the two fair young boys, to keep his promise made, and to please his subjects, and the ladies that made suit unto him to accept her from that time forth as his lawful wife, and to honor her," he masters his "obstinate rigor" and publicly acknowledges her,[10] in a way that seems emotionally and socially plausible, and could easily have been incorporated into the ending of *All's Well* if plausibility had been the playwright's intention. We have reason, similarly, to doubt Bertram's protestations of love for Helena just prior to her reappearance; perhaps he is only, once again, telling the King what he knows the King wants to hear, as he did earlier in the play when he made his politic recantation and agreed to marry Helena. It is true that he is described by the Second Lord as "chang'd almost into another man" (4.3.5) by the letter that informs him of Helena's death, but we see and hear nothing of this transformation; his only references to the event before Act 5 are the third and fourth items on his cluttered list of "sixteen businesses" dispatched in a night, having "buried a wife, mourn'd for her" (4.3.85–88). Barish seems in the right when he says that Bertram at the end of the play "remains the same Bertram as before . . . the same self-willed, self-satisfied adolescent of the earlier scenes, ready to trivialize all of his experience" (Pelican 25–26).

But if Bertram trivializes his experience—and if securing him as a husband is possible only because he is shallow and perverse—Helena along with him is responsible for undercutting the degree to which we can take truth, marriage, and love itself seriously in the play. It is certainly possible to regard her last deception as an exercise in futility if we do not accept at face value Bertram's protestations of love for her; what is the point of rescuing from an emotional dilemma a man who has next to no capacity for emotion in him to begin with? But this is to forget that a symptom of Bertram's shallowness is his fondness for riddles; it may not satisfy us that Helena engages his full attention with a riddle at the end of the play, but it seems to content him. And we have no right to ask whether this contentment will endure after the play has ended. The epilogue, spoken by the King, calls our attention to the fallacy of doing so by reminding us that "The King's a beggar, now the play is done; / All is well ended if this suit be won, / That you express content . . ." (1–3). To say that the play's ending is not romantically satisfying to the audience is not to say that it does not end as it should. Bertram has a wife who pleases him to the extent (however minimal) that he is capable of being pleased; Helena has the husband she desired from the start, however inferior we may think his talents and virtues when compared to her own. Had Bertram stood revealed at the end as a man of newfound sensitivity and discernment, we would certainly face another problem which his shallowness spares us: that of his accepting a woman who could subject him to such public humiliation as his wife does. And were Helena the saint she has sometimes been thought, she could hardly have been able to bring herself to satisfy the conditions set by Bertram's letter, but might instead, like Viola's imaginary sister, have pined away "like Patience on a monument" for love.

As it is, the only dilemmas left at the end of the play are those of the audience, which has always found it difficult to grant the King his suit; the characters all claim to be well-satisfied. The "problems" of this particular problem play are the ambivalent feelings it leaves us with, in particular our sense that the questions it has answered are not the questions it asked at the start. Many readers who search the play for some overriding principle that will reconcile its disparities point to the First Lord's judgment of Bertram, whose conduct toward Helena and Diana he finds as shameful as his conduct on the battlefield was exemplary: "The web of our life is of a mingled yarn, good and ill together; our virtues would be proud, if our faults whipt them not, and our crimes would despair, if they were not cherish'd by our virtues" (4.3.71–74). Barish tells us that the comment "is partly designed to mitigate . . . the severity of the

judgment we might otherwise be tempted to pass by forcing us
to recognize ourselves in Bertram" (Pelican 19). And there is no
reason why the comment should not similarly be applied to
Helena, for as a principle it seems general enough to cover any
dramatic character, overriding those conventions by which we
have come to insist upon psychological unity and coherent
behavior. The First Lord is doing more than pointing out a
paradox of human nature; he is also accounting for it, by
suggesting a symbiotic relationship between our virtues and
our flaws.

This complementary nourishment of opposites is also present in the play's other and more heavily emphasized principle,
as we hear it in its final reiteration: "All yet seems well, and if
it end so meet, / The bitter past, more welcome is the sweet"
(5.3.333–34). Suffering and joy, we are being told, require each
other, as do our virtues and our defects, and many other pairs
of opposites, in order to have meaning. In Shakespeare's
romantic comedies, the transcendence of quantitative thinking
is always maintained as an ideal, but there always exists a
calculus by which happiness must be bought, won, or paid for
after the fact. None of the plays is set in so uniformly auspi-
cious a clime, none of the heroes or heroines is conceived of as
so completely sympathetic, none of the endings is so free from
shadow that the answer to a mere riddle can satisfy us
completely. The claims and exigencies of the real world, with
its limitations and unfathomable complexities, are always present, however muted, to remind us that tricks, jokes, and
games rarely put an end to problems, but only allow us to
forget them for a while. At the end of this "problem play," the
real world is present by implication only. The paradox of *All's
Well That Ends Well* is that, regarded as a sealed, self-contained
dramatic structure, it is the tightest and least problematic of all
the plays, an end-stopped "fiction of concord," as Frank
Kermode might call it (59), but that few of us can regard it in
this way; only an audience of fanatical formalists could so drain
all emotional affect from its response. And so the sense of
dilemma persists in us, sharpened by the King's insistence that

dilemmas are not only nonexistent but inconceivable in the general rejoicing of the finale.

3

In *Measure for Measure*, we discover, the dilemmas of the audience grow to even greater proportions. One might become convinced of this without bothering to read the play, simply by skimming through the attempts of twentieth-century critics to come to terms with its themes, characters and genre, for no play in the Shakespearean canon has provoked more heated arguments or more disparate readings. L. C. Knights called *Measure for Measure* an ambiguous failure ("Ambiguity"); F. R. Leavis thought it one of Shakespeare's greatest plays (234–35). W. W. Lawrence found it "suffused with sympathy" (78); Una Ellis-Fermor spoke of the "dead disgust" of its world-view (259). For R. W. Chambers, Isabella is one of Shakespeare's noblest heroines (287); Harold C. Goddard, though he approved of her decision to refuse Angelo's demand, thought that she had "dropped from saintliness to beastliness" in the manner by which she reached it (442). Wilson Knight called her a "fiend" ("Gospels" 45), in contrast to the Duke, whom he elsewhere held to embody "the dignity and the power of a Prospero" (*Wheel* 79)—the same Duke whom Empson found in all respects "offensive" (*Structure* 283). While Roy W. Battenhouse and many others have read the play as an allegory of the Christian doctrine of atonement ("*Measure*"), E. M. W. Tillyard and the opposing school find it a secular and down-to-earth play, "acutely human and quite hostile to the tone of allegory" (129)—a play, says Roger Sale, that has "far more to do with a comic view of the social order than with Christian mercy" (57).

It is hard to believe that all these commentators are discussing the same work, but, in fact, the range and intensity of their disagreements is a valuable clue to the play's meaning and method. *Measure for Measure* is like the proverbial elephant that presented itself to six blind men as a wall, a rope, a tree, a fan, a spear and a snake, depending upon what part of it each had hold of; that the criticism of the play should group itself neatly into opposing schools of detractors and defenders is not surprising, for this tendency mirrors the play itself, in which the claims of justice and mercy, of "form" (2.4.12) and "blood" (15), to use its own terms, balance each other with the symmetry proclaimed by the title. Its Vienna is a city of extremes, populated, as far as we can tell, by the corruptly licentious and the puritanically repressed; the only professions represented in the play are prostitution, law, and the church, with ordinary family life all but invisible behind the jails, brothels, courts and convents in which the action takes place. License, as represented by Mistress Overdone, Pompey, and the gentlemen who gossip and snigger with Lucio in 1.2, is counterpoised by a rigid moralism centered around a contempt for, even a hatred of, the flesh that is reflected in Angelo's harsh sentences and Isabella's search for "a more strict restraint" (1.4.4) in the order of St. Clare.

In most cases, these moral extremes seem the product of personalities that gravitate naturally away from the middle ground. Angelo's conception of justice seems intemperate even when it is bolstered by his legal authority and the apparent sincerity of his convictions; in retrospect, it appears even more immoderate when he is revealed as a secret hypocrite and an extortionist. Lucio takes what at first seems a comparatively reasonable and even-handed view of sexual license—that it is an inherent part of man's nature, "impossible to extirp . . . till eating and drinking be put down" (3.2.102–03)—but his position forfeits much of its quality of common sense when it leads directly to his licentious slanders of the Duke.

Thus, when Claudio is sentenced to death for the crime of fornication, no precedent exists whereby he might take a balanced or moderate view of his predicament, and we find him oscillating between violent self-reproach and pathetic self-justification. During a single uninterrupted dialogue with Lucio, he describes his sentence as "just" (1.2.123) but accuses his sentencer of "tyranny" (163); he exonerates himself on the ground that he slept with Julietta "upon a true contract" (145)

but taxes himself with having taken "too much liberty" (125).
Throughout the play, Claudio alternates in this manner between guilt and indignation, between suing to live and seeking
to die; he compares himself, and all men, to "rats that ravin
down their proper bane" (129), and his sense of himself as a
victim of his own impulses, cursed by his self-destructive
nature, disposes him toward the dilemma under which he soon
labors.

Isabella describes similar oscillations, even before Angelo
poses for her the question that is at the center of the play's main
action. Her brother's offense, and his request that she plead for
him to Angelo, plunge her into a dilemma of emotional and
moral conviction which is immediately evident in the plea
itself:

> There is a vice that most I do abhor,
> And most desire should meet the blow of justice;
> For which I would not plead, but that I must;
> For which I must not plead, but that I am
> At war 'twixt will and will not. (2.2.29–33)

We have here, in her first dilemma, an opportunity to understand more fully her second, so it is worthwhile to discover, if
we can, just what it is that pulls her in opposite directions at
once. We cannot assume that the conflict in her is as simple or
straightforward as it has seemed to those critics who see her as
a woman torn between her moral principles and her love of her
brother, for both are open to question. There is little doubt that
she loathes sexual vice; clearly enough, that abhorrence is her
primary motive in entering a religious order that will isolate her
from men entirely. Given the squalor of Vienna's sexual
climate, it is possible to sympathize with her decision. But it
does seem that to Isabella, all sex is vicious; her own chastity
seems less a matter of conviction or principle than of a personal
"revulsion" (Geckle 62) against all human sensuality. In a
reaction against the Victorian tendency to idealize her, modern
criticism has lately focused upon Isabella's sexual dysfunction,
on whatever it is in her that requires the "strict restraint"

offered by the convent. Daryl F. Gless, in the most recent
full-length study of the play, notes that much about her,
including her name, suggests the passionate religiosity typical
of Spanish Catholicism (113), and indeed, if we examine the
imagery of certain of her less guarded speeches, we may feel
that she has more affinities with Crashaw's Saint Theresa than
with Saint Clare:

> . . . were I under the terms of death,
> Th' impression of keen whips I'ld wear as rubies,
> And strip myself to death, as to a bed
> That longing have been sick for. . . . (2.4.100–03)

Under the pressures of life in Vienna, the sexual impulse has
apparently been transformed in Isabella into a martyr's zeal; for
her (and for Claudio as well), sex and death are inextricably
wedded. The fact that Isabella's ethical principles grow out of
her emotional and psychological propensities hardly invali-
dates them, but it does make them seem more a matter of
personality than of piety, and this tends to lessen their authority for an audience struggling to discern where its sympathies
are meant to lie. If she is not "a thing enskied, and sainted"
(1.4.34), as Lucio (perhaps in mockery) called her, but only a
young, vulnerable, and quite human woman whose knowledge of and control over sexual desires is no more perfect than,
say, Angelo's, we are less likely to accept her as the play's
moral authority or *raisonneur*. Still, if we lose her services as a
guide through the play's moral thickets because we have begun
to regard her merely as one of its characters and not as a
spokeswoman for its author's religious views, it will be easier
in the long run for us to come to terms with what seems mean,
self-righteous or even repellent in her.

And if her moral credibility is undercut by these suggestions
of erotic obsession or religious fanaticism, her loyalties to her
brother are similarly open to question. There is no evidence
whatever in the play that she loves Claudio, pities him, or
comes to his defense for any other reason than that she is
unable to resist Lucio's demand that she do so. Certainly her

pleas to Angelo for Claudio's life, as we have seen, are notably lacking in conviction and enthusiasm, and Lucio more than once reproaches her for her timidity, urging her to renew her efforts: "Kneel down before him, hang upon his gown; / You are too cold" (2.2.44–45). This is a crucial indictment; we are reminded that Claudio chose her as his advocate precisely because "in her youth / There is a prone and speechless dialect, / Such as move men" (1.2.182–84). Isabella would not be completely wrong if she assumed that Claudio was in a limited and special sense pandering for her to Angelo; in any event, her coldness is her only defense, and an insufficient one at that, against the predicaments to which her sexual attractiveness subjects her. Her beauty is responsible for her coming under the domination first of Claudio and Lucio, who seek to employ it in Claudio's defense; next of Angelo, who is lustfully inflamed by it; and finally of the Duke himself, who is inspired by it to propose marriage to her. It is this continual subjugation to the will and desires of men that is the cause of all of Isabella's dilemmas in the play.

The consequences of her first dilemma are predictable enough: unable to commit herself wholly either to Claudio's cause or to the law that condemns him, she vacillates between pragmatic flexibility and moral outrage, depending upon what the moment seems to require. Interrupted by Lucio as she is about to enter the convent, she impatiently dismisses the predicament of Claudio and Julietta with "O, let him marry her" (1.4.49); faced with Angelo's intractability a short time later, she dismisses Claudio himself: "O just but severe law! / I had a brother then" (2.2.41–42). When Lucio chides her for her coldness, she borrows his own libertine defense of Claudio's conduct, asking Angelo, "Who is it that hath died for this offense? / There's many have committed it" (2.2.88–89), but when Angelo asks her to demonstrate her newly-adopted belief that unchastity is "rather . . . / A merriment than a vice" (2.4.115–16) by sleeping with him in exchange for Claudio's life, she once more reverses her position:

> O, pardon me, my lord, it oft falls out,
> To have what we would have, we speak not what we mean.
> I something do excuse the thing I hate
> For his advantage that I dearly love. (2.4.117–20)

Granted that her problem is insoluble to the extent that, as with all dilemmas, either alternative is disadvantageous in one way or another, what is important here is the way in which she tries to deal with it. Instead of making the hard but necessary choice dictated either by her principles or her familial obligations, she delays as long as possible, and by choosing first one alternative and then negating her choice in favor of the other, chooses neither. The result of this procrastination is that her first dilemma, left unresolved, allows Angelo to subject her to a second, which proves far more extreme:

> . . . I shall pose you quickly.
> Which had you rather, that the most just law
> Now took your brother's life, or, to redeem him,
> Give up your body to such sweet uncleanness
> As she that he hath stain'd? (51–55)

It is characteristic of Isabella that she ignores the question, refusing to confront or even acknowledge it until Angelo complains, a few speeches later, "Nay, but hear me, / Your sense pursues not mine" (73–74).

Angelo thereupon restates her alternatives and again demands a response: "What would you do?" (98). The choice he forces upon Isabella resembles a true *dubbio*—an occasion for extended debate, in the manner of the "questions" posed in Boccaccio's *Il Filocolo*—and for generations, critics of *Measure for Measure* have approached it as one, endlessly speculating upon the question itself, seeking its answer both within the play and outside it,[11] constructing justifications for both alternatives that either condemn Isabella's lack of compassion for her brother or praise her purity for refusing to make the sacrifice demanded by Angelo. These attempts are doubly futile. Being a dilemma, the question has no "right answer," and furthermore, the action of the play renders Isabella's choice irrelevant, since

Angelo intends to kill Claudio, and the Duke to save him, whatever she decides. Isabella's dilemma is a dramatic device for putting pressure on her, in order to show us how a woman who possesses a particular character-structure behaves when subjected to that pressure. Though few of us can refrain from wrestling with her dilemma along with her, we are more fortunate than she in this respect: we have far less invested in resolving it. Just as with Bassanio's dilemma of the ring in *The Merchant of Venice*, it is a mistake to assume that our understanding of *Measure for Measure* depends upon our deciding what Isabella should do, or what we should do were we in her predicament. Our attention ought therefore not to be occupied with the alternatives that she faces to the exclusion of what they dramatize: the process by which Isabella attempts to cope with the predicament they make for her.

The answer that she gives to Angelo appears at first glance forthright and unequivocal, but reveals itself when examined closely to be a demonstration of what Claudio earlier called her "prosperous art / When she will play with reason and discourse" (1.2.184–85):

> *Ang.* What would you do?
> *Isab.* As much for my poor brother as myself:
>   That is, were I under the terms of death,
>   Th' impression of keen whips I'ld wear as rubies,
>   And strip myself to death, as to a bed
>   That longing have been sick for, ere I'ld yield
>   My body up to shame. (2.4.98–103)

I have already commented on the sexual imagery in the speech, which makes figurative dying and literal death the same thing. The function of this modulation from the erotic to the fatal is to alter the hypothesis as Angelo has presented it: if she is being asked not to commit "sweet uncleanness" but to imagine herself under sentence of death, arguments that advance the veniality of sexual transgression no longer apply. The shift from sexual to literal dying is accompanied here by another significant alteration as well: from her own voice and *persona* to

Claudio's. She answers Angelo's question as if it had been put not to her but to an heroically idealized version of her brother. In her reformulation, it is not she who must choose between chastity and Claudio's life; it is Claudio who must choose between his own life and Isabella's. To her, the correct choice is obvious:

> *Ang.* Then must your brother die.
> *Isab.* And 'twere the cheaper way:
> 　Better it were a brother died at once,
> 　Than that a sister, by redeeming
> 　　him,
> 　Should die for ever. (104–08)

"The cheaper way": many critics have commented upon her tendency to employ the language of commerce "at unfortunate times" (Gless 113), here as a way of imposing a pat quantitative solution on a sticky qualitative problem.[12] By the end of the scene, she has recast the original dilemma to the point where the two alternatives are of such unequal weight as to make the choice, after a moment's computation, almost automatic: "Then, Isabel, live chaste, and, brother, die; / More than our brother is our chastity" (184–85). At the same time, however, she determines to do literally what she has already done rhetorically: avoid the consequences of her decision by referring the whole matter to Claudio, secure in her conviction

> That had he twenty heads to tender down
> On twenty bloody blocks, he'ld yield them up,
> Before his sister should her body stoop
> To such abhorr'd pollution. (180–83)

The following scene, in Claudio's prison cell, is surely one of the most perplexing and unpleasant in Shakespeare, especially since all its violence is verbal and emotional. Its tone is announced by the tasteless (and distinctly Metaphysical) joke that Isabella makes to her brother when she enters—a joke perfectly in keeping with her already demonstrated tendency to "play" with argument:

> *Claud.* Now, sister, what's the comfort?
> *Isab.*   Why,
>   As all comforts are: most good, most good
>   indeed.
>   Lord Angelo, having affairs to heaven,
>   Intends you for his swift ambassador. . . .
>   (3.1.53–57)

Nothing that Isabella says during the course of the play testifies quite so eloquently to her lack of empathy with Claudio's plight.[13] Her remark is addressed not to her brother as he is, a wretched and despairing man condemned to die, but to what she would have him be, a martyr who shares her own estimation of her virtue's pricelessness and his own life's worthlessness. Her version of Angelo's demand, as she here expounds it to Claudio, contains significant elisions and alterations of emphasis, so that it suggests no more than the vaguest of possibilities, an almost nonexistent loophole:

> *Claud.* Is there no remedy?
> *Isab.* None, but such remedy as, to save a head,
>   To cleave a heart in twain. (60–62)

Having failed to specify the remedy in question, she begins instead to impugn her brother's courage, inflating her chastity to "perpetual honor" and diminishing the remainder of his life to a mere "six or seven winters" (75–76). And such is her skill in playing with discourse that Claudio's first instinctive impulse is precisely the one she hoped for, a virtual paraphrase of her earlier impersonation of him:

> Think you I can a resolution fetch
> From flow'ry tenderness? If I must die,
> I will encounter darkness as a bride,
> And hug it in mine arms. (81–84)

"There spake my brother," she replies (85), and she is right: the tendency to approach death as a sexual encounter, at least in rhetoric, runs in the family. Having wrung from him this commitment to self-martyrdom, she clarifies for him at last what was up to now her dilemma, but is about to become his: "If I would yield him my virginity, / Thou mightst be freed!" (97–98). But as the possibility of avoiding his sentence takes root in his imagination, the patience born of hopelessness and abetted by the stoical preachings of the disguised Duke begins to drain away. First he echoes her earlier pleas to Angelo, musing, "Sure it is no sin, / Or of the deadly seven it is the least" (109–10); soon he progresses to "Death is a fearful thing" (116), followed by a long and vivid meditation on the body's decomposition and the soul's torment; finally, abjectly, he begs for life: "Sweet sister, let me live" (133).

Brother and sister are at this moment at utter cross-purposes,[14] each laboring under the false impression that the other's intention is to bring comfort. Claudio believes that he is being presented with a choice, but what Isabella has brought him is from her point of view a *fait accompli*, and his role, which he understandably mistakes, is merely to validate it for her. In the process of evading the consequences of her own dilemma, Isabella has constructed one equally cruel for Claudio: he may avoid his sentence if he is craven enough to ask her for his life, but if he makes such a request, he is, by her standards, unfit to live:

> *Isab.* O you beast,
>   O faithless coward! O dishonest wretch!
>   . . .
>   Die, perish! Might but my bending down
>   Reprieve thee from thy fate, it should proceed.
>   I'll pray a thousand prayers for thy death,
>   No word to save thee. (135–46)

And the result of this tirade, paradoxically but predictably, is to incline him once again toward death: "I am so out of love with life that I will sue to be rid of it" (171–72), he tells the Duke.

Here, at the moment of Isabella's exit from Claudio's cell, the play undergoes what Tillyard called a "change in its nature" (130) that shifts our attention from the problems of Claudio and Isabella to the purposes of the Duke. Largely an observer for the first two acts, the Duke now assumes the task of directing the course of the action, exerting over it such unwavering jurisdiction that he seems to Battenhouse and others more than human, a literal embodiment of divine Providence. What he proposes is to cut the Gordian knot of all the play's dilemmas, releasing not only Claudio and Isabella from their predicaments but also Mariana, who has not yet entered the action. To Isabella the disguised prince makes an extravagant and unexpected promise:

> . . . A remedy presents itself. I do make myself believe
> that you may most uprighteously do a poor wrong'd
> lady a merited benefit; redeem your brother from the
> angry law; do no stain to your own gracious person; and
> much please the absent Duke. . . . (198–203)

This is a solution so all-encompassing that it will solve problems of which neither Isabella nor the audience is yet aware. It is the sort of solution that we have come to associate with the actions of comedy and romance, and, just as in the case of *All's Well That Ends Well*, it raises problems of generic classification for those who, like Theodore Spencer, take *Measure for Measure* to be made of "basically tragic material" (184).[15] Much recent criticism has attempted to dispose of this new difficulty by showing that the play is "comedy throughout" (Bennett 24), but the question remains moot, for, again as with *All's Well*, the more one manipulates definitions of genre the looser they become, until finally they can accommodate any dramatic structure one cares to propose.

For our purposes, the most telling feature of the Duke's "remedy"[16] is that it consists essentially of the answer to a riddle: Mariana, at the end of the play, is married but lacks a husband because, though she knows him, he "knows not that ever he knew me" (5.1.187).[17] The riddle is generated by Shakespeare's second bed-trick, through which the Duke purposely confuses the identities of Isabella and Mariana in order to bring light, order and justice out of the ensuing revelations. The Duke's focus is quite explicitly upon the power of this device to blunt the double-edged sword of Isabella's dilemma, relieving her of the consequences attached to either of its alternatives: the substitution of Mariana for Isabella in Angelo's bed "not only saves your brother, but keeps you from dishonor in doing it" (3.1.236–37), he explains for the second time, and even a third: "by this is your brother sav'd, your honor untainted, the poor Mariana advantag'd, and the corrupt deputy scal'd" (253–55)—all this repetition designed to underscore the point that nobody's problem, however small, will be left without "remedy" and to lobby for the dubious principle that "the doubleness of the benefit defends the deceit from reproof" (257–58).

But the bed-trick makes new problems for the audience, as it did in *All's Well That Ends Well*, and it does not quite solve the old ones. Claudio's life is not saved by this device, for Angelo fails to keep his bargain with Isabella after he believes she has kept it with him, and the Duke is forced to scramble for some other means of preventing the execution. It is true that Mariana, whom Angelo had once contracted to marry, gains a husband by consummating their union, but that Angelo himself should thereby be "scaled"—i.e., weighed or judged, and by extension punished—gets us close to the fundamental problems with which the ending of the play has been taxed. The Duke's justification for the questionable ethics involved in uniting sexually two persons not wed in public ceremony— "He is your husband on a pre-contract: / To bring you thus together 'tis no sin" (4.1.71–72)—demolishes the legal basis for Claudio's execution, collapsing the central theme of the conflict between the letter of the law and the spirit of justice. In addition, of course, it bears an unwholesome resemblance to the pandering that was and is at the center of Vienna's licentiousness, the original and most serious problem that the Duke set out to solve. And finally, the "remedy" represented by the bed-trick fails to address the emotional breach that has opened between Isabella and Claudio, who left each other on terms of the most extreme bitterness on her part and guiltiness on his, couched in their rancorous dialogue in his cell—a conversation that proves to be, in fact, the last words they speak to each other in the play.

These problems are not different in kind from the ones that arose from Helena's manipulations in *All's Well That Ends Well*. What is different is the fact that Helena was forced to adopt questionable devices because she was powerless; she had no influence over Bertram except what he provided her by his letter, which dictated to her the terms upon which he would accept her as his wife. The Duke, by contrast, possesses power that, even if it does not transcend the sphere of the temporal, as Battenhouse suggests, is sufficient for him to have accomplished instantly, by fiat, what he chooses to effect secretly and tortuously. "Craft against vice I must apply" (3.2.277) he soliloquizes, but he never explains why he might not have reappeared in his true identity and, shedding his craft with his disguise, freed Claudio, condemned Angelo, and arranged whatever marriages he liked at the end of the third act instead of at the end of the fifth.

From a purely practical point of view, nothing would have been lost had he done so, and much would have been gained: since the Duke's absence and his appointment of Angelo as his deputy were responsible for many of the difficulties now in need of redress, it would surely have been to his and everybody else's advantage to clear them up as simply and quickly as possible. But the Duke's point of view is not practical; it is esthetic. The "craft" with which he intends to combat vice soon reveals itself as a form of stagecraft, through which he imposes upon the action a resolution whose form owes more to the conventions of drama than to the laws of Vienna or the needs and deserts of its citizens. That his material is intractable and unsuitable to the genre he has selected for it does not deter him. In order to bring about an ending replete with dramatic revelations of identity, stunning reversals of fortune, and a multiplicity of marriages, he is prepared to have the convict Barnardine executed, not because the law demands his death but because the Duke requires his head in order to deceive Angelo. To the Provost, he sends a letter of explanation that succinctly expresses the dramatic formula upon which the denouement of a romantic comedy with a surprise ending is based: "Put not yourself into amazement how these things should be," he advises him; "all difficulties are but easy when they are known" (4.2.204–06).

Similarly, his motive in withholding from Isabella the fact that Claudio lives is a conventional one, shared by other providential figures in Shakespearean comedy and romance. It rests upon the principle that gratification deferred or achieved laboriously is more satisfying than that which comes easily or swiftly: " . . . I will keep her ignorant of her good, / To make her heavenly comforts of despair, / When it is least expected" (4.3.109–10). Thus the Duke joins the company of the King in *All's Well That Ends Well*, who concluded that play with another version of that principle: "The bitter past, more welcome is the sweet" (5.3.334). And among its other members may be found Prospero, whose reason for interposing himself between Ferdinand and Miranda is based on the same tenet: "They are both in either's pow'rs; but this swift business / I must uneasy make, lest too light winning / Make the prize light" (*The Tempest* 1.2.451–53). Many other examples could be adduced from the Shakespearean canon, including one delivered by the god Jupiter, who declares, in *Cymbeline*, "Whom best I love I cross; to make my gift, / The more delay'd, delighted" (5.4.101–02). Frye points out that all such human and divine controllers share with Shakespeare himself a playwright's perspective; each is "a projection of the author's craftsmanship" (*Natural* 69). But the maladroitness of the Duke in *Measure for Measure* sets him apart from these other surrogate dramatists. Operating by a set of theatrical conventions wholly inappropriate to the characters upon whom he imposes them and to the setting in which the action takes place, he brings the plot to a conclusion that satisfies nobody but himself and, just possibly, Mariana. It might be said of the Duke, as Frye remarked about Shakespeare, that "he seems to have been so absorbed in the theatrical process as to be largely indifferent to anything outside it" (*Natural* 22), but it should be added that this preoccupation, which undoubtedly contributed to Shakespeare's success as a playwright, is largely responsible for the Duke's shortcomings as a governor.

The Duke's dramatic inspiration comes to fruition in the labyrinthine fifth act, when he stages, in effect, two plays, one inside the other. First, in concert with Mariana and Isabella, he exposes the villainy of Angelo through the solution of the bed-trick riddle; then, acting alone, and with his former fellow-players now his audience, he presents his *coup de theatre* by producing Claudio alive. The latter production, though performed publicly at the Viennese court, is really directed at an audience of one: Isabella, whom it is designed both to entertain and to instruct. Since she is deficient in compassion, she must be taught to embrace mercy and humility by being won, through Mariana's offices, to plead for Angelo's life—after which, presumably, she will be entitled to those "heavenly comforts of despair" that the Duke intends to provide her by producing Claudio alive.

But throughout the scene, the Duke finds himself wrestling for control of the stage with Lucio, whose continual interruptions all but vitiate the effect of Mariana's riddles, exploding dialogue intended as mysterious and gnomic into farce:

> *Mari.* Pardon, my lord, I will not show my face
>   Until my husband bid me.
> *Duke.* What, are you married?
> *Mari.* No, my lord
> *Duke.* Are you a maid?
> *Mari.* No, my lord.
> *Duke.* A widow then?
> *Mari.* Neither, my lord.
> *Duke.* Why, you are nothing then: neither maid, widow,
>   nor wife?
> *Lucio.* My lord, she may be a punk; for many of them are
>   neither maid, widow, nor wife.
> *Duke.* Silence that fellow. (5.1.169–81)

Lucio's answer to the riddle is every bit as good as the Duke's, however "wrong" in the technical sense it is, and, given the moral climate of Vienna, it seems in some ways more fitting. There is no silencing Lucio; untile is arraigned for slander, he continues to treat riddles as opportunities for comic repartee. The spontaneity and brevity of his answers makes Mariana's exposition seem ponderous and studied by comparison:

> *Mari.* My lord, I do confess I ne'er was married,
> And I confess besides I am no maid.
> I have known my husband, yet my husband
> Knows not that ever he knew me.
> *Lucio.* He was drunk, then, my lord, it can be no better.
> *Duke.* For the benefit of silence, would thou wert so too. (184–89)

Lucio's ironic commentary has the same tone, and serves the same function, as the heckling of *Pyramis and Thisbe* by Theseus's court in the last act of *A Midsummer Night's Dream*: it makes the romantic machinery look cumbersome and the romantic vision seem absurd. So does the Duke's unfortunate reminder that the original corruption of Vienna remains, impervious to "remedy" by the means he has chosen to employ; despite the strict laws that Angelo has attempted to enforce, it is still a city of "faults so countenanc'd, that the strong statutes / Stand like the forfeits in a barber's shop" (319–21), thanks largely to the Duke's own predilection for dispensing amnesty and inculcating a general spirit of forgiveness, which, however well-suited they might be to more benign settings such as Belmont, Athens or Illyria, simply serve in Vienna to maintain the status quo of its licentiousness.[18]

At the root of the difficulty are the marriages that take place at the Duke's insistence, and particularly his paradoxical conception of them as instruments of both pleasure and punishment—a variation on the alliance between death and sexual pleasure earlier articulated by both Isabella and Claudio. Lucio regards his enforced betrothal to a whore whom he at some earlier time had got with child and then abandoned as nothing else than his sentence for talking out of turn, an impression that the Duke does not contradict:

> *Lucio.* Marrying a punk, my lord, is pressing to death,
>   whipping, and hanging.
> *Duke.* Slandering a prince deserves it. (522–23)

To the extent that we receive comic satisfaction from seeing the
tables turned on Lucio, we may remain relatively untroubled
by this event; at least it lessens the population of Vienna's
stews by one, and since Lucio has been from the first the play's
exponent of comic tough-mindedness, much in the manner of
Gratiano in *The Merchant of Venice*, it would be inappropriate to
weep for him now. But the case is different when Angelo is
made to suffer the same fate—when his marriage to Mariana is
presented to him, and to us, as the wages of his sin:

> *Ang.* Immediate sentence, then, and sequent death,
>   Is all the grace I beg.
> *Duke.* Come hither, Mariana.
>   Say: wast thou e'er contracted to this woman?
> *Ang.* I was, my lord.
> *Duke.* Go take her hence, and marry her instantly. (373–77)

In the general amnesty that follows, Angelo's death sentence
is commuted, but his only remaining speech in the play shows
us how little he is delighted by this change of fortune: " . . . I
crave death more willingly than mercy: / 'Tis my deserving, and
I do entreat it" (476–77). Perhaps Lucio was only indulging in
characteristic hyperbole when he called his marriage a fate
worse than death, but there is no reason to question Angelo's
sincerity in saying much the same thing. Of course, the cause
of his penitential despair is about to be lifted from him when
the Duke produces Claudio unharmed, but if this event pro-
cures in Angelo any change of mood or heart, we do not see it
or hear it; neither he nor any other character on stage makes
any vocal response to the unmuffling of Claudio.

Presumably, what the Duke expects at the end of his play is
something like the recognition scenes in *Twelfth Night* or *The
Winter's Tale*, in which seemingly miraculous resurrections
produce joy and astonishment in those who witness them. But
he has miscalculated his audience, particularly Isabella, whose

feelings about Claudio's death are more complicated than he realizes. He assumes her to be in a state of "despair" concerning her brother's death; we recall that her last words to him were a condemnation more enthusiastic than Angelo's: "I'll pray a thousand prayers for thy death, / No word to save thee" (3.1.145–46). We are reminded similarly of her difficulty in mustering any real conviction when she sued to Angelo for Claudio's life at the beginning of the play, and of the fact that her plea for Angelo's life at the end is not so much a request for mercy as a legal justification of Claudio's execution: "Let him not die. My brother had but justice, / In that he did the thing for which he died" (5.1.448–49), she argues, with what Ernst Schanzer calls "the finesse of a seasoned attorney" (101). It would seem just as likely that the sight of her brother might produce shame and remorse in her as joy, but the text offers no help on that point, for, like Angelo, she does not audibly respond to Claudio's appearance at all; the reader, or director, is left to draw or stage his or her own conclusions.[19]

Similarly absent from the play is any hint of response on her part to the Duke's proposal of marriage, which even he recognizes to be unsuited to the occasion: "Give me your hand and say you will be mine, / He is my brother too. But fitter time for that" (492–93). So powerful are the conventions that associate the endings of comedies with marriage that at least one critic takes Isabella's silence as a more or less formal assent, speaking of her "decision to abandon the rule of St. Clare and marry the Duke" (Gless 211). But it is more consistent with her behavior throughout the play if we regard her silence at the end as evidence of her being in the grip of yet another dilemma, pulled by the Duke's importunings in one direction and by her desire for "a more strict restraint," which the events of the play could hardly have weakened, in the other. It is not unlikely that she might assent to the proposal, of course, since she has in similar situations invariably done what those in authority have expected of her, but the play ends before any such resolution actually occurs.

The roots of comedy's conventional ending in marriage go

back to the Greek *komos*, in which the emotional emphasis is upon the festive aspects of the union, its function as a guarantee of regeneration and a celebration of nature's role in human affairs. What is absent from the conclusion of *Measure for Measure*, even more so than from the ending of *All's Well That Ends Well*, is a sense of festival. Whatever misgivings the concluding marriage of the earlier play may have inspired in us, at least the participants were, for the moment, willing; here, enthusiasm for the nuptials is expressed by Mariana and the Duke alone. Gless tells us that our personal feelings about these marriages are "peripheral, if not illegitimate, matters of concern. We are not normally invited to ask probing questions about the psychological compatibility of partners who marry at the end of romantic and symbolic narratives" (233–34). This is true, but we are not normally *inclined* to ask such questions, either; romantic and symbolic narratives usually arrange matters so that the issue of compatibility does not arise. It arises here because *Measure for Measure* does not seem romantic and symbolic enough, despite the Duke's efforts—because the participants in the three proposed marriages keep calling attention to their personal inclinations, however idiomatic or at odds with the larger structure into which the Duke demands they be integrated. The marital convention as Shakespeare employs it is always liable to cause us some difficulties; A. D. Nuttall no doubt speaks for many among us when he says, "The disparity between the absolute, indissoluble character of the bond and the casualness with which it could be formed must always have been too much to hold in one's head" (56). But *Measure for Measure* pushes the disparity further than any other play of Shakespeare's, so that the only way to accept it is to form a new conception of what we mean when we speak of the ending of a comedy as festive.

Northrop Frye, as usual, formulates the question more succinctly than anyone else:

> Does anything that exhibits the structure of a comedy have to be taken as a comedy, regardless of its content or our attitude to that content?

The answer is clearly yes. A comedy is not a play which ends happily: it is a play in which a certain structure is present and works through to its own logical end, whether we or the cast or the author feel happy about it or not. The logical end is festive, but anyone's attitude to the festivity may be that of Orlando or Jaques. (*Natural* 46)

It is hard to quarrel with this formulation, except to point out that those who see a degree of overlap between happy endings and festive ones have the weight of tradition on their side; Frye himself notes, "Comedy is . . . the name of a structure, yet it has a predominating mood which is festive" (*Natural* 49). In the case of *Measure for Measure*, though, it is not quite sufficient to call it a comedy because "a certain structure is present" without noting that it is present solely at the pleasure of the Duke; it does not so much work through to its own logical end as obey his will, the logic of the play being, as many generically-oriented critics have argued, tragic or ironic or in some other way opposed to the comic.

As in the case of *All's Well That Ends Well*, the final dilemma of *Measure for Measure* is that of the audience, though it is in this case shared by several of the characters. For them, as for us, it is a dilemma of emotions that contradict each other, but from our perspective it is more: if we find ourselves unable to respond to the conclusion of the action in the way that the Duke wants us to, we may recognize that our difficulty has to do with his inability to satisfy expectations that he himself has raised. It is not that he has failed to give us a comedy, at least not if we take Frye's last word on the subject to heart: "The festive ending of a comedy represents what the audience normally regards as on the whole a desirable solution to the action" (*Natural* 130). Compared to the conclusion that would have ensued had the Duke not intervened, his solution is indeed "on the whole desirable." But he seemed to promise throughout the play, by action and word, that he would provide a panacea, a "remedy" for every difficulty. Whether the conventions of the genre mandate it or not, we are led in *Measure for Measure* to expect something we do not get: a solution that is all-encompassing and in its own way perfect, like the answer to a prayer or the fulfillment of a dream.

The problematic ending of *Measure for Measure* brings us back to our original distinction between dilemma and riddle. *The Merchant of Venice*, *All's Well That Ends Well* and *Measure for Measure* share a common structural pattern: each moves from a setting associated with (or at least evocative of) the world inhabited by the audience, the "real" or "everyday" world, into (or at least in the direction of) a domain associated with fantasy, dream, and the fulfillment of wishes, whose characteristic obstacle is not the insoluble dilemma but the soluble riddle. In generic terms, this journey has sometimes been called the movement from tragedy to comedy, but neither this nor the the previous description is quite adequate. It is true that the initial settings of all three plays are places where a major character is faced with imminent death, but since in each case the movement in the direction of tragic suffering is quickly arrested, the result might better be termed, because of its incompleteness, ironic. Similarly, the term *comic* is itself unable to express or fully define the domain of riddles, a fact recognized by most critics, who distinguish certain of Shakespeare's plays that contain them as romances or romantic comedies.

But this formulation creates a further difficulty: the terms *romance* and *comedy* are often used in the critical literature as if they were interchangeable instead of merely overlapping. Thus Josephine Waters Bennett speaks of the law against fornication in *Measure for Measure* as "a comic device . . . like the beanstalk in the fairy tale" (19) and Hal Gelb of motifs such as "the quitting of a particular society, disguise, and the enforcement of arbitrary laws" as "comic devices" (19), though all are readily found in any number of romances that lack comic overtones. Comedy and romance share a common border, but at their farthest extremes, romance approaches the seriousness of tragedy, while comedy takes on the hard-boiled flippancy of the ironic, where empathy with the emotional and spiritual life of the characters is suppressed. Comedy *per se* puts external obstacles in the path of lovers—usually in the form of parental opposition or some arbitrary law that is imposed upon them from without. When the feelings of the lovers themselves become the obstacle to their union, as in the case of *All's Well That Ends Well* and *Measure for Measure*, we are moving in the direction of romance and its recognition of more profound emotional and spiritual possibilities.

The central problem of the "problem plays" is that their comic and romantic elements are at war with each other. The competing influences may most readily be defined by examining the properties of the riddles more closely, for though riddles are a motif common both to comedy and romance, their functions in the two genres are not identical. Riddles in romances are an elliptical means of revealing and testing character; that is what Siemon means when he says that Bassanio solves the riddle of the caskets because he is a true lover, not because he is good at games. The would-be solver of a romantic riddle is usually aided by some higher power, such as love, intuition, or providence. Helena, like Bassanio, has the inspiration of love at her disposal, as well as a demonstrated command of the semi-miraculous talents by which she cured the King; the Duke of Vienna, who invents Mariana's riddle and also proclaims its solution, possesses credentials that have convinced some critics, as has been noted, of his association with the powers of divinity.

Comic riddles, by contrast, we expect to view as games, as showcases for the display of wit and cleverness, as devices for demonstrating mastery, usually at someone else's expense. To the extent that we regard the riddles in these three plays as comic, we will find it difficult to believe them capable of solving any serious problems. And in each case, as we have seen, comic elements intrude themselves, elbowing aside the fragile romantic mood that attaches itself to the riddles when they are first posed. In *The Merchant of Venice*, Bassanio seems to arrive at his answer as much by calculation as by the intuition of a true lover, and Portia, even as he contemplates his choice, is planning a comical ploy by which to seize advantage over him, in the form of a riddle disguised as a dilemma. In *All's Well That*

Ends Well, Bertram's delighted astonishment at the end puts the focus not on Helena's power to inspire love in him but on her virtuosity as a trickster, which seems to him her most lovable trait. In *Measure for Measure*, if one doubts the Duke's providential nature, his riddles become little more than staged effects, theatrical simulations of wit (and uninspired ones, at that) which address not the real problems of the play but only those artificial ones created by the Duke at the outset in order that he may dispose of them at the end.

The effect of this competition between dramatic genres— whispered in *The Merchant of Venice*, spoken in *All's Well That Ends Well*, and shouted in *Measure for Measure*—is that they neutralize each other. The result is that the comic and romantic visions become a dilemma for the audiences of these plays, asserting claims upon our belief and our feelings that are at once very similar and diametrically opposed. In the later two plays particularly, our instinct may tell us that the riddles are being rung in as a kind of diversion, a substitute for the solutions to the real problems. Those problems are dilemmas, and they remain with us long after the riddles have been answered.

NOTES TO CHAPTER TWO

[1] According to Barber, "The dramatic point is precisely that there is no signal" (174); several earlier critics have suggested the contrary. Perhaps the inclination to view the song as a clue is a natural one, for without some precisely demarcated instruction to Bassanio, it is difficult to tell just when and how he discovered that the world was filled with false appearances.

[2] See Bernard Knox's compelling argument in "Sophocles' Oedipus," discussed in Chapter 1.

[3] Neil Carson is one of several critics who argue that Bassanio's willingness to take risks is evidence of his faith in divine providence (168–77).

[4] Leo Salingar discusses the marked similarities between the choosing scenes of the two plays in *Shakespeare and the Traditions of Comedy* (318).

[5] Lawrence Danson illustrates the modern tendency among commentators when he refers to *The Merchant of Venice* as "the most scandalously problematic of Shakespeare's plays" (*Harmonies* 2).

[6] It is interesting that Kermode's discussion of Shakespeare's endings is restricted to the tragedies, for his argument works equally well here. Another

temporal dichotomy that applies is the distinction (derived from Mircea Eliade) made by Norman O. Brown in *Life Against Death* between archaic time, which is "cyclical, periodic, unhistoric" and modern time, which is "progressive (historical), continuous, irreversible" (274). Though Helena does not quite leave the King with a sense of time that is "ahistoric" or endless, his earlier conception of time is exactly "modern" in the sense used above, and he might therefore be included among the "philosophical persons" at whom Lafew's sneers, who, through their scientific materialism and calculative propensities, make spiritual and religious mysteries "modern and familiar."

⁷ John Arthos refers to "something in her nature that is making its demands and ruling her even while she thinks she will never possess what it demands" (114).

⁸ Walter N. King asks why we should not accept Shakespeare as "depicting men and women as they behave inconsistently in everyday life rather than as they behave in traditional romantic story" (33).

⁹ Nevill Coghill, though, argues that at some point during their marriage, after the play's conclusion, Bertram is likely to reproach Helena for her deceit (72).

¹⁰ William Painter, "Giletta of Narbona," *The Palace of Pleasure* (qtd. in Appendix, *All's Well That Ends Well*, Arden edition [152]).

¹¹ In particular, I have in mind representatives of that approach to moral and religious issues in Shakespeare's texts which seeks to locate the solutions to such problems as these in what they identify as the received Christian doctrine of Shakespeare's age. Roy W. Battenhouse's "*Measure for Measure* and the Christian Doctrine of Atonement" is the best-known example of its application to this play.

¹² Terence Hawkes suggests that Vienna as it is depicted in the play is a place of "rational assessment in which prices are fixed for moral commodities" (94).

¹³ Mark Taylor offers a contrasting interpretation that is plausible: that Isabella's joke "shows her nervousness about trying to justify the unjustifiable, her awareness that Claudio might not be easily convinced that she has done the right thing, and thus that perhaps she has not done the right thing" (letter to the author, 19 January 1987).

¹⁴ Anthony Caputi notes, of this and the play's other extended scenes of debate, that "all end in unresolved states of conflict; characters meet, talk, discover differences of opinion, discuss their differences, and part only after having heightened the tension expressed in their disagreement" (88–89).

¹⁵ For arguments constructed along approximately the same lines, also see Harriet Hawkins, *Likenesses of Truth in Elizabethan and Restoration Drama* and David L. Stevenson, *The Achievement of Shakespeare's* Measure for Measure.

¹⁶ "Remedy"—or its absence—is peculiarly central to *Measure for Measure*.

The word occurs more frequently than in any other play (eight times); seven of the occurrences are in 2.1 and 3.1 (the prison interview); five of the occurrences involve the phrase "no remedy."

[17] The riddle is almost identical to that offered by Diana in 5.3 of *All's Well That Ends Well*, discussed earlier.

[18] Hal Gelb attempts to clarify the difference between the earlier plays and *Measure for Measure* when he suggests that the Duke goes wrong because "he is not dealing with folly but with evil" (32).

[19] Admittedly, much that occurs in a Shakespearean recognition scene may be embedded in the subtext; delight and amazement might as likely be the cause of a character's silence at such a moment as bafflement and dismay, and the scene in question is often staged so that both Angelo and Isabella mime their satisfaction with the way events have turned out. But the absence of definitive text here opens the way for the converse interpretation, for which there is, in Shakespeare's plays, some precedent: in *Macbeth*, when Malcolm triumphantly disavows his confessions of vice to Macduff, the latter's silence is not evidence of tacit approval but is explicitly identified as the product of a contradiction between "welcome and unwelcome things at once" (4.3.137–39). See the following discussion in Chapter 5.

3

"O Well-Divided Disposition!":
The Dilemmas of Tragic Love

1

The speaker of Sir Thomas Wyatt's sonnet "They flee from me," lamenting his mistress's "new-fangleness" (line 19)—the modern fashion of sexual promiscuity that encouraged women to "range, / Busily seeking with a continual change" (6–7)[1]— placed himself in a line of male lovers stretching back through two centuries of English and Italian lyric poetry. Espousing the traditional values of constancy and sincerity, they found themselves at the mercy of worldly temptresses who scornfully derided such sentiments as being old-fashioned, irrelevant and even absurd. The lover of Sidney's "With how sad steps, 0 moon, thou climb'st the skies!" elaborates this conceit by comparing heavenly love to earthly:

> Then, ev'n of fellowship, O moon, tell me,
>> Is constant love deemed there but want of wit?
>> Are beauties there as proud as here they be?
> Do they above love to be loved, and yet
>> Those lovers scorn whom that love doth possess?
>> Do they call virtue there ungratefulness? (9–14)

It is as though lovers and their mistresses had come to inhabit different (though contiguous) worlds. In the well-known companion poems of Christopher Marlowe and Sir Walter Ralegh, "The Passionate Shepherd to his Love" and "The Nymph's Reply to the Shepherd," the swain and his beloved speak to each other across the gulf that separates the shepherd's conventionally pastoral realm, that timeless landscape of "valleys, groves, hills, and fields" (3) whose delights are those of "May morning" (22), from the nymph's time-bound world, where, she points out, the simple pleasures of nature "Soon break, soon wither" (15). What is striking about these disillusioned ladies is the self-absorption, the sophistication, and in particular the intellectuality implicit in their approach to love. They are apt to offer assessments of passion's faulty logic: to Ralegh's nymph, romantic ardor seems "in folly ripe, in reason rotten" (16); to Sidney's sublunary coquettes, constancy is mere "want of wit." These cerebral leanings herald the emergence of the Metaphysical mode, with its ironic perspective, cynical tone and relatively realistic setting—a mode that represented a contrast, even a challenge, to the older Petrarchan tradition. But because for a time the two modes co-existed, the range and variety of the lyric poem at the end of the sixteenth and beginning of the seventeenth century in England was remarkable; every form of erotic impulse, from the spontaneously ardent to the coolly calculated, could be expressed and accommodated.

Many of the problems in the "problem comedies" stemmed from a similar conflict of genres: the comic vision, struggling to express itself in its romantic aspect, was repeatedly undercut by an essentially ironic realism. When we turn, as we now shall, to *Othello* and *Antony and Cleopatra*, we shall find the counterpart of this struggle in the sphere of tragedy. The opposition between the two alternative conceptions of love described above produces a characteristic dilemma in these plays: what romance calls "constant love," irony dismisses as "want of wit." But before we turn to the plays themselves, it will be instructive to examine these two conceptions of love singly, insofar as it is possible (given their propensity to call each other into being) to isolate them. We may locate the first of them in the poems of Shakespeare, who, conveniently for us, was the most romantic poet of his age when it suited his purposes to adopt that mode. Thus, if one reads—in whatever order—the sonnets, *The Rape of Lucrece* and *The Phoenix and the Turtle*, one becomes aware of an emergent ideal of romantic love uncompromised by those elements of irony that prolifer-

ate in the poems of his contemporaries and immediate successors. It is an ideal of such fervor and intensity that it may seem
to some modern readers an embarrassment (particularly when
it is love between men that is being idealized). As Sonnet 116
defines it, it is a conception of love as a state of almost
preturnatural constancy:

> Let me not to the marriage of true minds
> Admit impediments; love is not love
> Which alters when it alteration finds,
> Or bends with the remover to remove.
> 0 no, it is an ever-fixed mark
> That looks on tempests and is never shaken;
> It is the star to every wand'ring bark,
> Whose worth's unknown, although his highth be taken.
> Love's not Time's fool, though rosy lips and cheeks
> Within his bending sickle's compass come,
> Love alters not with his brief hours and weeks,
> But bears it out even to the edge of doom.
>   If this be error and upon me proved,
>   I never writ, nor no man ever loved.

The poem, and the conception of love it embodies, may be
considered independently of the sonnets that surround it—at
least, independently of the spurious homosexual/heterosexual
controversy that still obscures the meaning of the sequence as
a whole.[2] Love does not, in this sonnet, take different forms
and varieties depending upon its object; it is a single, discrete
entity, but so rare that it can be defined in the poem only by its
more familiar shadow or imitation, that which passes for love
in the world but is not. If it can be seen to "alter" or "remove"
when it meets with alteration or removal, it exposes its essential falseness. This is an extreme and uncompromising view of
love, to be sure, one that seems almost a guarantee of heart-
break and loneliness; the fate of Dickens's Miss Havisham in
Great Expectations demonstrates its likely results. But the true
lover's compensation for a life of inevitable disappointment is
the state of certitude, the security of personal identity, that love

confers: it is the "mark" or "star" by which the lover can navigate throughout his or her life.

The possibility of achieving such a rapport with another human being is, in Shakespeare's poems, remote. If marriage is only to exist between "true minds," and if by "true" is meant an unblinking constancy to which only death can put an end, the institution of wedlock as it exists in an imperfect world seems an unpromising vehicle for it. Certainly none of the other sonnets makes provision for a marriage of true minds so conceived; where marriage is contemplated in the preceding poems, it is primarily a medium whereby the beauty of a young man may be reproduced for future generations to marvel at. Among all of Shakespeare's lovers, in fact, only one pair merge their individual identities completely:

> Reason, in itself confounded,
> Saw division grow together,
> To themselves yet either neither,
> Simple were so well
>   compounded:
>
> That it cried, "How true a twain
> Seemeth this concordant one!
> Love hath reason, Reason none,
> If what parts, can so remain."
> (*The Phoenix and the Turtle* 41–48)

Romeo and Juliet never quite reach this state of perfect union; neither do Rosalind and Orlando, Beatrice and Benedick, Antony and Cleopatra or Viola and Orsino. For one thing, the personalities of even the most ardent lovers in the plays remain too distinct for the requisite submersion of selfhood to occur, though admittedly this is less true in the late romances than in the early plays; Ferdinand and Miranda come about as close as human lovers might to resembling the concordant twain of the poem. Particularly where a love-heroine has wit (and the wit of Portia, Viola and Rosalind has distinct affinities with that of Ralegh's cynical nymph), love cannot hope to confound reason, but must co-exist with it. Requited love in its purest form—that unworldly, almost unrealizable ideal defined by "the marriage of true minds" and embodied in the union of the phoenix and the turtle—is a relatively rare occurrence in Shakespeare compared to examples of unrequited love, which are far more numerous and obvious. The normative state of the true lover is closer to that described in those sonnets in which the speaker maintains that though he is played false by the object of his love, his love itself will remain constant to the point where it is destructive of his self-interest: "Such is my love, to thee I so belong, / That for thy right myself will bear all wrong" (13–14) concludes the lover in Sonnet 88, and again, in 92, "Thou canst not vex me with inconstant mind, / Since that my life on thy revolt doth lie . . ." (9–10).

Such is the romantic ideal of love in Shakespeare. But that is not the only mode of love that he could conceive; Northrop Frye calls the sonnets "a poetic realization of the whole range of love in the Western world, from the idealism of Petrarch to the ironic frustrations of Proust" (*Fables* 106). Those frustrations inform some of the best, and best-known, of Shakespeare's poems, and it would be both possible and convenient to illustrate the ironic conception of love that is diametrically opposed to the one we have been discussing by referring to, say, Sonnet 129 ("Th' expense of spirit in a waste of shame"), a poem of characteristically Jacobean self-disgust, or in Sonnet 138 ("When my love swears that she is made of truth"), which is as witty, intellectually playful, and emotionally detached as any Metaphysical lyric. Instead, however, let us return to Donne, whose "Songs and Sonnets" are recognized by most readers as the authoritative voice of amatory disillusionment at the beginning of the seventeenth century. "Go and catch a falling star" is representative:

> . . . Ride ten thousand days and nights
>   Till age snow white hairs on thee;
> Thou, when thou returns't, will tell me
> All strange wonders that befellthee,
>   And swear
>   Nowhere
> Lives a woman true, and fair. (12–18)

This is of course an ancient and traditional complaint, a potential dilemma of love, as the Wife of Bath's bridegroom discovered when forced to choose between a foul but true wife and a false but fair one. But Donne adapts conventional plaints like this one to his own modern purposes, turning it inside out in "Woman's Constancy," whose speaker postulates an amazing series of increasingly tortured but ingenious excuses by which his mistress might justify breaking her newly-made oaths to him. And lest we should imagine this lover to be merely a cleverer version of the constant gallant who inhabits the lyrics of Wyatt, Sidney and Shakespeare, bemoaning his outcast state even before he occupies it, the last quatrain sets us straight:

> Vain lunatic, against these 'scapes I could
>   Dispute and conquer, if I would,
>   Which I abstain to do,
> For by tomorrow I may think so too.
>   (14–17)

Thus is the ideal of constancy eroded into a mere conceit, a joke at its own expense. The emotional conviction of Sonnet 116 seems in comparison to the "new-fangleness" of Donne's lovers a bit archaic. If inconstancy is the ruling fashion of the day, true love is not only rare but aberrant, a virtual bar to courtship: "I can love any, so she be not true" (9), exclaims the impatient lover of "The Indifferent." To be sure, the lover and the poet are not the same man; the rhetorical question that follows—"Will no other vice content you? / Will it not serve your turn to do as did your mothers?" (10–11)—suggests, by the extremity of his bitterness, that Donne may be satirizing the cynicism of his *persona* as well as speaking through it. But the voice of that *persona* is an appropriate vehicle for satire because it speaks in a recognizable accent of the times, expressing the age's quest for "love's sweetest part, variety" (19) and its concomitant mystification (mingled with contempt) at those surviving relics of a bygone age, "some two or three / Poor

heretics in love . . . / Which think to 'stablish dangerous
constancy" (23–25).

It might be assumed that the fashion of inconstancy and
sexual experimentation in these poems was merely a literary
convention, not a reflection of actual social practices, but
apparently, the poems had some significant basis in fact.
Lawrence Stone tells us that female promiscuity among the
aristocracy had become a matter of serious concern by the end
of the sixteenth century:

> Although it was only under the rule of the tolerant (and homosexual)
> James I that the sexual morality of the court reached its nadir and
> became a public scandal, the situation had evidently been deteriorating
> in the latter years of Queen Elizabeth, despite her anxiety to prevent
> her entourage from enjoying those sexual pleasures which she had
> deliberately denied herself. As early as 1603 Lady Anne Clifford
> reported that "all the ladies about the court had gotten such ill names
> that it was grown a scandalous place." . . . Ben Jonson summed up the
> moral tone of the court when he remarked, "'tis there civility to be a
> whore." (504)

The reference to Jonson is particularly apt. If the emotional
ambience of Shakespeare's sonnets prefigures that of his romantic comedies, the dramatic equivalents of Donne's love
lyrics are the realistic "city comedies" of Jonson, Marston and
Middleton, in which recognizable London types—courtesans,
shopkeepers, cutpurses and impoverished gentlemen—practice on each other a variety of sexual and financial gulleries.[3]

Because both Shakespeare's and Donne's lyrics are short,
permitting space for the development of only a single conceit,
the perspective of any given poem tends in most cases to be
unified: either romantic or ironic, but seldom a mixture of the
two. In a more lengthy narrative poem such as *The Rape of
Lucrece,* however, Shakespeare gives us an intimation of what
we can expect in the mature love-tragedies when romantic
idealism and ironic realism collide.

These qualities are personified, respectively, by the chaste
Lucrece and her unscrupulous ravisher Tarquin. Lucrece is
presented to us as the archetype of the virtuous wife, "a

peerless dame" (21) whose very goodness inflames Tarquin's ardor. In creating her both true and fair, Shakespeare did not entirely rebut Donne's skeptical belief that these qualities were not to be found in the same woman, for in the stanzas devoted to the coexistence of Lucrece's beauty and virtue, they are shown to be antagonistic: they "strived / Which of them both should underprop her fame" (52–53), contending with each other in a "silent war" (71):

> This heraldry in Lucrece' face was seen,
> Argued by beauty's red and virtue's white;
> Of either's color was the other queen,
> Proving from world's minority their right;
> Yet their ambition makes them still to fight,
>   The sovereignty of either being so great
>   That oft they interchange each other's seat. (64–70)

While this paradox does not reflect any division or contention in Lucrece's guileless mind—"She touch'd no unknown baits, nor fear'd no hooks" (103)—it inspires in Tarquin a dilemma: he is "madly toss'd between desire and dread" (171). He debates long with himself before he can overcome his scruples, and then he does so by a sophistical and fallacious process of reasoning by which "what is vile shows like a virtuous deed" (252). As he nears Lucrece's chamber, he is

> Full of foul hope, and full of fond mistrust;
> Both of which, as servitors to the unjust,
> So cross him with their opposite
>   persuasion,
> That now he vows a league, and now
>   invasion. (284–87)

From first to last, dilemma is one of the central motifs of *The Rape of Lucrece*, for Tarquin not only conquers Lucrece's body but in so doing infects her with his state of psychological ambivalence. Before the rape occurs, he poses for her a *dubbio*, not unlike the one presented to Isabella by Angelo: if she will submit tamely, he will allow her to live, and her dishonor may remain a secret; if she struggles, he will kill her and fabricate evidence of adultery between her and a servant. But without waiting for a reply, he impatiently ravishes her and then, in a post-coital change of heart, spares her life. Now the dilemma is hers: she must decide "To live or die which of the twain were better, / When life is sham'd and death reproach's debtor" (1154–55). Lucrece's beauty has betrayed her by attracting Tarquin's attention, but it is her exquisite conscience that completes her ruin. She is aware that a case can be made for her innocence—"Though my gross blood be stain'd with this abuse, / Immaculate and spotless is my mind" (1655–56)—and she is further aware that in purely moral terms, suicide is her "soul's pollution" (1157). But despite these powerful persuasions, with which her husband, her father, and the assembled nobility of Rome agree, she chooses to die by her own hand. The arguments against suicide seem to acquire for her, suddenly and mysteriously, a facile, self-serving quality even as she rehearses them. Both the expression on her face and the objection on her tongue testify, at the moment before her death, to an infusion of almost Metaphysical cynicism:

> . . . with a joyless smile she turns away
> The face, that map which deep impression bears
> Of hard misfortune, carv'd in it with tears.
> "No, no, "quoth she, "no dame hereafter living
> By my excuse shall claim excuse's giving."
> (1711–15)

Both the disclaimer and the smile transport us to the world of Donne, where lovers are always on the lookout for a handy excuse, and where all arguments, particularly those that seem cogent and logically impeccable, are suspect. It may be assumed that the intellectual and emotional counterpart of her physical pollution is a newfound disillusionment, a tendency to think the worst of men and to find confirmation of this misanthropy in the misleading beauty of their outward appearances. As she examines a portrait of Sinon, the Greek who

brought the wooden horse to Troy, she muses on the relationship between surfaces and what underlies them:

> "It cannot be," quoth she, "that so much guile"—
> She would have said, "can lurk in such a look";
> But Tarquin's shape came in her mind the while,
> And from her tongue "can lurk" from "cannot" took:
> "It cannot be" she in that sense forsook,
> And turn'd it thus, "It cannot be, I find,
> But such a face should bear a wicked mind."
>   (1534–40)

And it would seem plausible that this pessimism should
extend itself to include a concomitant self-doubt and self-
loathing, generalized into an indictment of women as well as
men. But there is equal reason to assume that her suicide
represents not so much a way of resolving her dilemma as
simply an escape from having to deal with it; she dies so as not
to have to choose between two alternative views of herself. The
state of being in such a dilemma is intolerable to her, and death
a means of deliverance from "the deep unrest" (1725) in which
her soul finds itself.

At the end of the poem, her suicide is criticized by her father,
her husband, and her husband's friend Brutus, who sees in her
not a romantic martyr but simply "a wretched wife" who
"mistook the matter so, / To slay herself, that should have slain
her foe" (1826–27). The poem ends not with a celebration of
Lucrece's chastity or an appreciation of her moral and emotional dilemma, but with a recital of the narrowly political
consequences of Tarquin's act: his fall from office and subsequent banishment. To read The *Rape of Lucrece* is thus to move
in a direction analogous to the journey from Belmont to Venice:
an action that is personal, timeless and semi-allegorical becomes impersonal, historical and realistic. And such a movement is seen to encompass within it another movement: from
the state of moral certitude and emotional constancy in which
we find Lucrece at the beginning of the poem to the state of

dilemma in which first the subtle Tarquin and later the fallen Lucrece struggle.

Dilemmas, then—both in *The Rape of Lucrece* and in the later love-tragedies—are the price that Shakespeare's tragic lovers pay for inhabiting, or even acknowledging, the fallen world, where it may be doubted that truth is on every shepherd's tongue, and where it is to be assumed that both male and female virtue and beauty are often found separately but never together. Sonnet 116 identifies true love with an emotional certitude that, though it is no guarantee of happiness, "is never shaken." But when love of this sort is subjected to the deforming pressures of "real" or "modern" life, in an atmosphere of urban sophistication whose distinguishing feature is the withering irony of a Donne or a Crashaw, the dilemmas of love begin to appear.

That appearance, however, comes surprisingly late in the Shakespearean canon. With the exception of *The Merchant of Venice*, they do not figure to any significant extent in the early comedies. In *A Midsummer Night's Dream*, for instance, Hermia has no difficulty in distinguishing between Lysander and Demetrius, though to our eyes they must appear almost identical if the joke about love is to work. When her father forces upon her a choice that is potentially a dilemma—marry a man she does not love, or marry no one at all—she chooses death or confinement in a nunnery without the least hesitation. She looks at Lysander with the eyes of love, and though the play is filled with jokes at the expense of lovers' judgment (as when it is grotesquely parodied in the chemically-induced passion of Titania for the ass-eared Bottom), the milieu of Athens is sufficiently connected with the magical woods surrounding it to permit love to flourish. The play's *eiron*, Puck, calls mortal lovers fools, but the lovers never hear this judgment and would not be swayed by it if they did. Those who control the play's two worlds are themselves lovers—Theseus and Hippolyta who rule in Athens, and Oberon and Titania who preside over the supernatural groves. Old Egeus, the

Plautine *senex* who embodies the conventional claims of reality upon romance, cannot argue those claims persuasively since he has at his disposal not wit but only an arbitrary temporal law, which Theseus as arbitrarily suspends at the end of the play.

Nor do the dilemmas of love appear to any important extent in *Romeo and Juliet*. The conditions favorable to their growth do exist there; Verona is a far more familiar, accessible, and mundane place than Athens, Illyria, Belmont or the court of Duke Frederic, and in the persons of the Nurse and Mercutio we have articulate representatives of anti-romantic rationalism. The Nurse's advice to Juliet on the subject of Romeo's banishment is an implicit rebuttal of Sonnet 116's view of love:

> *Jul.* What say'st thou? Hast thou not a word of joy?
>   Some comfort, nurse.
> *Nurse.* Faith, here it is.
>   Romeo is banished, and all the world to nothing
>   That he dares ne'er come back to challenge you;
>   Or if he do, it needs must be by stealth.
>   Then, since the case so stands as now it doth,
>   I think it best you married with the County.
>   O he's a lovely gentleman!
>   Romeo's a dishclout to him. . . . (3.5.211–19)

In other words, "Bend with the remover to remove." But Juliet utterly disregards this worldly and practical advice, and seeks another remedy of the Friar—one more to her liking and in keeping with her temperament, involving as it does a magic potion, a symbolic death and rebirth, and an ultimate reunion with Romeo. Of course the Friar's magic fails, or *Romeo and Juliet* would be known to us not as Shakespeare's first love-tragedy but as the love-comedy that either preceded or followed *A Midsummer Night's Dream*, depending upon its date of attribution. But it fails by the narrowest of margins; for all its realism, its bustling servants, political intrigues, and ridicule of love, Verona is capable of supporting, without much strain to our sense of what is plausible, a narrative of romantic passion.

2

When we move from the Verona of *Romeo and Juliet* to the Venice of *Othello,* we cover a distance far greater than a map of Italy would suggest; in fact, nothing in Shakespeare's earlier work or in contemporary travel literature quite prepares us for it. *Othello's* Venice is neither the carnival-city pictured by Shylock, where capering fools with varnished faces affright the air with their revelings, nor the center of pleasure, commerce and culture, of gorgeous palaces and more gorgeous courtesans, with which English travelers inflamed their countrymen's imaginations.[4] The play gives us no glimpses of Tintoretto at work, no Doge's palazzo or Villa d'Este gleaming above the Grand Canal, certainly no glamorous courtesan in the person of Bianca, who is merely "A huswife that by selling her desires / Buys herself bread and clothes" (4.1.94–95). Rather, it is a city whose *ethos* suggests Padua or even Geneva, a place where law and logic reign, a center of epistemological thought[5] and empirical investigation—a city of questions, as it was in *The Merchant of Venice,* but not the same kinds of questions. Was Desdemona enchanted by Othello? What is the destination of the Turkish fleet? Has Othello cuckolded Iago? Has Cassio? Does Cassio love Desdemona? Who began the brawl between Cassio and Montano? Why did Desdemona marry Othello? Is she honest? What is important here is not the answers to the many questions given explicit and detailed consideration by the characters during the course of the play, but the weight of discussion given over to the *means* of answering them, to the criteria for establishing truths of various sorts, so that even scenes that do not contain trials (and many do) take on the flavor of legal seminars or even philosophical colloquia.

˙Philip McGuire notes that two scenes in particular—1.2 and 1.3—are largely devoted to debates of this sort, first over Brabantio's claim that Othello has bewitched Desdemona and second on the question of the Turkish strategy. Each is a demonstration of men grappling with questions through the formal employment of logic, though with varying success.

Brabantio's conclusions are incorrect because he reasons from a faulty premise regarding Othello's suitability as a lover:

> Damn'd as thou art, thou hast enchanted her,
> For I'll refer me to all things of sense,
> If she in chains of magic were not bound,
> Whether a maid so tender, fair, and happy,
> So opposite to marriage that she shunn'd
> The wealthy curled darlings of our nation,
> Would ever have, t' incur a general mock,
> Run from her guardage to the sooty bosom
> Of such a thing as thou—to fear, not to delight!
> Judge me the world, if 'tis not gross in sense,
> That thou hast practic'd on her with foul
>   charms,
> Abus'd her delicate youth with drugs or
>   minerals
> That weakens motion. I'll have't disputed on,
> 'Tis probable, and palpable to thinking.
>   (1.2.63–76)

Later, before the Duke, Brabantio extends his hypothesis to include not only Desdemona but all women, even "all rules of nature" (1.3.101), which seem, in his view, to prohibit such a match. But the Duke properly rejects his argument by pointing out the fallacy that underlies it:

> To vouch this is no proof,
> Without more wider and more overt test
> Than these thin habits and poor likelihoods
> Of modern seeming do prefer against him.
>   (1.3.106–09)

And Desdemona is sent for, in order that her direct testimony may supply evidence that is more conclusive than the unsupported resort to what is merely "probable."

In the second instance, we have even a clearer view of the Senate "enacting the human ability to discriminate between what seems to be and what is" that McGuire calls the play's "cognitive norm" (200). The first reports of the Turkish galleys are "disproportioned" (1.3.3)—one hundred and seven galleys sighted, one hundred forty, two hundred—yet these inconsistencies are seen, correctly, to be irrelevant:

> 2. *Sen.* . . . though they jump not on a just accompt
> (As in these cases where the aim reports,
> 'Tis oft with difference), yet do they all confirm
> A Turkish fleet, and bearing up to Cyprus
> *Duke.* Nay, it is possible enough to judgment.
> I do not so secure me in the error
> But the main article I do approve
> In fearful sense. (1.3.5–12)

A report that the Turks are making for Rhodes instead of Cyprus is shrewdly discounted by a senator on grounds of improbability: "This cannot be / By no assay of reason; 'tis a pageant / To keep us in false gaze" (1.3.17–19). And so it proves; by weighing "what is possible to judgment" more skillfully and with better sense than Brabantio was able to do, the senators divine the Turkish plan and act to save the interests of Venice. These two examples, McGuire concludes, "affirm that reasoned judgment can accurately know the nature of persons and the meaning of events" (200). And examples drawn from Iago's conversations with Roderigo concerning Desdemona and from his temptation of Othello could be adduced to support the view that "reasoned judgment" is the definitive mental act of Venetians in the play, continually brought to the fore so as to capture our attention.

But to what end? What purpose might there be in setting a tragedy of timeless romantic passion in a late-Renaissance center of logic, argument and inquiry? Part of the answer lies in the fact that Venice is Othello's adopted home, the foreign culture to which he has voluntarily emigrated and to which he attempts to assimilate himself, both by serving the state and by penetrating its social structure in what Brabantio considers a grossly presumptuous manner. Venice is set in opposition, implicitly, with Othello's Moorish homeland, and by extension with the exotic and adventurous life he led before his embrace of Italianate culture. Of Othello's Moorishness, there are several divergent views. In the opinion of Roderigo and Iago, Othello is "an extravagant and wheeling stranger" (1.1.136), "an erring barbarian" (1.3.355–56). Othello himself, naturally, holds a different conception of his origins:

> . . . I fetch my life and being
> From men of royal siege, and my demerits
> May speak, unbonneted, to as proud a fortune
> As this that I have reach'd. . . . (1.2.21–24)

But whether viewed sympathetically or not, Othello's Moorishness is always an issue; we are never permitted to forget that his impulses, assumptions, and modes of thought are not those of a native Venetian.

Robert B. Heilman, in *Magic in the Web*, has made the best case for the view that Othello's tragedy is precipitated by his abandonment of his true roots (which are in magic and romance, not in scientific empiricism) in his attempt to embrace a culture both foreign and inhospitable to him. This attempt makes Othello feel from the start a bit provincial, and his self-justifications are often tinged with apology: " . . . little of this great world can I speak / More than pertains to feats of broils and battle" (1.3.86–87) is a characteristic admission. But, though it is impossible to conceive of him engaging in the sort of frivolous chatter with which Iago tries to entertain Desdemona at the quayside, it is not witty conversation but just those tales of "broils and battle" that attracted her to Othello; he won her, he says, with accounts "of most disastrous chances: / Of moving accidents by flood and field" (1.3.134–35).

It is not until the third act, however, that Othello's Moorish past and character come into conflict with the practical, problem-solving perspective of Venice. This occurs when Iago initiates his temptation, for Iago, who "thinks like a rigorous geometrician" (Spivack 427), is the character who best exemplifies the techniques of rationalism. If there is critical unanimity on any point concerning him, it is here. His motives may be cloudy or even nonexistent, but that his methods are those of the calculator, the logician, the empiricist, there is little doubt;

more than anyone else in the play, he is, as Heilman calls him, "the self-conscious possessor of brain-power" (*Magic* 222).

But for all his familiarity with the tools of intellectual inquiry, Iago is virtually indifferent to truth. He may, in his delvings, superficially resemble the diligently inquisitive senators we looked at earlier, but his investigations have been rightly called by Wylie Sypher "a perversion of scientific curiosity and ingenuity" (*Ethic* 113). He is not so much a rationalist as a parodist of rationality; if he owes allegiance to any established school of thought, it is to philosophical skepticism at its most extreme. Iago deals not with what is but with what might plausibly be maintained; with what is likely, apparent, or arguable:

> I hate the Moor,
> And it is thought abroad that 'twixt my sheets
> H'as done my office. I know not if't be true,
> But I, for mere suspicion in that kind,
> Will do as if for surety. (1.3.387–90)

Truth and possibility are hardly worth differentiating: "That Cassio loves her, I do well believe't; / That she loves him, 'tis apt and of great credit" (2.1.286–87). Though he claims that his suspicions of Emilia "gnaw [his] inwards" (2.1.297), he never makes any attempt to ascertain whether they are justified or not. More an artist than a scientist, he spends much of his time constructing scenarios for Othello and himself, coherent narratives into which the known facts may be comfortably fitted but which are themselves fictions. As with Brabantio, the stuff of Iago's mentality is what is "probable, and palpable to thinking"—hypotheses about human affairs and human nature based upon the arbitrary assumption that the mental processes of men and women are entirely logical and therefore predictable and mechanical, a system of counterpoised pressures and reciprocal forces. Iago draws his pictures of the human mind with a draftsman's compass: "If the beam of our lives had not one scale of reason to poise another of sensuality, the blood and baseness of our natures would conduct us to most prepost'rous conclusions" (1.3.326–29). In the same vein, he exclaims of Cassio, " . . . do but see his vice, / 'Tis to his virtue a just equinox, / The one as long as th' other" (2.3.123–25). It is into this geometric and quantitative system of hypothesis, induction, and plausible but fallacious conclusion that he inducts Othello.

Iago's "minimizing naturalism" (*Magic* 212) is not new to us. It is the voice that speaks to us from Donne's lyrics, here proclaiming, in the reigning fashion both of the play's world and of the audience's, Iago's cynicism, his persistent and nihilistic irony, his fondness for argument that is ingenious and specious in equal proportion. Iago is the Metaphysical consciousness made flesh, and nowhere more recognizably than in the view of love for which he proselytizes throughout the play. Not merely the behavior of Othello and Desdemona but that of minor characters as well supports his thesis that love is infirmity, dotage and folly: Roderigo is a "sick fool . . . / Whom love hath turn'd almost the wrong side out" (2.3.51–52); Bianca's attachment to Cassio is "the strumpet's plague" (4.1.96). His materialistic conception of human nature predictably determines his conception of love as amounting to nothing more than "a lust of the blood and a permission of the will" (1.3.334–35).

And the cynicism that informs this view is, if not embraced by Othello from the start, a by-product of his gradual assimilation of Venetian mores. The romantic intensity of his love for Desdemona comes on occasion to be tempered by irony or undercut by self-conscious embarrassment, as when, after unabashedly proclaiming his love for her when they are reunited in Cyprus, he apologizes for his rhetorical excesses: "I prattle out of fashion, and I dote / In mine own comforts" (2.1.206–07). This excuse is offered to Desdemona, but it is Iago, not she, who regards love as dotage, and who displays for us and for her the witty fashion in which Venetians discuss it in their scene on the quayside, before Othello's arrival. Though Desdemona for the moment tolerates Iago's amusing scurrility, his portrait of women as "Saints in your injuries,

devils being offended, / Players in your huswifery, and hus-
wives in your beds" (2.1.111–12) can hardly correspond to her
own perspective; she explains that she entertains it simply in
order to pass the time and distract herself from fears for
Othello's safety: "I am not merry; but I do beguile / The thing
I am by seeming otherwise" (2.1.122–23). Finally, she dismisses
Iago's wit as a collection of "old fond paradoxes to make fools
laugh i' th' alehouse" (2.1.138–39). There is no reason to doubt,
however, that Iago is voicing a felt conviction, to the extent that
he can be said to hold convictions or to feel anything; at any
rate, his slanders are consistent with everything else he says
about women in the play—of a piece with his suspicions of
Emilia, and of all women, including Desdemona:

> Her eye must be fed; and what delight shall she have to
> look on the devil? When the blood is made dull with the
> act of sport, there should be, again to inflame it, and to
> give satiety a fresh appetite, loveliness in favor, sympa-
> thy in years, manners, and beauties—all which the Moor
> is defective in. Now for want of these requir'd conve-
> niences, her delicate tenderness will find itself abus'd,
> begin to heave the gorge, disrelish and abhor the Moor;
> very nature will instruct her in it and compel her to some
> second choice. (2.1.225–35)

It may be objected here, of course, that he is speaking for
effect, merely attempting to persuade Roderigo of what he
knows to be an unlikely eventuality in order to practice upon
him. But when does Iago not speak for effect? The question of
whether he believes what he says is beside the point, for him
and therefore for us. The view that he expresses of female
depravity is cogent, coherent and consistent; it is what the play
gives us as Iago's view of women. Inconstancy, the burden of
Donne's lyrics, is Iago's text as well—inconstancy as a necessary feature of human appetite is what makes romantic love as
Shakespeare describes it in Sonnet 116 inconceivable for him.
As Spivack notes, " . . . nothing engrosses him so much as the
subject of love or receives from him so mordant a negation. The
marriage of true minds, or, for that matter, any level of love

above sexual appetite, is exactly what he does not believe in" (426).

What Iago offers in its place is, as ought by now to be clear, ironic self-consciousness and a cynical misogyny by which Venice comes to be identified with sophistry, amorality, and reason perverted by wit: Desdemona herself is to Iago "a super-subtle Venetian" (1.3.356) and becomes to Othello later "that cunning whore of Venice" (4.2.89). Iago rails about his native city in just the tones of complaint found in contemporary English sermons : "In Venice they do let God see the pranks / They dare not show their husbands; their best conscience / Is not to leave't undone, but keep't unknown" (3.3.202–04). And in Emilia's tongue-in-cheek justification of adultery we hear the familiar accents of Metaphysical ingenuity:

> *Des.* Beshrew me, if I would do such wrong For the whole world.
> *Emil.* Why, the wrong is but a wrong 'i th' world; and having the world for your labor, 'tis a wrong in your own world, and you might quickly make it right.
>
> (4.3.78–82)

It is one of Emilia's functions in the play to propound that view of women to Desdemona that Iago forces upon Othello: women, she says, have "affections, / Desires for sport, and frailty" (4.3.100–01), and will serve men as men serve them. It is the attitude expressed by the male lover in the song of "Willow" that Desdemona sings: "'If I court moe women, you'll couch with moe men'" (4.3.57). The point, however, is always to contrast Desdemona's own character and practice with these unflattering assumptions; whatever the common understanding of women is in Venice, she has no need of Emilia's sophistries, never deserves the song's condemnations. Desdemona possesses, as Heilman says, "an un-Venetian ignorance of the world" (*Magic* 209) that Othello shares, and it is this very innocence in them that permits Iago to deceive them with such thoroughness and ease.

Othello, who is prepared to see as a shortcoming the fact that he lacks "those soft parts of conversation / That chamberers

have" (3.3.264–65), certainly does not regard his wife at the
start of their marriage as a typical member of a corrupt society,
but is aware of the gulf between his own self-confessed
rudeness and the courtliness of her social milieu. Iago, therefore, has something to work with that is already in Othello,
which may help to explain why Othello so soon abandons faith
as a viable principle of love and as an imperative of his own
conduct. At the first warning against jealousy that Iago gives
him, Othello proclaims himself a man whose reason and pride
compel him to engage in just what Sonnet 116 defines as the
behavior of the false lover—he will bend with the remover to
remove: "I'll see before I doubt; when I doubt, prove; / And on
the proof there is no more but this—/ Away at once with love
or jealousy!" (3.3.190–92).

Here is an Othello who has modelled himself on Iago: a man
of empirical judgment who can by an act of will subdue passion
to reason, whose self-interest is never undermined by the
dotage of love. In accounting for the scope of the influence that
Iago exerts on Othello, scholars have resorted to a variety of
explanations: Iago is the object of an unconscious homosexual
attachment on Othello's part (Hyman 101); Iago represents for
Othello "the shared rudeness of male speech and male knowledge" that he abandoned when he married Desdemona (Rogers 140); Iago draws his power from sources that are more than
human, from wellsprings of allegorical convention that provide
him with a unique advantage over goodness and innocence
(Spivack). There is truth in all these formulations. But it is also
true that Othello is predisposed to view himself as ingenuous
and unsophisticated, and, out of a wish to correct what he
takes to be this defect, assents to what seems to him the
orthodox Venetian doctrine of woman's frailty as preached by
Iago. For all his pride, we have seen that there runs deep in
Othello a current of self-doubt, a recognition that by the
standards of contemporary discourse he is "Rude . . . in
speech" (1.3.81), that his age, his complexion, and his origins
argue against Desdemona's loving him according to "rational"
standards. Even in affirming his faith in her, he discounts his

own worth: "Nor from mine own weak merits will I draw / The smallest fear or doubt of her revolt, / For she had eyes, and chose me" (3.3.187–89). But if she chose him with her eyes, she must soon, as Iago predicts, observe the "daily beauty" of Cassio (5.1.19), for eyes are the organs of sense, of a love that is primarily appetitive. Eyes perceive appearances, and appearances are (notwithstanding the whole theoretical basis of empiricism) invariably false and misleading, according to the conventions of love: destructive "fancy" is bred not in the heart or in the head but "is engend'red in the eyes, / With gazing fed . . ." (*Merchant* 3.2.63–67).

Othello is thus predisposed to look for, and to give, "reasons" for Desdemona's love, reasons that from the start have something weak and unconvincing about them; there is a kind of anticlimax about "She lov'd me for the dangers I had pass'd, / And I lov'd her that she did pity them" (1.3.167–68). If that were really the source of Desdemona's love, it might easily be confused with the sensation-seeking that Brabantio says is foreign to his daughter's nature. In fact, Desdemona gives an account of her love for Othello that makes clear its independence of any such visual stimuli as the "rosy lips and cheeks" that Sonnet 116 numbers among the casualties inflicted by time: "My love doth so approve him," she says, "That even his stubbornness, his checks, his frowns—/ . . . have grace and favor in them" (4.3.19–21). True love is, in *Othello*, what it is in Shakespeare's early love plays. Desdemona's position is almost identical with that of Hermia, Olivia, or Juliet, in that all four women have at their disposal suitors who represent, by the worldly standards of reason and personal advantage, superior alternatives to the men they love. Hermia and Juliet might have kept within the good graces of their fathers had they married Demetrius and Paris, and what is more significant, *our* eyes cannot discover just what makes those worthies inferior to Lysander and Romeo. *Twelfth Night* presents a slightly different situation but a similar conclusion: Orsino shares with Olivia just those qualities of birth, age, and fortune that all the marital handbooks of Shakespeare's time recommend, yet she chooses, for reasons of the heart, a husband who is perhaps younger than she and slightly her social inferior. What makes the case of Desdemona unique is that her choice between Othello and Cassio exists only in the minds of Iago and Othello, not in her own; before she met Othello, she rejected the rich and favored suitors whom she might have chosen with her father's blessing, and after it, is so far from contemplating any sexual alternative to Othello that she finds even the *concept* of adultery improbable.

Alone among the major characters of the play, Othello is gripped by a dilemma, which in the end destroys him and Desdemona. Neither Iago nor Desdemona is so afflicted. Why this should be so is implicit in those several differences among the three characters that we have already discussed, but it may be useful to examine them again in the specific context of dilemmas.

When Desdemona is called upon to testify before the Senate at her husband's trial, Brabantio poses a traditional *dubbio* for her:

> *Bra.*　　　　Come hither, gentle mistress.
> 　Do you perceive in all this noble company
> 　Where most you owe obedience?
> *Des.*　　　　My noble father,
> 　I do perceive here a divided duty:
> 　To you I am bound for life and education;
> 　My life and education both do learn me
> 　How to respect you; you are the lord of duty;
> 　I am hitherto your daughter. But here's my husband;
> 　And so much duty as my mother show'd
> 　To you, preferring you before her father,
> 　So much I challenge that I may profess
> 　Due to the Moor, my lord. (1.3.179–89)

The content of the speech recalls Cordelia's reply to Lear, though its tone, of course, is less irritable and it is more diplomatically phrased. Only Desdemona's tact accounts for the internal conflict suggested by the phrase "a divided duty." In fact, there is no contradiction in her mind between filial and

connubial love; she gives her allegiance entirely to her husband, as her notion of duty demands and as love dictates. The
romantic conception of marital love completely encloses Desdemona (as it does not Othello), and love preserves her, as it
preserves all "true minds," from the agonies of uncertainty.
Love is an absolute here, a state of unity and consistency, and
it does not admit of the dualism implicit in dilemmas.

The state associated with dilemmas throughout the play is
not love but jealousy. In fact, as Iago uses the word, jealousy is
almost a synonym for dilemma: a condition of incertitude, a
double vision of the love object as simultaneously true and
false:

> O, beware, my lord, of jealousy!
> It is the green-ey'd monster which doth mock
> The meat it feeds on. That cuckold lives in bliss
> Who, certain of his fate, loves not his wronger;
> But O, what damned minutes tells he o'er
> Who dotes, yet doubts; suspects, yet strongly loves!
>   (3.3.165–70)

Though he himself claims at least twice during the play to
inhabit such a state, it has been argued persuasively that Iago,
if he does in fact doubt Emilia's honesty, is spared the pangs of
a jealous lover: "He has no emotion other than the pleasure of
his work," asserts Spivack, "because he has no affinity to
anyone or anything that could provoke him to any other
emotion" (31). Iago's position in relation to his wife otherwise
resembles Othello's quite closely, as it seems designed to do: it
is the focus of Iago's plan that he shall be "even'd with him,
wife for wife" (2.1.299), and so he is, killing Emilia just minutes
after Othello has killed Desdemona. But though he may crave
symmetry, he has, as we have seen, none of Othello's need for
certainty, and this alone—his ability to tolerate the state of not
knowing the truth about his wife's supposed relations with
Othello and Cassio (indeed, his virtual indifference to the truth
or falsity of any of his suppositions)—is sufficient to protect
him from experiencing the pangs of jealousy, which is another

way of saying that he is insulated from the possibility of finding himself in a dilemma of love. For Iago is in no sense a lover; he will not "bend with the remover to remove" because there is nothing, not even a "love [that] is not love," for him to remove. He and Desdemona are at opposite reaches from each other in matters of the heart: one is a true lover and the other is not a lover at all. And because their positions are equally extreme, neither is in any danger of being trapped in those middle regions where dilemmas exist.

Othello, however, even before he becomes the victim of Iago's manipulations, is just the stuff of which dilemmas are made. When we hear him exclaim impatiently that "passion, having my best judgment collied, / Assays to lead the way" (2.3.206–07), we recognize, as does Iago, a predisposition to view himself as a battleground for competing psychic influences, coupled with a compulsive desire for certainty in all things. Othello's demand for knowledge, his avidity for getting to the bottom of questions (in this case, the causes of the quarrel between Montano and Cassio), causes him to embrace with fervor the Venetian method of inquiry: problems are to be solved by the application of logical reasoning to empirical data. But in so doing, he turns his back on the mode of judgment that made him choose Desdemona for a wife and Cassio for a lieutenant in the first place, and that is most movingly illustrated by the powerful argument of Desdemona's sleeping kiss: "O balmy breath, that dost almost persuade / Justice to break her sword!" (5.2.16–17), he exclaims. Yet he resists, deafening himself to that persuasion in preference to what he has come to regard as a more substantial kind of evidence, rejecting, as Heilman puts it, "the magical powers of love" (*Magic* 209) in favor of a barren and abstract logic.

Thus Terence Hawkes seems right in the main when he argues, "The gradual poisoning of the intuitive world of Desdemona by the rational world of Iago constitutes the main theme of the play" (107). But we must not think the play so loaded in favor of love's ineffable intuition that the scientific method is to be regarded as worthless. Had Othello more thoroughly assimilated the valid techniques of rational inquiry, he might have been aware of the flaws in his method—in particular, his willingness to regard the weight of evidence as cumulative, so that several incidental facts, each in itself merely suggestive, aggregate for him into an irrefutable case for Desdemona's dishonesty. It is partly Iago's tutelage that encourages him in this error of accumulation; the most insubstantial piece of evidence against Desdemona is Cassio's "dream," which is itself hearsay, and false hearsay at that, but Iago persuades Othello that it "may help to thicken other proofs / That do demonstrate thinly" (3.3.430–31). And having adopted this dangerous principle, Othello loses no time in applying it; Desdemona's handkerchief in Cassio's hand, he says, "speaks against her with the other proofs" (3.3.441). Thus Othello is guilty of what I have been calling, in my discussions of earlier plays, the quantitative fallacy; beginning with *The Merchant of Venice*, would-be lovers who attempt to weigh love by counting and measuring (like Othello's countryman, the Prince of Morocco), are doomed to failure. Even apart from Iago's misdirection, though, jealousy itself is sufficient to make impossible the sort of objective and dispassionate reasoning Othello attempts, for it warps the perceptions and distorts any scale of values. Iago counts on it: "Trifles light as air / Are to the jealous confirmations strong / As proofs of holy writ" (3.3.322–24), he says. And when Desdemona protests that she never gave Othello cause for jealousy, Emilia's reply shows that she shares her husband's view of jealousy's power:

> But jealous souls will not be answer'd so;
> They are not ever jealous for the cause,
> But jealous for they're jealous. It is a
>   monster
> Begot upon itself, born on itself. (3.4.159–62)

So jealousy is a perversion of love and an aberration of the reason; the two opposites come together in it. It is a perversion (perhaps it would be more accurate to call it a travesty) of love because, like love, it is causeless and immune to reason; it is like reason in that its operations are essentially those of mind. It is logic without proportion, induction without common sense, and its conclusion is an abstraction, removed from life, truth, and faith.

The act of thinking in *Othello* is seldom performed without some emotional influence coming into play, and thus potentially introducing a source of interference into the operation of logic; Othello's repeated demands of Iago—"What dost thou think?" (3.3.104), "Show me thy thought" (116), "By heaven, I'll know thy thoughts" (162)—elicit from Iago a valid caution: "Utter my thoughts? Why, say they are vild and false, / As where's that palace whereinto foul things / Sometimes intrude not?" (136–38). Othello's greatest mistake, from an epistemological point of view, is in attempting to separate, to compartmentalize, love and logic; the ambivalence that shadows the act of "thinking" is never more apparent than in Othello's explicit description of his dilemma to Iago:

> By the world,
> I think my wife be honest, and think she is not;
> I think that thou art just, and think thou art not.
> I'll have some proof. (384–86)

Here are two faiths, one true and one false, indistinguishable to the man who holds them because he has mistaken them for theorems. Where Desdemona was able without apparent effort to discriminate between her duty to her father and to her husband, Othello lacks her sense of proportion; he gives equal weight to the claims of his wife and those of a man who, if more than a servant, is less than a friend. His "irritable reaching after fact and reason" (Sypher, *Ethic* 118), his demand for "ocular proof," is born of an understandable but tragic failure to trust the promptings of nature, the instincts of love. If Heilman is correct in saying that he has betrayed those instincts, justice is served, for now they betray him: they tell him that Iago is as loyal to him as Desdemona is. It is a circumstance that Sonnet 116 does not allow for. The sonnets contain a love triangle that superficially resembles Iago-Othello-Desdemona, but nowhere in those poems is the love of a friend and mistress described as mutually exclusive. In this most romantic of all tragedies, Metaphysical cynicism and misogyny align themselves against true love to the point where, with Othello at the fulcrum, they balance exactly.

Othello leaves us with a tidy summation of himself—he is the loyal servant of the Venetian state who "lov'd not wisely but too well" (5.2.344). He overlooks (though we should not) that crucial element in his character, his need for absolutes. Wandering between the security of unquestioning love that is Desdemona's and the faithless pragmatism that is Iago's, Othello searches vainly for certainty throughout the play. Ironically, he boasts on more than one occasion that he has found it:

> Like to the Pontic Sea,
> Whose icy current and compulsive course
> Nev'r feels retiring ebb, but keeps due on
> To the Propontic and the Hellespont,
> Even so my bloody thoughts, with violent pace,
> Shall nev'r look back, nev'r ebb to humble love,
> Till that a capable and wide revenge
> Swallow them up. (3.3.453–60)

Of all his self-delusions, this is the most pitiful; a short while later, after reiterating it—"No, my heart is turn'd to stone; I strike it, and it hurts my hand" (4.1.182–83)—he dissolves in tears: "But yet the pity of it, Iago! O Iago, the pity of it, Iago!" (195–96). More than any other characteristic, his determination never to waver, his need to keep "compulsive course," accounts for the relative ease with which Iago seduces him; what more could Iago ask of his victim than a man whose motto is "To be once in doubt / Is once to be resolv'd" (3.3.179–80)?

Perhaps we should not blame Othello too much for his inability to see through Iago's deceptions; Emilia, who knows Iago better than Othello does, and knows moreover that Desdemona's handkerchief is in his possession, is similarly unable to divine that the "busy and insinuating rogue"

(4.2.131) practicing upon Othello is her husband. Of the failure of his lover's instinct, of his faith, Othello is more culpable, though there, too, some extenuation is possible: it is not so much that his faith in Desdemona wavers as that it is neutralized by the new intellectual perspective that he persuades himself to adopt, whose concrete form is his faith in Iago's skepticism.

Othello's real weakness is that he would rather be certain that Desdemona is untrue than not know what to believe. Othello's dilemma—from the point at which Iago begins his seduction in Act 3 to the point at which Othello rejects the persuasions of Desdemona's beauty in Act 5—causes him anguish so insupportable that he builds of hearsay, conjecture and hypothesis the engine of his own and Desdemona's destruction.

3

No play of Shakespeare's more explicitly or ostentatiously directs our attention toward the dilemmas of its central characters than *Antony and Cleopatra*. The term appears constantly in the critical literature,[6] and where it does not, it is clear that the modern view of Antony, in particular, has incorporated or made use of the concept. He is "humanum genus . . . torn between his desire for worldly power and his love for a queen who insists that it is 'paltry to be Caesar'" (Rose, Introduction 3); he is "caught between what he tells Cleopatra, and in part believes, and what he tells himself about her, and in part believes" (Ornstein, "Ethic" 41); he is "both a weakly vacillating general entrapped by the flesh and a heroic soldier who transcends himself in becoming a lover" (Dorius 314); he is a man compelled "to choose between the opposed values represented by Cleopatra and Octavius or not to choose between them" (Markels 8)—a choice between dilemmas, as it were. Nor is Antony perceived as being alone in his predicament; it is shared by Enobarbus, Cleopatra, Octavia (who fails Antony out of a "statuesque hesitation between heart and tongue"

[Markels 34]) and, inevitably, the audience itself, required "simultaneously to believe and disbelieve" what it sees of Antony (Adelman 28).

These dilemmas of character, in the modern critical tradition, have their foundation in the emotional, cultural, and moral alternatives of Rome and Egypt. If Antony is torn between Caesar and Cleopatra, goes the argument, it is because Caesar and Cleopatra are linked with those settings. And indeed, the settings have been so conceived as to represent polar opposites in the manner of Venice and Belmont in *The Merchant of Venice*. Rome is the city where judgment, reason and calculation reign, Alexandria the home of passion and intuition. Rome is the immutable, unyielding place whose imagery associates it with rock and earth, in distinction to aqueous Egypt, where things "discandy" (4.12.22). Rome is masculine and Egypt feminine but, these generative possibilities notwithstanding, Rome is sterile while Egypt is fertile beyond all measure. Above all, Rome is seen as the sphere of public life, of duty, self-denial and ceremony; Egypt, the private sphere, is associated with pleasure, impulse, and self-indulgence. If Antony must choose between these two systems of value and belief, "held in tenuous balance because they are presented as having equally compelling merit," it is no wonder that William Rosen sees Antony's analogue not in his patron Hercules but in Odysseus, "who, in his seventeenth year on Calypso's island, was so torn between the equally powerful demands of judgment and passion that he could not remain on the island, yet could not depart homeward" (125).

But in recording these multitudes of oppositions, dualities and paradoxes, few of the commentators cited have made much of the fact that the fundamental dilemma of the play cuts across the public-private axis as if it did not exist.[7] It appears both in Rome and Egypt; it afflicts lovers and politicians alike, because it is deeply rooted in the human psyche, at a point below the differentiations of individual temperaments. We first hear of it in Antony's meditation on the death of Fulvia:

Thus did I desire it.
What our contempts doth often hurl from us,
We wish it ours again. The present pleasure,
By revolution low'ring, does become
The opposite of itself. She's good, being gone. . . .[8]

(1.2.122–26)

This "pattern of the presence known too late" (Adelman 48) we might call the Dilemma of Necessary Alienation: attraction diminishes with proximity and increases with distance, temporal and spatial, so that human beings, by an inevitable, cyclical process that is part of their nature, love those whom they lack and weary of those whom they possess. And this principle applies equally to the specific case and to the general: Antony deduces from his own condition that of "Our slippery people, / Whose love is never link'd to the deserver / Till his deserts are past" (1.2.185–87). In Rome, Caesar says almost the same thing when he tries to account for the resurgence of Pompey's popularity:

It hath been taught us from the primal state
That he which is was wish'd, until he were;
And the ebb'd man, ne'er loved till ne'er worth love,
Comes dear'd by being lack'd. (1.4.41–44)

Paradoxically, though with equal perversity, men may love those whom it is in their interest to love: " . . . the hated, grown to strength, / Are newly grown to love" (1.3.48–49) remarks Antony of Pompey. But the result, as with all dilemmas, is stasis, whether it is in a political context or an erotic one, the similarity brought home by the almost identical imagery used to describe two such situations—first, when Caesar stigmatizes the populace as being "Like to a vagabond flag upon the stream, / [which] Goes to and back, lackeying the varying tide, / To rot itself with motion" (1.4.45–47), and next when Antony speaks of the divided loyalty of Octavia, torn between husband and brother, who is thus become like "the swan's down feather, / That stands upon the swell at the full of tide, / And neither way inclines" (3.2.48–50).

This psychological mechanism comes into play not only in Antony's relations with Fulvia but in his relations with Caesar as well. Presumably, it underlies Enobarbus's accurate prediction regarding the new alliance forged in Act 2: "that which is the strength of their amity shall prove the immediate author of their variance" (2.6.128–30). Love and loathing are reciprocal, and may be expected to alternate with each other at regular intervals. This almost invariable condition of human nature, though it does not call into question the existence of those many antitheses recorded earlier, does undercut the importance of the polarity of Rome and Egypt as a means of coming to terms with character in the play. We cannot isolate Antony's private passions from his feelings of duty and honor; we cannot bisect him into a Roman and an Egyptian component (though both Cleopatra and Enobarbus do this on occasion), nor can we isolate his own mental processes from those of the other characters. Men will be men, whether choosing leaders or lovers. To formulate Antony's dilemma as a simple choice between the values of two cultures fails to take this basic human trait into account.

The temptation to apply the principle inherent in "she's good, being gone" to Antony's treatment of Cleopatra is hard to resist, particularly as his peregrinations during the first half of the play seem to invite this interpretation; in Alexandria, at the start of the play, a "Roman thought" strikes Antony: "These strong Egyptian fetters I must break, / Or lose myself in dotage" (1.2.116–17), he exclaims, and immediately makes sail, but once in Rome, his first speech to his second wife—"The world and my great office will sometimes / Divide me from your bosom" (2.3.1–2)—lays the groundwork for his departure, and shortly we hear a new resolve that contradicts the original one: "I will to Egypt; / And though I make this marriage for my peace, / I' th' East my pleasure lies" (39–41). "Dotage" is transformed into "pleasure" by the width of the Mediterranean, it would seem, and many critics, whether they have connected it with Antony's posthumous devotion to Fulvia or with Rome's new devotion to Pompey, see in Antony's love for

Cleopatra little more than "a constant and vehement oscillation, an unbroken to-and-fro between positive and negative" (Holloway 69), expressed in the vicious circle of his leavetakings and returnings.

But for Antony, Cleopatra is more than another Fulvia. It is certainly true that, like Fulvia, "she's good, being gone," but the converse is manifestly false. It is Cleopatra's particular genius that familiarity with her breeds not contempt but the desire for greater familiarity: "Other women cloy / The appetites they feed, but she makes hungry / Where most she satisfies" (2.2.235–37). In this special way, at least, they are perfectly matched—the woman who quickens appetite by feeding it and the man whose "bounty . . . grew the more by reaping" (5.2.86–88). It is true that he leaves her, and more often determines to leave her, when he momentarily takes a Roman view of her and himself, and sees not a "famous pair" but an aging witch and an old dotard. But even in those moments of negation, amidst his exasperation and even anger at Cleopatra, there is never a hint of satiety and weariness. The defects of her character, which might make any other woman "cloy," are part of what Enobarbus calls "Her infinite variety" (2.2.235); she is Antony's "wrangling queen! / Whom everything becomes—to chide, to laugh, / To weep" (1.1.48–50). Antony ponders, leaves, returns; at times he loves Cleopatra more, or more intensely, than at other times. But he never ceases to love her, nor does he, like the Antony of Dryden's version of the play, love anyone else.

It is not obvious how Rome, through its personification in Caesar, can exert sufficient force upon Antony to balance the attraction Cleopatra holds for him. It is usually thought that his love for her is counterpoised by a set of feelings that make up the opposite of love—his sense of public duty doing battle with his passion, his Roman conception of manliness (which identifies his earlier greatness with his capacity to deny his appetites) reasserting itself against his newly-acquired Egyptian fondness for self-indulgence, the commander who ate berries and tree bark with his soldiers sporadically disavowing the libertine who now breakfasts on eight boars roasted whole. But, though attractive, it is a misleading assumption that such an opposition is what runs the play. As we have seen, there is a single dynamic operating in both public and private life whereby "The present pleasure, / By revolution low'ring, does become / The opposite of itself" (1.2.124–26). Cleopatra may be outside this principle of human perversity, but since it applies in other cases—Antony's marriages to Octavia and Fulvia, for example, and Rome's fickleness with regard to Pompey the Great and his son—we ought to be examining not Antony's sense of duty or his Roman heritage but instead his personal relationships with Octavius and Cleopatra if we wish to discover what it is that summons him periodically from the latter to the former.

What we discover is not the expected oppositions and contrasts but a surprising similarity.[9] Consider the following description of what awaits Antony in the coming war with Caesar:

> *Ant.* Say to me, whose fortunes shall rise higher,
>   Caesar's or mine?
> *Sooth.* Caesar's.
>   Therefore, O Antony, stay not by his side.
>   Thy daemon, that thy spirit which keeps thee, is
>   Noble, courageous, high unmatchable,
>   Where Caesar's is not; but near him, thy angel
>   Becomes a fear, as being o'erpow'r'd: therefore
>   Make space enough between you.
>   . . .
>   If thou dost play with him at any game,
>   Thou art sure to lose; and of that natural luck,
>   He beats thee 'gainst the odds. (2.3.16–28)

Since Cleopatra's hold over Antony is of precisely the same kind, we may say that the peculiar dilemma of Rome's greatest hero is to live out his fate situated between the only two mortals in the world who can consistently get the better of him. His defeat at Actium is as much the result of Cleopatra's actions as of Caesar's; further, their effect on Antony is identical, as Enobarbus knows. Fearing Cleopatra's influence, he tells her, "Your presence needs must puzzle Antony" (3.7.10), and so it does. When she flees, Antony, "The noble ruin of her magic" (3.10.18), follows. When she reproves him for doing so, his answer calls to mind the Soothsayer's warning concerning the advantage enjoyed by Caesar: "O'er my spirit / Thy full supremacy thou knew'st. . ." (3.11.58–59).[10]

The mechanics of Antony's subjugation to Octavius are not made as explicit as in the case of Cleopatra's power over him; the Soothsayer only suggests that the law of averages ceases to apply to games of chance played between them, and that Antony's innate superiority is not enough to overcome the odds against him. In the case of Cleopatra, whose "infinite variety" Enobarbus credits as the source of her hold over Antony, we see that it consists in part of a studied unpredictability, a conscious refusal to bend to Antony's will or expectation. This tactic informs her instructions to her handmaid:

> See where he is, who's with him, what he does.
> I did not send you. If you find him sad,
> Say I am dancing; if in mirth, report
> That I am sudden sick. (1.3.2–5)

She treats him similarly in the next scene when Antony announces to her the death of Fulvia. The dilemma Cleopatra forces upon him here is a microcosm of his predicaments throughout the play: should he weep for Fulvia, he would invite reproach for not loving Cleopatra, but when he does not weep for her, Cleopatra can reproach him all the same: "Now I see, I see, / In Fulvia's death, how mine received shall be" (1.3.64–65). Since daily life with Cleopatra is a continuing dilemma for Antony, it is not surprising that she should describe him as a man of two minds:

> *Cleo.* What, was he sad, or merry?
> *Alex.* Like to the time o' th' year between the extremes
>   Of hot and cold, he was nor sad nor merry.

Cleo. O well-divided disposition! Note him,
　　Note him, good Charmian, 'tis the man; but note him:
　　He was not sad, for he would shine on those
　　That make their looks by his; he was not merry,
　　Which seem'd to tell him his remembrance lay
　　In Egypt with his joy; but between both.
　　O heavenly mingle! Be'st thou sad or merry,
　　The violence of either thee becomes,
　　So does it no man's else. (1.5.50–61)

Whether purposely or not, she has misunderstood Alexas's report. If Antony were sad and merry at once, perhaps we could call his disposition "well-divided," though Antony himself might regard such a state as resembling his plight after Actium, when he accuses his hairs of mutiny, "for the white / Reprove the brown for rashness, and they them / For fear and doting" (3.11.13–15). But in fact, Antony is indeed, at their first parting, "nor sad nor merry;" he is reduced to a state where ambivalent emotions thwart and cancel each other. The great attraction Cleopatra holds for Antony is the paradox of her character: she makes hungry where most she satisfies. But when the contradictions of this paradox present him with a dilemma, no unified response is possible for him because what he is being asked to respond to is itself contradictory and antithetical. Sadness and merriment have neutralized each other in Antony, and this foreshadows the Antony we next see in Rome, steeped in "a Lethe'd dullness" (2.1.27). Adelman has a point when she suggests that the only way out of Antony's predicament is drink (21), except that stupefaction is not an escape from dilemma, but merely an alcoholic counterpart of the dilemma-state itself.

All of Antony's dilemmas, then, may be viewed as personal ones, for his relationships with both Cleopatra and Caesar are presented to us in personal terms. Moreover, in one respect at least, Cleopatra and Caesar involve Antony in the same dilemma, for, as we have said, Antony binds himself most strongly to those with whom he cannot successfully compete. The source of Caesar's hold over Antony is not the same as Cleopatra's—Caesar, largely because his temperament is proof against emotional distraction, is able to concentrate his energies more effectively, while the same cannot be said of Cleopatra—but their effect on Antony is almost identical. Cleopatra instructing her diver to place a salt fish on Antony's hook, turning the news of Fulvia's death to her own advantage, putting her tires and mantles on him while she filches his sword, all find their counterparts in Caesar's irresistible challenge to fight at sea and his scornful refusal to meet Antony in single combat. Antony's fate may thus be said to be the product of two inescapable facts: it is not in his nature to ignore the provocations and challenges of Caesar and Cleopatra, and it is not in his power to overcome them.

Caesar's singlemindedness, coupled with the coldness of his humour, immunizes him against the distractions of love. In this, he is alone among the play's major characters; Antony, Cleopatra, Enobarbus and Octavia all face love's dilemmas in one form or another—and the forms are several, for love in this play is more various than in any other work of Shakespeare's. This is perhaps inevitable, given the worldliness of the protagonists; their maturity and experience, though hardly precluding "romantic love" between them, preclude a love that is solely or uniformly romantic. D. J. Enright complains

> that critics are always pressing toward extremes, so that one party sees the essence of romantic love where the other sees falsehood, rhetoric, strain. . . . The implication of the objections brought by some critics is that there is only one sort of love possible between man and woman, and this is the sort we witness in the case of Romeo and Juliet. (74)

What sort of love is it, in particular, that we find in *Romeo and Juliet*? The Friar describes for us, in typically Elizabethan terms, the passions of lovers whose defining characteristic is their youth:

> These violent delights have violent ends,
> And in their triumph die, like fire and powder,
> Which as they kiss consume. The sweetest honey
> Is loathsome in his own deliciousness,
> And in the taste confounds the appetite.
>
> (2.6.9–13)

The "fire and powder" of *Romeo and Juliet* is not absent from *Antony and Cleopatra*, and, indeed, we have already heard from Enobarbus that Cleopatra's deliciousness does not confound the appetite: "she makes hungry / Where most she satisfies." But the multiple perspectives from which love is seen here are nothing like the earlier play's unified view. That is why critics so inclined (like Robert Ornstein and, more recently, Jonathan Dollimore) have been able to find support for readings that dwell upon the lovers' shortcomings, particularly Antony's. Ornstein points out the strained hyperbole of Antony's early declarations of passion (notably the speech beginning "Let Rome in Tiber melt" [1.1.33ff]), his several references to Cleopatra as mere "pleasure" or "sport," and the fact that when they are apart, though her every thought and speech concern him, Antony never mentions her name and is irritated when others do (41). It is possible to make a case for the view that Cleopatra loves Antony more than he loves her simply by noting his many public disavowals of her when they are apart (as when in Rome he speaks of the "poisoned hours" [2.2.90] that bound him from his duty) and contrasting them with Cleopatra's preoccupation with him during his absences. Indeed, Antony's inner conflict is far more apparent, for he is in Caesar's grip as well as hers. But there are moments when she, too, appears to waver: "Let him for ever go—let him not, Charmian—/ Though he be painted one way like a Gorgon, / The other way 's a Mars" (2.5.115–17). And later, her wavering becomes the central issue of the play. The possibility (impossible to be certain of) that Antony is correct when he charges that her fleet has deserted at the second battle of Actium because she has struck a bargain with Caesar, Seleucus's contention that she has reserved half her fortune for her own use even as she claims to be preparing for suicide, and her careful inquiries into Caesar's plans for her all suggest that she is still debating her future course of action and might decide to outlive Antony by more than a few hours.

It is easy, then, to indict these lovers if we set for them standards derived from *Romeo and Juliet,* from "Let me not to the marriage of true minds . . ." or from *The Art of Courtly Love.* But audiences are not bound to apply such standards. The love of Antony and Cleopatra seems a shared experience both in its sublimity and in its departures from sublimity. Antony's passion for Cleopatra is by turns heroic ("the nobleness of life / Is to do thus" [1.1.36–37]), mundane ("What sport to-night?" [47]) and, in Caesar's view, casual ("Let's grant it is not /Amiss to tumble on the bed of Ptolemy" [1.4.16–17]); Cleopatra's love for Antony ranges from the bawdy ("O happy horse, to bear the weight of Antony!" [1.5.21]) to the connubial ("Husband, I come!" [5.2.287]), to the transcendent (" . . . if there be, nor ever were one such, / It's past the size of dreaming" [5.2.98–99]). The standards by which we judge a love so various and mutable must be derived not from a single external source but from the internal evidence, of many kinds, that the play presents to us.

One such standard is provided by the behavior of Enobarbus and Octavia, whose failure to resolve their own love-dilemmas sets a norm that both Antony and Cleopatra far surpass. An important function of Octavia's in the play is to act as Cleopatra's foil in this respect—to embody a potential alternative, but one in which Shakespeare's Antony, unlike Dryden's, has no interest. Antony has no difficulty in choosing between connubial and illicit love, for, if Enobarbus is correct, it is precisely Octavia's wifely virtues that make her deficient in his eyes:

> *Eno.* . . . Octavia is of a holy, cold, and still
> conversation.
> *Men.* Who would not have his wife so?
> *Eno.* Not he that himself is not so; which is Mark
> Antony. He will to his Egyptian dish again. Then
> shall the sighs of Octavia blow the fire up in
> Caesar. . . . (2.6.122–27)

And so it proves. The necessity of Cleopatra's ingenuity is dramatized for us by the failure of Octavia's ingenuousness; her pliancy and obedience hold no attraction for Antony. Her

virtues are not presented in such a way as to justify her conduct
or damn Antony's when his inevitable departure occurs, for,
submissive as she is, her allegiance is divided at the start
between her husband and her brother. We need only remember Desdemona's speech on her divided duty to be aware of
Octavia's shortcomings here: in Julian Markels's words, "she
exhibits a legalistic Roman impersonality just when it most
behooves her as a wife to show a bit of Egyptian warmth" (34).
Her farewell to her brother has as much feeling in it as anything
she says to Antony—as Antony notes when he compares her to
the feather on the tide, which "neither way inclines."

The dilemma that afflicts Octavia when the eventual fall-
ing-out occurs between her brother and her husband is predictable:

> *Oct.*   A more unhappy lady,
> If this division chance, ne'er stood between,
> Praying for both parts.
> The good gods will mock me presently
> When I shall pray, "O bless my lord and husband!"
> Undo that prayer by crying out as loud,
> "O, bless my brother!" Husband win, win brother,
> Prays, and destroys the prayer, no midway
> 'Twixt these extremes at all. (3.4.12–20)

Octavia will have to choose—something Desdemona never
considered doing; she will have to alter when she alteration
finds. The perfection of her dilemma testifies to the imperfection of her marital bond: she owes obedience to Antony
because she is his wife, and she is his wife because she owes
obedience to her brother.

Antony's advice to her is to solve her dilemma not by
emotional but by intellectual means:

> When it appears to you where this begins,
> Turn your displeasure that way, for our faults
> Can never be so equal that your love
> Can equally move with them. (33–36)

Such a solution is not practical, however. It is as difficult for Octavia as it is for us to determine the justice of the quarrel, but that is beside the point; when did true love move with the deservings or faults of the loved one? Antony's advice only points up the futility of Octavia's position, which is as much due to her own shortcomings as to Antony's.

The situation of Enobarbus is both more interesting and more complicated. He too is an analogue of Cleopatra; it is the depth of his commitment to Antony, the composition of his loyalty and its relation to competing loyalties, that is being measured. In Octavia's case, the commitment was largely formal; in Enobarbus's case, it is far deeper. Throughout the play, two qualities, which distinguish him from many of the other Romans, have been notable in him: his impatience with the hypocrisies of political maneuvering and his superior understanding of the life of sensuous fulfillment. What is interesting is that these qualities pull against each other, the first displayed by the satirical sensibility we hear in his comment on Antony's first meeting with Caesar—" . . . if you borrow one another's love for the instant, you may, when you hear no more words of Pompey, return it again" (2.2.103–05)—and the second revealing the romantic imagination that produces the great description of Cleopatra at Cydnus. Two systems of belief, two perspectives, two rhetorics clash in Enobarbus as he observes what appears to him "A diminution in our captain's brain" (3.13.197). Cleopatra's favors to Thidias provide Enobarbus with what he takes to be a precedent for leaving Antony—"Thy dearest quit thee" (65)—but the image preceding this conclusion contains a clear though implicit self-indictment: "Sir, sir, thou art so leaky / That we must leave thee to thy sinking" (63–64) tells us that Enobarbus equates himself with vermin.

Opposed to his conception of limited Roman self-interest is more than pure sentiment: Enobarbus loves Antony, but in addition owes him loyalty. It is possible to argue, he knows, that "The loyalty well held to fools does make / Our faith mere folly" (42–43), but he also knows that such an objection can easily be countered by a shift of perspective:

> . . . yet he that can endure
> To follow with allegiance a fall'n lord
> Does conquer him that did his master conquer,
> And earns a place i' th' story. (43–46)

There will be more to say later of "the story," a preoccupation shared by Antony, Cleopatra and Caesar. For the moment, it is sufficient to point out the multiplicity of voices debating within Enobarbus's mind as the ironic and the romantic, the rational and the emotional, struggle for mastery of his will. The most compelling argument is finally the practical one, which induces Enobarbus to desert Antony, and that fact is itself a comment on the status of practicality in the play, for Enobarbus's decision to leave Antony is the wrong one, and proves fatal to him.

In a play in which love seems so often studied, so often compromised, so easily diluted by self-interest or self-absorption, perhaps the single most spontaneous gesture is the death of Enobarbus. Even, or especially, is this so when it is weighed against the suicides of Antony and of Cleopatra, neither of which is achieved, like Enobarbus's demise, by "swift thought" (4.6.34) alone. When this Roman soldier succumbs to a broken heart, all the conventions of romance testify to the intensity of his love for Antony, and that is why the fact of his desertion does not contradict our final impression of an attachment as genuine and powerful as any in the play. It is the misfortune of Enobarbus's life that he comes to appreciate the depth and constancy of his love for his commander too late to save him from his error.

Surely, then, both Enobarbus's and Octavia's failures to resolve their dilemmas successfully—Octavia because she cannot choose, Enobarbus because he chooses wrongly—offer a comment on the attempts of *Antony and Cleopatra* to resolve theirs, illustrating for us the twin perils of inaction and misguided action. Enobarbus teaches us, by his mistake, what the right course must be for them, and he shows us that the infinite variety of love cannot be rejected by an act of will, simply because it is marked by a quality that makes it unusual or difficult to recognize. That quality, which more than any other differentiates love in Antony and Cleopatra from its counterparts among the earlier love-plays, is its self-consciousness. Enobarbus's temptation to "follow with allegiance a fall'n lord" in order to "earn a place i' th' story" is a recognition of the historical dimension of the action in which he plays a role. So inevitable is it that posterity will record the doings of all concerned that anonymity is not even to be thought of; Enobarbus is moved, at the moment of his death, to provide his survivors with his own epitaph:

> O Antony,
> Nobler than my revolt is infamous,
> Forgive me in thine own particular,
> But let the world rank me in register
> A master-leaver and a fugitive. (4.9.18–22)

Nowhere is the inverse relationship between public and private life in this play made more evident than in the tension between the personal meaning of this event and its larger dimension— between Enobarbus's hope of forgiveness by Antony and his certainty of a shameful reputation in the eyes of the world.

This conception of the world as a "register" pervades Antony's thought as well, as we see quite early in the play. It is "the nobleness of life" for him and Cleopatra to embrace publicly, he proclaims,

> when such a mutual pair
> And such a twain can do't, in which I bind,
> On pain of punishment, the world to weet
> We stand up peerless. (1.1.37–40)

Many critics have commented upon Antony's self-consciousness. Richard L. Nochimson has argued that "his primary concern is with his image and his self-image" (106), and even Paul A. Cantor, who sees in Antony an embodiment of the new spirit of Imperial Rome, which fostered an interest in private lives and private satisfactions at the expense of the traditional Republican emphasis on public life and duty, admits that "one cannot conceive of Antony and Cleopatra restricted to private lives and still retaining their identities" (150). Antony's consciousness of his "remembrance" prevents him at times from acting upon any unconsidered impulse, or even upon rational considerations of the moment, forcing him to stage-manage his life from the perspective of posterity. And there is more here than his awareness of public scrutiny; the whole justification of his and Cleopatra's conduct rests upon the world's acknowledging that, when ranked with other famous lovers, they are without equal. But if public opinion is part of the foundation on which their love rests, it may be subversive as well. Antony knows that a significant portion of the world thinks them ignoble, as he admits to a messenger from Rome:

> Speak to me home, mince not the general
> tongue;
> Name Cleopatra as she is call'd in Rome.
> Rail thou in Fulvia's phrase, and taunt my faults
> With such full license as both truth and malice
> Have power to utter. (1.2.105–09)

"Both truth and malice"—for the moment, in Antony's view, they are interchangeable, but when, as often happens, they are at odds, the question of which takes precedence is much on his mind. On more than one occasion we find him living for posterity almost in defiance of his present interests and inclinations, as when he says of his enemy Pompey, who has "laid strange courtesies" upon him, "I must thank him only, / Lest my remembrance suffer ill report; / At heel of that, defy him" (2.2.155–57). Throughout the play, Antony's consciousness of living in the eye of public opinion and of future history leads him to express his emotions in terms of others' views of him. "I have offended reputation, / A most unnoble swerving" (3.11.48–49) he frets after Actium, but soon he reassures himself and Cleopatra: "I and my sword will earn our chronicle. / There's hope in't yet" (3.13.175–76).

Antony's "remembrance"—the judgments of future generations, shaped by the various histories and biographies that will be produced after his death—is a silent but tangible presence in the play. By no means all of these texts, of course, are what people conventionally take to be "histories." When Enobarbus is tempted to ignore reason, following Antony into defeat in order to earn "a place in the story," he uses the word *story* in its purest etymological sense; Tom F. Driver notes that for the Romans, a *historia* was "a narrative of past events . . . so that it came to mean merely an account, a tale, or a story"—the emphasis shifting from "the enterprise of discovering truth" to "the literary (or oral) form in which the inquiry is finally cast" (7). More recently, Hayden White has made explicit the view implied by Driver that no real distinction exists between the products of historians and those of dramatists and poets, telling us that "the best grounds for choosing one perspective on history rather than another are ultimately aesthetic and moral rather than epistemological" (xii).

White treats the historical work "as what it most manifestly is: a verbal structure in the form of a narrative prose discourse," containing "a deep structural content which is generally poetic, and specifically linguistic, in nature." This he terms "the metahistorical element," which gives his study its title (ix). Shakespeare's play might itself be considered a kind of "meta-history," in which the poetic and linguistic structures are not unwilled or unconscious on the part of the writer, as White suggests is the case with many historians, but manifest and overt. Certainly, *Antony and Cleopatra* is one of the most influential in a series of historical texts that have shaped Antony's "remembrance" for the modern world, a series that includes all the accounts on which Shakespeare may have drawn—Adelman mentions, in addition to North's Plutarch, those of Horace, Spenser, Garnier, Samuel Daniel and many more (53)—as well as those that followed, like Dryden's *All for Love* and Shaw's *Caesar and Cleopatra,* both of which are at once revisions of Shakespeare's play and historical commentaries in their own right. But *Antony and Cleopatra,* more than any of these, continually scrutinizes the status of its own and its characters' versions of a given set of historical events, and is thus not only a "history" of Antony, Cleopatra and Octavius but an investigation into the processes of history-making and history-writing. Adelman usefully suggests that "part of the experience of the play consists in deciding the meaning of a known narrative," so that the audience's familiarity with the various traditional interpretations of that narrative is indispensable to its own understanding of it (53).

Thus the self-consciousness of the play's major characters is perfectly consistent with the self-consciousness that is the play's dominant mode. And the omnipresent imperative of living one's life in and for the public eye is that what the public inevitably requires—and what, in the views of Driver, Adelman and White, historians of all kinds necessarily provide—is an account that imposes a distinct, unified and recognizable pattern upon the disorderly flux of discrete events, the raw material from which "stories" are made. The artistic processes of simplification and rearrangement tend to produce, at their most extreme reach, succinct and shapely epitaphs such as Enobarbus's self-characterization as "A master-leaver and a fugitive" or Othello's as "One that loved not wisely but too well," or even Malcolm's dismissal of Macbeth and Lady Macbeth as "this dead butcher and his fiend-like queen." In such cases, because as spectators we are privy to the secrets of these characters to an extent denied to "posterity," we may have a sense that much is being left unsaid, that such reductive economy of speech, although (or because) it leads to neatly-turned phrases, is inadequate to express the complexity of these individuals. But in *Antony and Cleopatra,* we are dealing not only with eulogies or epitaphs—though these are important, since they are the rhetorical form in which the characters themselves tend to work, as it were—but with the shape of the narrative as a whole. The artistic processes of elision, distortion and rearrangement are apparent at this level as well, along with other traditional means of ordering material employed, according to White, by historians and dramatists alike:

Providing the "meaning" of a story by identifying the kind of story that has been told is called explanation by emplotment. If, in the course of narrating his story, the historian provides it with the plot structure of a Tragedy, he has "explained" it in one way; if he has structured it as a Comedy, he has "explained" it in another way. Emplotment is the way by which a sequence of events fashioned into a story is gradually revealed to be a story of a particular kind. (7)

White's categories of the modes of emplotment used by historians are derived from Northrop Frye's Theory of Genres, which brings us back to the continuing debate among *Antony and Cleopatra's* critics over the predominant genre of the play. This debate perhaps originated in Plutarch's paraphrase of the Alexandrians, who said "very gallantly and wisely, that Antonius shewed them a comical face, to wit, a merry countenance: and the Romans a tragical face, to say, a grim look" (44). Several modern critics appear to assume that being able to classify the play in this way will allow us to choose among the varieties of conflicting interpretations that it makes available to us. Thus, Reuben Brower tells us that Shakespeare has suppressed the problematic aspects of Antony's character as Plutarch recorded them—his cruelty, his lustfulness, and particularly his dying "miserably," in a "cowardly" fashion—in order to make Antony, along with Cleopatra, a fit subject for tragedy (350). And Jonathan Goldberg agrees; Antony, he says, "is never more himself than when he plays that particular Roman part that Brutus plays in his final scene, suicide" (166). But Jonathan Dollimore finds Antony descending into "bathos" when "he resolves on suicide only to bungle the attempt . . . [and] suffers the indignity of being dragged up the monument" (211); Dollimore wholeheartedly adopts Philo's view that the love between the protagonists is mere "sexual infatuation," tracing it to Antony's anxiety over his political and sexual loss of power (217). Nochimson sums up this school of thought when he suggests that Shakespeare took "the tragic element inherent in the story of Cleopatra and Antony and reduced it" to something less than tragic—that the play's "ironic view" is closer to that of *Troilus and Cressida* than to such tragedies as *Macbeth* (100).

Adelman, though, instead of attempting to resolve the play's dilemmas by settling upon one or the other alternative, insists upon an overview that recognizes and preserves the contradictions: "The play is a series of conflicting judgments passed upon the protagonists themselves," she says, none of which can be absolute (25–26). For her, the play seems to encompass all the genres *except* irony: "The Roman world is bound by the limitations of time and death characteristic of tragedy; the Egyptian world has the essential disregard for time and death characteristic of comedy. And in the end, the lovers seem almost to escape into the profoundly comic world of the romances" (176).

Whatever the generic recipe followed by Shakespeare, it is not merely the critics but the characters themselves who attempt to define the artistic principle that shapes their story. The word they employ, however, is not *genre* but the broader term *decorum,* which applies equally to rhetoric, to plays, and to human events in which "comeliness, seemliness; fitness, decency, neatness, propriety, grace" (McAlindon 7) are called for. Of the three appearances of the term in Shakespeare's plays, two occur in *Antony and Cleopatra:* Iras prays that Isis "keep decorum" by giving a knave a knavish fortune (1.2.74), and Cleopatra explains to Proculeis "That majesty, to keep decorum, must / No less beg than a kingdom" (5.2.17–18). Our attention is thus directed forcefully toward an ideal of consistency and homogeneity that Antony's "divided disposition" and Cleopatra's "infinite variety" cannot accommodate. Antony in particular, as Shakespeare gives him to us, is by turns vain, courageous, petty, magnanimous, fluent, inarticulate, manly and effeminate; the Antony that history will record must be smoothed into a "heavenly mingle" that will reconcile all these seeming inconsistencies, as the Alexandrians did through the image of Antony's tragic and comic masks, and as Plutarch finally did as well by presenting us with an Antony whose early greatness was genuine but who at the end of his life was "so ravished and enchanted with the sweet poison of [Cleopatra's] love" (58)[11] as to forfeit much of his credit.

Hence Antony's final dilemma. Under the pressure exerted upon him by his consciousness of historical scrutiny, the contradictions of his life are thrown into new and sharper relief as his death approaches. At the play's emotional nadir, after the second defeat at Actium, Antony compares his substance to cloud or water; he complains that he "cannot hold this visible shape" (4.14.14). But *some* shape must appear; a form will be imposed upon his life by posterity if he cannot dictate one while still living, so he casts himself, as he prepares for death, in the familiar and conventional role of the constant lover betrayed:

> I made these wars for Egypt, and the Queen,
> Whose heart I thought I had, for she had mine—
> Which whilst it was mine had annex'd unto't
> A million moe (now lost)—she, Eros, has
> Pack'd cards with Caesar's, and false-play'd my glory
> Unto an enemy's triumph. (15–20)

This speech and others like it present a crux of interpretation. It may be objected that to regard this utterance as a piece of conscious role-playing, packaged in rhetoric designed to appeal to the waiting ears of posterity, is to read a quite-unwarranted cynicism into Antony's motives; why should we not rather call this speech a heartfelt expression of Antony's pain and grief cast in the slightly hyperbolical form that is dictated by his character and that constitutes the play's predominant style? But the suggestion that Antony's rhetoric is not to be taken as spontaneous or artless originates with Cleopatra, who early in the play protests that Antony is untrue both in leaving her and in protesting his love for her as he does so:

> Nay, pray you seek no color for your
>   going,
> But bid farewell, and go. When you sued
>   staying,

> Then was the time for words; no going then;
> *Eternity was in our lips and eyes,*
> *Bliss in our brows' bent; none our parts so poor*
> *But was a race of heaven.* They are so still,
> Or thou, the greatest soldier of the world,
> Art turn'd the greatest liar.
>
> (1.3.32–39; emphasis added)

The italics indicate the lines in which Cleopatra is quoting *verbatim* or paraphrasing (and in the process parodying) a speech or a mode of speech that she attributes to Antony before the play proper has begun. Though it resembles in a general way other speeches of his that we have heard, such as "Let Rome in Tiber melt," hearing it foregrounded in this manner—issuing from Cleopatra, in the present context of rancor and discord between them—has the curious effect of undercutting not only the speech in question, which we have not heard, but also the very similar protestations of his love for her with which we are familiar. If Cleopatra is to be believed, making such speeches has become a habit of his, which further dilutes their effect. To Antony's claim that "the nobleness of life / Is to do thus [*embracing*]—when such a mutual pair / And such a twain can do't . . ." (1.1.36–38), her reply is "Excellent falsehood!" (40), which connects quite solidly with her point in quoting him to himself: that all such speeches will be proven false retroactively if Antony leaves her. And vows made to her own lovers in "her salad days" are treated in exactly the same manner by Charmian in a later scene:

> *Cleo.*   Did I, Charmian,
>   Ever love Caesar so?
> *Char.*   *O that brave Caesar!*
> *Cleo.* Be chok'd with such another emphasis!
>   Say "the brave Antony."
> *Char.*   *The valiant Caesar!*
> *Cleo.* By Isis, I will give thee bloody teeth,
>   If thou with Caesar paragon again
>   My man of men.

Char.   By your most gracious pardon,
   I sing but after you.
                    (1.5.66–73; emphasis added)

Thus the tendency to speak for attribution is not limited, on the part of either *Antony and Cleopatra*, to shaping utterances for "remembrance"; what they say to each other, and what they have said to other lovers in the past, is apt to lack spontaneity and sincerity, or is at the least subject to later revision. This familiar form of rhetorical dissimulation provides the foundation for their more explicitly "historical" messages, their conscious attempts at image-making. And we are forcefully reminded of the relationship of *Antony and Cleopatra* to the "real" persons and events that it treats of by such references as these, which direct our attention to that shadowy realm in which they live their offstage lives, a realm halfway between the play's fictive world and our own historical one.

At any rate, the large number of speeches early in the play that have a conscious purpose beyond communication of a state of mind, and that call attention to the fact,[12] have the effect of sensitizing the audience to the speeches Antony makes as his death approaches, pointing up their potentially self-serving aspect and damping their emotional affect. The speech in which Antony casts Cleopatra as *la belle dame sans merci* and himself as her latest victim utterly ignores the complexity of her character; similarly, it takes no account of his own earlier glory except to record its conversion into shame. It is both incomplete and inaccurate; its only virtue is its conciseness. Fortunately, his ensuing reconciliation with Cleopatra permits him to revise it, but the new version, though almost equally brief, is not conspicuously closer to the truth:

    The miserable change now at my end
    Lament nor sorrow at; but please your thoughts
    In feeding them with those my former fortunes
    Wherein I liv'd, the greatest prince o' th' world,
    The noblest; and do now not basely die,

> Not cowardly put off my helmet to
> My countryman—a Roman by a Roman[13]
> Valiantly vanquished. (4.15.51–58)

Our immediate response to this may be that it surpasses the truth by as much as the earlier speech fell short of it. When Cleopatra determines to kill herself "after the high Roman fashion" (87), she reminds us of the esthetic shortcomings of Antony's own "fashion" of suicide, about which he himself commented, "I have done my work ill" (4.14.105): the trick played on him by Eros, who, as Antony steels himself to receive the killing thrust, stabs himself instead; Antony's failure to dispatch himself cleanly and his inability to persuade anybody else to finish the job for him; the comic ambiguity in the crowd's exclamation at the sight of him being "heaved" up to the monument: "A heavy sight!" (4.15.40).[14] These details are present in Plutarch's *Life*, but are presented as relatively trivial misfortunes; in the play, particularly in performance, they threaten to transform Antony's death scene into Theatre of the Absurd. The texture of his death, like that of his life, is imperfectly human, full of flaws that threaten the integrity of the fact itself. And we should be aware that the epitaph proposed by Antony's final speech is not one that posterity is obliged to accept; it may be the earlier version that is adopted. It was, after all, Antony himself who, in an earlier incarnation, argued, "The evil that men do lives after them, / The good is oft interred with their bones" (*Julius Caesar* 3.2.75–76)—though of course the principle that men come to admire those whom they lack will work in Antony's favor, as it did in Pompey's. At any rate, Antony's final dilemma is a choice he is powerless to make because it must be a posthumous one: between alternative versions of his life that exclude each other but that can be supported equally well by the facts as they are known at his death.

The choice is determined by the actions of Cleopatra, who has her own dilemma to resolve. Her consciousness of role and reputation is as highly developed as Antony's, and is if anything more concretely imagined: where Antony conceives of history's judgments abstractly, in terms of "remembrance" and "report," for Cleopatra history is recorded by the actors, those "brief chronicles of the times," as Hamlet called them (2.2.524), who will represent her to the "Mechanic slaves / With greasy aprons" (5.2.209–10) that make up the popular Roman audience. Unlike modern scholars, she does not doubt which dramatic genre will be chosen for her story:

> The quick comedians
> Extemporally will stage us, and present
> Our Alexandrian revels: Antony
> Shall be brought drunken forth, and I shall see
> Some squeaking Cleopatra boy my greatness
> I' th' posture of a whore. (216–21)

This perspective is grimmer than anything Antony envisions; at their worst, his self-portraits had about them a certain defeated dignity not incompatible with tragedy, but Cleopatra can readily imagine the two of them as stock figures of Roman farce. In order to effect the requisite generic transformation, she first sets about creating a new Antony, who will have nothing about him to interest the "comedians":

> His legs bestrid the ocean, his rear'd arm
> Crested the world, his voice was propertied
> As all the tuned spheres, and that to friends;
> But when he meant to quail and shake the
>   orb,
> He was as rattling thunder. (82–86)

That she is consciously limning, in the manner of a playwright, an image of Antony in the heroic mold, she is well aware: "Nature wants stuff / To vie strange forms with fancy" (97–98), she admits. Along with Antony's, she must rehabilitate her own image, and here, fancy alone will not accomplish her purpose. Action is required, so she is "again for Cydnus" (228)—where, in Enobarbus's description of her, the irreducible note of her own splendor and greatness was first struck.

The images that accompany her suicide tell us that her infinite variety is being replaced by a unified and coherent presentation of self whose very seamlessness will allow no opportunity for comical revision: "I am marble-constant" (240), she exclaims. By an act of will, she purges her nature of what is unwanted: "I am fire, and air; my other elements / I give to baser life" (289–90).

Caesar, whose intention to lead Cleopatra in triumph provokes her to her final display of greatness, becomes the final arbiter of her place in history and of Antony's.[15] That is fitting, for no other character has set more store by ceremony, has been less impulsive or more aware of the eyes that watch events on the stage of public life. Even after the quarrel with Antony has become intolerable, Caesar insists upon according his rival the eminence to which he is entitled. Indeed, he makes Antony's eminence part of his grievance, as when he exclaims to Octavia, who has returned alone from Athens,

> The wife of Antony
> Should have an army for an usher, and
> The neighs of horse to tell of her approach,
> Long ere she did appear; the trees by th' way
> Should have borne men, and expectation fainted,
> Longing for what it had not; nay, the dust
> Should have ascended to the roof of heaven,
> Rais'd by your populous troops. But you are
>   come
> A market-maid to Rome, and have prevented
> The ostentation of our love, which, left unshown,
> Is often left unlov'd. (3.6.43–53)

For Octavius Caesar, love is identical with, or at least does not exist independent of, public display. But more important, this speech gives us an indication of Caesar's tastes in the matter of historical judgment and dramatic perspective. Cleopatra is correct in believing that Caesar means to display her as a conquest in Rome; Dolabella admits as much to her, and we have heard Caesar lay plans to prevent her suicide, "for her life in Rome / Would be eternal in our triumph" (5.1.65–66). But she mistakes the temper of the man if she believes he wishes to see her and Antony scorned and demeaned—both because this would demean his own victory, and because his regard for Antony's greatness, and the fame it deserves, is genuine: "The breaking of so great a thing should make / A greater crack" (14–15) he exclaims at the news of Antony's death. It is consistent with Caesar's regard for decorum that Decretas should omit the messiness of Antony's suicide from his official report:

> . . . that self hand
> Which writ his honor in the acts it did
> Hath, with the courage which the heart did lend it,
> Splitted the heart. (21–24)

And where Caesar had earlier reviled Antony as being "not more manlike / Than Cleopatra" (1.4.5–6), he now sets about the task of safeguarding Antony's reputation:

> . . . let me lament,
> With tears as sovereign as the blood of hearts,
> That thou, my brother, my competitor
> In top of all design, my mate in empire,
> Friend and companion in the front of war,
> The arm of mine own body, and the heart
> Where mine his thoughts did kindle—that our stars,
> Unreconciliable, should divide
> Our equalness to this. (5.1.40–48)

Though the speech serves Octavius in its equation of his greatness with Antony's,[16] it serves Antony too. All that is missing from it is any mention of Cleopatra. Given Octavius's leanings toward the epic and tragic, there is little possibility of Antony's being remembered as an effeminate dotard, but if Cleopatra wishes to secure her own "place in the story," she will have to demonstrate her worthiness. That is what her suicide is designed to do, and what it does. Whatever triumph

Caesar has planned for her, she triumphs over him in the end, and he is forced to admit it: "Bravest at the last, / She levell'd at our purposes, and being royal / Took her own way" (5.2.335–37).

Caesar's final and presumably definitive version of the "story" is one in which Enobarbus, as might be expected, plays no part, and from which Octavia, as might not be expected, is similarly omitted: Caesar's sense of decorum proves stronger than his fraternal obligation, and in his view, Cleopatra has earned the right to replace his sister, whose claim on Antony was only, after all, a legal one. Cleopatra, he says, "shall be buried by her Antony; / No grave upon the earth shall clip in it / A pair so famous" (358–60). The speech closely approximates Antony's original premise: that when such a "mutual pair" as they embrace, sensuality is transformed into "the nobleness of life." The rest of Caesar's summation, with which the play ends, is not a record of events; there is no mention of battles, marriages, alliances, scandals, or even persons. Instead, it consists of a precise delineation of the uniformly tragic perspective from which the love of Antony and Cleopatra may shine to best advantage:

> High events as these
> Strike those that make them; and their story is
> No less in pity than his glory which
> Brought them to be lamented. Our army shall
> In solemn show attend this funeral,
> And then to Rome. Come, Dolabella, see
> High order in this great solemnity. (360–66)

Thus are the contradictions of Antony's nature soldered up; thus is his life knitted together posthumously by the mutual actions of Cleopatra and Caesar. "Pity," "glory," "great solemnity"—the terms apply, at the end, equally to Antony's Roman and Egyptian careers. In life he found it necessary to divide himself between the two, but beneath the apparent opposition of Rome and Egypt there existed from the first a current of human nature that was the same, and at the end of the play, in

Caesar's elegy, the public and the personal "mingle" and appear at last as one.

Notes

¹ All quotations from non-Shakespearean poems in this chapter are taken from *Renaissance Poetry*, ed. Leonard Dean.

² Douglas Bush has remarked: "One often could not say, and does not need to say, whether an individual sonnet is concerned with love for a man or a woman; one supreme example is 'Let me not to the marriage of true minds / Admit impediments'" (Introduction, *Shakespeare's Sonnets*, Pelican Shakespeare, 15).

³ On the correspondence between Jacobean city comedy and Metaphysical poetry, see Joseph G. Price, *The Unfortunate Comedy: A Study of* All's Well That Ends Well *and Its Critics*, Chapter 1.

⁴ Perhaps the best-known English description of Venice in the period is contained in *Coryat's Crudities* (which, admittedly, appeared in 1611, several years after Shakespeare's two Venetian plays).

⁵ Says Rosalie Colie, "Except for *Hamlet*, *Othello* is the most epistemological of Shakespeare's tragedies, an examination of the relation between truth and expressing the truth" (241).

⁶ Maurice Charney, in his discussion of *Antony and Cleopatra*, speaks of tragedy's being based on significant choices in situations which have some elements of a "moral dilemma" about them (*Shakespeare's Roman Plays* 115). Janet Adelman uses the term in a somewhat different context, to describe the dilemmas not of the protagonists but of the audience. She argues that "the stage action necessarily presents us with one version of the facts, the poetry with another. This is the dilemma inherent in much dramatic poetry, and the more hyperbolical the poetry, the more acute the dilemma" (*The Common Liar* 103).

⁷ Paul A. Cantor (*Shakespeare's Rome: Republic and Empire*) is among the minority of critics who reject the symmetrical opposition of Rome and Egypt as spurious. The more genuine antithesis, he asserts, is that between the older values of the Roman Republic and those of the Empire, which came to replace them.

⁸ We have encountered a phrase almost identical to "she's good, being gone" in *All's Well That Ends Well*, where the King describes the predicament into which Helena's supposed death has thrust Bertram:

> . . . love that comes too late
> Like a remorseful pardon slowly carried,
> To the great sender turns a sour offense,
> Crying, "That's good that's gone." (5.3.57–60)

⁹ In the view of Jonathan Dollimore, Octavius and Antony are similar in that both are masters of "realpolitik" (*Radical Tragedy* 280ff); he finds their relationship to be characterized by the struggle for power, a struggle he sees in every relationship in the play. This view seems to me to have some merit, but I do not share his admiration for Antony's political skills, as my own argument will make clear.

¹⁰ James E. Siemon wonders whether *spirit* in this context refers to "his quintessential self or his demon," but in either case, he continues, the word is linked in both speeches with Antony's "subjugation to another" ("The Strong Necessity of Time" 319).

¹¹ Adelman, surveying historical recollections of Antony, summarizes the majority opinion as follows: "a good soldier but a weak man who made himself servant to a woman, though his noble death usually redeems him to some degree" (56).

¹² Perhaps the most interesting example is the conversation in which Enobarbus and Agrippa quote/paraphrase/parody Lepidus's habits of courtly flattery:

> *Agr.* 'Tis a noble Lepidus.
> *Eno.* A very fine one. O, how he loves Caesar!
> *Agr.* Nay, but how dearly he adores Mark Antony!
> *Eno.* Caesar? Why, he's the Jupiter of men.
> *Agr.* What's Antony? The God of Jupiter.
> *Eno.* Spake you of Caesar? How! The nonpareil!
> *Agr.* O Antony! O thou Arabian bird!
> *Eno.* Would you praise Caesar, say "Caesar": go no further.
> *Agr.* Indeed, he plied them both with excellent praises.
>
> (3.2.7–14)

¹³ Reuben Brower in *Hero and Saint* notes a significant revision of Plutarch by Shakespeare: where Plutarch paraphrased Antony's dying words as "now he was overcome, not cowardly but valiantly, a Romane by an other Romane," Shakespeare drops "an other" and thus gives us an Antony defeated only by himself, not by Caesar. "Through this slight omission . . . the peculiar 'nobility' of his death is given precise expression," says Brower (350).

¹⁴ On the perspective taken toward Antony's suicide I agree with the views discussed earlier of Dollimore, though I resist his conclusion that Antony is throughout the play a pathetic, masochistic, and thoroughly unheroic figure.

¹⁵ Adelman notes: "The victor will frequently be granted the privilege,

temporarily at least, of writing his own version of history." But in her view, "it is a version that makes Cleopatra eternal in the posture of a whore" (54), a reading with which I shall disagree.

[16] Antony at one point vehemently denies Caesar's claim to soldiership equal to his own: Caesar, he says, "Dealt on lieutenantry, and no practice had / In the brave squares of war" (3.11.39–40).

4

"To Be, or Not To Be":
Hamlet and the Dilemmas of Existence

In the last scene of *Hamlet*, Horatio proclaims his affinity with the world of *Antony and Cleopatra*: "I am more an antique Roman than a Dane" (5.2.341), he insists, preparing, like Antony's servant Eros, to demonstrate his fealty by preceding a beloved leader in death. And when Hamlet prevents Horatio's suicide, it is because, like Antony, the prince is at the moment of his own death preoccupied with his place in history: "O God, Horatio, what a wounded name, / Things standing thus unknown, shall I leave behind me!" (344–45), he cries. Horatio must live to report him and his cause "To the unsatisfied" (339).

Though *Hamlet* is the earlier of the two plays by six or seven years, the gulf between the "mingle" of human character and experience on the one hand and the decorous reordering and simplifying of motives and events by the judgments of history on the other is, if anything, wider here than it is in *Antony and Cleopatra*. Caesar's epitaph for Antony omits both the perplexed and human lover whom we have occasionally glimpsed and the demigod whom Cleopatra has imagined, but his tragic and dignified portrait is both accurate and recognizable as far as it goes. Fortinbras's summation of Hamlet, though, is almost entirely a piece of *post hoc* revisionism:

> Let four captains
> Bear Hamlet like a soldier to the stage,
> For he was likely, had he been put on,
> To have prov'd most royal; and for his passage,

The soldiers' music and the rite of war
Speak loudly for him. (395–400)

In terms of the effect Hamlet's actions will have upon Denmark after his death, there is both logic and justice in the military honors decreed for him by Fortinbras. But for the audience, which has been receiving from Hamlet throughout the play accounts of his motives that are dominated by his hatred of his uncle, his mingled yearning and revulsion for his mother, his obsession with the processes of death and disease and his philosophic skepticism concerning the nature of man, the universe, and reality itself, it is very late to begin thinking of him as a hero in an exclusively military mold. To conceive of the prince essentially as a simple patriot who gave his life in the service of his country may serve both his "remembrance" and Fortinbras's political purposes, but it distorts the perspective from which both he and we have viewed the events of the play. Though one effect of revenging his father's murder has certainly been to restore legitimacy to the throne and wholesomeness to Denmark, these concerns have seemed, throughout much of the action, peripheral to the far more subjective focus of Hamlet's thoughts, ambitions, and desires.

Thus the gap between the perspectives from which the protagonist's life may be viewed is greater in *Hamlet* than it was in *Antony and Cleopatra*. The number of perspectives is greater as well. It is only at the end of the play that Hamlet becomes anxious about the possible divergence of his life as he has lived it and as history will record it, but from the first he has been preoccupied with similar and equally fundamental distinctions: between the world and the stage, between life and death, between life and afterlife. What is more significant, these appear to him not simply as alternative points of view that may be taken toward the same set of events but rather as alternative modes of existence, each in its own way as fundamentally "real" as the others.

Hamlet's preoccupation with existence—which he conceives not as a given state of being but rather as a series of conscious choices—leads us inevitably to the most famous passage in the Shakespearean canon, the fourth soliloquy. It is difficult to think freshly about the meaning of "To be, or not to be"; its familiarity seems to wrench it loose from its conceptual and narrative contexts in the play, so that, for audience and actor alike, it has become a set piece.[1] Nonetheless, this must be our starting point, for when Hamlet identifies his choice between the alternatives of being and non-being as a "question" (3.1.55), the word possesses just the force and meaning that it had in Boccaccio's *Il Filocolo*: a dilemma. There are, though, both for Hamlet and ourselves, significant difficulties in formulating and identifying the alternatives it presents, partly because the language in which they are expressed is ambiguous and partly because they are formulated in two different ways, in quick succession:[2]

> To be, or not to be, that is the question:
> Whether 'tis nobler in the mind to suffer
> The slings and arrows of outrageous fortune,
> Or to take arms against a sea of troubles,
> And by opposing, end them. (55–59)

The logic of syntax tells us that "To be" should be synonymous with "to suffer the slings and arrows of outrageous fortune" and "not to be" with "to take arms against a sea of troubles." If that is so, "to be" is for Hamlet a state of passive endurance at fortune's mercy, while "not to be"—suicide—is by contrast active, dynamic, a way of mastering troubles and fortune alike. But this reading contradicts Hamlet's original formulation. At the time of his first interview with his father's ghost, "to be" was anything but a state of indifference or immobility; he was impatient for the name of his father's murderer so that he might "with wings as swift / As meditation, or the thoughts of love, / . . . sweep to [his] revenge" (1.5.29–31). And we should also note that the metaphor intended to express Hamlet's domination over misfortune, "to take arms against a sea of troubles," conjures up instead an image of futility, almost of absurdity—a man in armor doing battle with the waves—

which itself soon gives way to the analogy with that most passive of living states, sleep. Living and dying, then, seem much the same thing—states of helpless suffering. It hardly seems possible to distinguish between "those ills we have" and "others that we know not of" (3.1.80–81).[3]

Thus it is not surprising that Hamlet's dilemma "puzzles the will" (79). Unable to choose between two states of immobilization, he remains immobilized, as "the native hue of resolution / Is sicklied o'er with the pale cast of thought" (83–84). Thought cannot resolve Hamlet's dilemma, for thought has created it. "Hamlet's world," Maynard Mack proposes, "is in the interrogative mood" (49), and the distinctive shape of Hamlet's countless interrogatories is self-determined: it is his particular habit of mind to transform his questions, his choices, and his resolutions into alternatives that mirror each other, simultaneously opposite and identical. A "craven scruple / Of thinking too precisely on th' event" (4.4.40–41) turns what for less exacting minds might be answerable questions—whether or not the Ghost's accusation is founded, for example—into Hamlet's dilemma of death-in-life or life-in-death.

Why this should be so—why Hamlet's mental processes should lead him repeatedly into intellectual impasse—is itself a difficult and complicated question, one whose answer will have to be arrived at after a somewhat roundabout journey. A convenient place to start is at Hamlet's favorite metaphor. His determination to perform his father's command and his reluctance to do so, his dislike of Claudius and his recognition of his own kinship with his uncle, his attraction to his mother and his revulsion against female perfidy—indeed, almost all of what he says, thinks and feels in the play about the paradoxes of his own character and the world in which he lives is expressed through that great Elizabethan commonplace, the metaphor of the world as a stage. It has long been recognized that acting (performing a deed) and acting (playing a role) are as "knotted and combined" in Hamlet's brain as the locks on his head; that Claudius, who goes through the motions of ruling from his brother's throne, is as much a "player-king" as the monarch in

The Murder of Gonzago.[4] Almost no one who has written on this aspect of *Hamlet* has failed to note the implications of Hamlet's indignant denial that his grief for his father's death consists only of "actions that a man might play" (1.2.84), or of the triple pun in his reference to his skull as "this distracted globe" (1.5.97), or of his calling his father's commandment "the motive and the cue for passion" (2.2.561), to note but a few instances. And it seems equally clear that his "antic disposition" is at least in part an assumed role, as is the conventional figure he portrays for Ophelia, the complaining lover who appears again in a list of such character-types that he enumerates later in the play when he describes the repertoire of the travelling players, which includes "his Majesty," "the adventurous knight," and "the humorous man" (2.2.320–25).

Nor are all the shows of Hamlet's devising. The Ghost "with solemn march" going "slow and stately by" (1.2.201–02), the player's impersonation of Pyrrhus, the "loosing" of Ophelia and later of Gertrude to Hamlet by Polonius, the performance at court of *The Murder of Gonzago*, Ophelia's mad songs and later her funeral, at which Laertes's "phrase of sorrow / Conjures the wand'ring stars and makes them stand / Like wonder-wounded hearers" (5.1.255–57), the dueling scene in which Hamlet and Laertes "play" with each other,[5] and finally Fortinbras's calling "the noblest to the audience" (5.2.387) of Hamlet's last role, which ends with the prince borne "like a soldier to the stage" (396)—all are microcosms of the play itself, dramas in miniature watched attentively by more than one audience.

What has not been so thoroughly studied, however, is the place to which Hamlet assigns himself upon the world-stage of Denmark. Our first piece of information on that subject comes when, at the close of his first meeting with his father's spirit, he makes the following promise: "Remember thee! / Ay, thou poor ghost, whiles memory holds a seat / In this distracted globe" (1.5.95–97). The "globe" is both his skull and (implicitly) the world, held in relation to each other by the unspoken middle term, the theater in which the first performance of *Hamlet* was played—though unlike that Globe, the theater that is his mind is, in the two senses of a second pun, "distracted."[6] But what is most important here is that Hamlet apparently conceives of himself not as an actor in that playhouse but as a member of the audience; his memory holds not the stage but merely a seat among the other watchers and listeners as it observes and records the spectacle presented to it.

This conception of his essential self as a spectator has a significant bearing on the question of why he is unwilling, or unable, to "sweep to [his] revenge." For it is the role of spectators to remain physically passive, no matter how emotionally responsive they may be to what they see and hear. The two states are, in fact, inversely proportional to each other, according to Norman N. Holland, who writes, "Activity in the inner world and activity in the outer seem mutually exclusive" (74). When we watch a play, Holland continues, "what is actually happening 'out there' feels as though it were happening 'in here'" as long as the dramatic frame remains intact, and this process of "introjection" acts as a restraint to prevent us from physically intervening in what we have come only to witness. It is only when the frame is breached that a spectator of sound mind may behave like the woman who, at a performance of John Osborne's *Look Back in Anger* in New York some years ago, rushed from her seat onto the stage and struck one of the actors with her umbrella because his character had been abusing his wife (96).

Of course, it is possible to think of an audience's physical quiescence not as a psychological inhibition, as Holland does, but merely as a piece of social decorum, or an arbitrary convention of behavior associated with going to plays—and not all plays at that. S. L. Bethell notes the various historical shifts in the audience's relationship with, or distance from, the actors and the action:

> At a standard performance of Ibsen, the audience remains passively receptive, whilst in another two-dimensional world, beyond the orchestra pit, within a picture-frame and behind footlights, the actors create a vivid illusion of actual life. In the Elizabethan, or the modern

experimental theatre . . . the audience are vividly aware of acting in
progress, and the communication, through their co-operative goodwill,
of a piece of dramatic art. (32)

Even so, communicating one's goodwill comes somewhat
short of leaping onto the stage. But in *Hamlet*, a court play, a
ghostly progress, a funeral and several other quasi-dramatic
spectacles or performances are interrupted by spectators; indeed, from more than one character we hear the curious
implication that the conventional passivity of audiences is
somehow shameful, that there is something like cowardly
paralysis in keeping one's place and watching others act. Thus
Horatio, describing Marcellus and Bernardo at the ghost's
appearance, tells Hamlet: "they, distill'd / Almost to jelly with
the act of fear, / Stand dumb and speak not to him"
(1.2.204–06). And a short time later Polonius asks Claudius, in
order to justify his interference between Hamlet and Ophelia,

> what might you,
> Or my dear Majesty your queen here, think,
> If I had play'd the desk or table-book,
> Or given my heart a winking, mute and dumb,
> Or look'd upon this love with idle sight,
> What might you think? (2.2.134–39)

Where action seems called for, Marcellus and Bernardo are
capable only of "the act of fear," which freezes them, and
Polonius's motionless and insensate table-book recalls Hamlet's other metaphor for his memory, a "table" or notebook
(1.5.98). Then there are those stars that stand like "wonder-
wounded hearers" above the spectacle of Hamlet and Laertes
grappling in Ophelia's grave, and the courtiers who later fail to
separate the same antagonists at the king's command but
instead "look pale, and tremble" at Hamlet's bloody performance, and are "but mutes or audience" to the "act" of revenge
(5.2.334–35). To fear or to wonder is to stand dumb; the
emotions that make men tremble also make them mute.

Hamlet, then, at the beginning of the play, is oriented
toward it precisely as we are: he watches it as he would a

dramatic spectacle, moved but unmoving, just as we do. Anne Righter has argued that the later sixteenth century witnessed the popularization of the self-contained play, which cut the audience off from its traditional participatory role (41). To an extent, Shakespeare restores the dynamic of co-operation between spectator and performer in *Hamlet*, for, while we hardly participate in the same way as do the actors, the most important character in the play demonstrates by word and action that in some sense he participates with us. Perhaps all this partly accounts for the extraordinary empathy audiences have always felt for him, which made Coleridge exclaim, "I have a smack of Hamlet myself, if I may say so" (67), and Hazlitt, similarly, "It is we who are Hamlet" ("Characters" 32). Nor are we moderns exempt: Jan Kott suggests that the play is a mirror in which we see ourselves reflected (58), and Harry Levin tells us "that Hamlet means so many things to so many men because he invites them to put themselves in his place" (6). The contemporary critic who has most thoroughly explored this connection is Stephen Booth, who places the uncanny conjunction of Hamlet and the audience very early in the play: at Hamlet's first entrance, and with his first speech, which is addressed to us, "Hamlet takes the audience for his own, and gives himself to the audience as its agent on the stage. Hamlet and the audience are from this point more firmly united than any other such pair in Shakespeare, and perhaps in dramatic literature" ("Value" 150). Hamlet interprets the action of *Hamlet* for us in his soliloquies as he interprets the action of *The Murder of Gonzago* for the court in his asides. The dilemma of being and non-being, then, is partly a function of his simultaneous existence in two realms: Denmark and England,[7] the play-world and the real world, the actor's space and the spectator's. Until Hamlet chooses between these residences, he will be unable to act.[8]

It is to a large extent Hamlet's own doing that we should feel this special kinship with him, at least during the first half of the play. Hamlet continually invites us to put ourselves in his place, never more clearly than in the early speech in which he claims to his mother that he possesses a reality more profound than that of the "seemers" who counterfeit upon the stage or at the court of Denmark. Hamlet has, he claims, "that within which passes show" (1.2.85), an existence independent of whatever roles have been dictated for him by circumstances, by other people, by providence (and, implicitly, by the playwright who conceived him). Literally, this ought not to be true; Hamlet, however more complex a character than Gertrude, Rosencrantz, Guildenstern, Osric or Polonius, ought not to be any more "real" than they—ought not to exist, any more than they can, independent of Shakespeare's conception of him or of the actor's representation of him. And yet here he is, claiming for himself just such an ontological superiority, disdainfully cutting himself off from the play and insisting upon his right to watch it from our vantage point, the privileged, omniscient position of the "real" spectator.[9]

One result of this identification is that it dramatizes Hamlet's predicament for us—it allows us to experience his dilemma as if it were our own, as Booth implies when he calls *Hamlet* "the tragedy of an audience that cannot make up its mind" ("Value" 152). Has it ever occurred to any of us at a performance of the play to rise from our seats and leap to his aid? None of the critics who inveigh against his so-called procrastination has undertaken to rid Denmark of Claudius themselves, or even to shout a warning to the trusting Hamlet that the foils have been tampered with. That is because they are aware that they are watching not a fellow man struggling with an awful task but "a fiction . . . a dream of passion" (2.2.552), as Hamlet describes it. Hamlet's "problem" is that he has exactly the same fictive conception of Claudius that we have: not a true or real king but a player-king, "A king of shreds and patches" (3.4.102), and that, like us, because he sees Claudius from the perspective of a spectator, his instinctive responses are those of a spectator as well. Before he can bring himself to act against Claudius, then, Hamlet must find a way to act with him; though he feels so little kinship with his uncle, he must abandon the detachment that informs him, truthfully but not helpfully, that Claudius is but a walking shadow, and descend to the realm of shadows by becoming a player himself.

This descent Hamlet begins to accomplish through the medium of the play-within-a-play, where theatrical metaphors crystallize the relationship between reality and illusion that is at the heart of his dilemma. When the players appear, writes Maynard Mack,

> we have suddenly a situation which tends to dissolve the normal barriers between the fictive and the real. For here on stage before us is a play of false appearances in which an actor called a player-king is playing. But there is also on the stage, Claudius, another player-king, who is a spectator of this player. And there is on the stage, besides, a prince who is a spectator of both these player-kings, who plays with great intensity a player's role himself. And around these kings and that prince is a group of courtly spectators . . . and they, as we have come to know, are players too. And lastly there are ourselves, an audience watching these audiences who are also players. Where, it may suddenly occur to us to ask, does the playing end? (56)

Where indeed? Mack's question (and of course it is Shakespeare's and Hamlet's question as well) moves the focus of our attention away from the vehicle of the world/stage metaphor to its tenor. It leads us from our consideration of the ways in which the stage represents the world to the ways in which the world (Denmark or England, depending upon one's point of view) resembles a playhouse. Booth has noted, "*Hamlet* was of course born into the culture of Western Europe, our culture, whose every thought—literary or nonliterary—is shaped by the Platonic assumption that the reality of anything is other than its apparent self" ("Value" 152). And this is, broadly speaking, true. But the question of where the playing ends would not have been asked in a theater much before the end of the sixteenth century, by which time a new vision of reality—more relativistic, more subjective, more self-conscious—had begun to appear, for audiences during the Middle Ages and the early Tudor era simply were not encouraged to watch themselves as they watched plays, or to reflect upon the metaphysical significance of doing so.

By contrast, the world-view of the early seventeenth century, that amalgam of Platonism, skepticism and rationalism, was a culture in which the world/stage metaphor flourished. Without the assumption that the senses do not give an accurate account of reality, it would have been impossible to conceive of the world as a show without substance. But as we have seen, in employing this metaphor Shakespeare does more than simply accept what had become a commonplace assumption; *Hamlet* is not merely a depiction of the age's figurative conception of reality but an investigation into reality's nature and of the means by which it could be apprehended. The play is a critique of the limitations of empirical rationalism, not in the comic/romantic vein of *All's Well That Ends Well* but in that what Soellner calls the "relativistic and skeptical spirit" (40) which derived principally from Montaigne.

The ontological and epistemological questions that underlie Hamlet's dilemma—what is real, and how may we know it?—are introduced with the appearance of the ghost and the summoning of Horatio to validate its existence by empirical means: "Before my God," he exclaims, "I might not this believe / Without the sensible and true avouch / Of mine own eyes" (1.1.56–58). Horatio is one of several characters who place their trust in the data of sense perception. He is accustomed to living in the daylight world of shadowless substance, in which objects and events are what they seem. With him are Claudius, who never dreamt that evidence of his crime might come to light by other than natural means; Polonius, who pledges his life that his observations of Hamlet's behavior have led him to correct conclusions as to its cause; and Gertrude, who, because she can neither see nor hear the ghost of her husband in her chamber, assumes unquestioningly that her son, who seems to be conversing with the air, is mad. In her, says Maynard Mack, "we have the imperturbable self-confidence of the worldly world, its layers upon layers of habituation, so that when reality is before its very eyes it cannot detect its presence" (52).

The same might be said, in fact, of almost every character in the play except Hamlet, who knows better. Yet his own conception of reality and the senses is complicated and self-contradictory. On one hand, he is the play's spokesman for the position that the essences of things are hidden by their appearances: "There are more things in heaven and earth, Horatio, / Than are dreamt of in your philosophy" (1.5.166–67) he tells his friend, referring to the "natural philosophy" taught at Wittenberg which presumably (though anachronistically) includes such intellectual novelties as Galileo's doctrine of Primary and Secondary Qualities. It is Hamlet who says to the skull in the graveyard, "Now get you to my lady's chamber, and tell her, let her paint an inch thick, to this favor she must come" (5.1.192–94). Thus Hamlet apprehends reality not with his eyes but with his inward vision, the "prophetic soul" (1.5.40) that informs him, not logically but infallibly, of the true state of affairs. He hates Claudius long before the ghost tells him why he should, and, while he lacks literal foreknowledge of the final trap, he has a premonition of it—"such a kind of gain-giving, as would perhaps trouble a woman" (5.2.215–16). The rationalism of a Polonius—composed equally of reliance on sense-data and on the precedents of authority and experience—is a faulty index to the altered world of Denmark, "out of joint" both temporally and spatially and no longer governed by the traditional laws of physics, psychology or morality. Only Hamlet possesses the sixth sense necessary to pick one's way through it. Of the five physical senses, not sight but smell comes closest to apprehending reality, and it is with his nose that Hamlet perceives the "things rank and gross in nature" that make up the unweeded garden in which he lives (1.2.136).

Yet, on the other hand, Hamlet's admiration for the rationalistic and empirically-inclined Horatio is boundless, despite the fact that his friend's stoical temperament apparently cuts him off from the uncanny presentiments that unerringly instruct Hamlet throughout the play. Hamlet's chief ambition is to achieve and maintain a state of reason, as if reason were all that stood between men and those lustful and murderous passions that have turned his mother and his uncle, in his view, into beasts. However, the mechanism by which he comes to know who and what his enemies are is fueled by Hamlet's own passions, and the "rashness" by which he finally accomplishes his purpose could not exist without them.

Moreover, though at times he hardly bothers to distinguish between what he sees with his corporeal eyes and with his inward vision—as when he startles Horatio by claiming that he sees his father before him in his "mind's eye" (1.2.185)—he often places a trust in appearances that is clearly unwarranted. In the closet scene, for example, the contrast between Claudius and King Hamlet with which he chastises his mother is a visual one and nothing more. Charles R. Forker is correct in claiming that Hamlet, now fully engaged in theatrical enterprise, is seeking to dramatize the differences between the two brothers (226), but it is hardly likely that Claudius's portrait, whether upon the wall or in Gertrude's locket, depicts his uncle as Hamlet describes him: "like a mildewed ear, / Blasting his wholesome brother" (3.4.64–65). Hamlet appears to have abandoned his earlier conception of Claudius's evil as a hidden, inner essence, belied by his smiling face. It may be wondered, too, whether Hamlet's description of his father's visage— "Hyperion's curls, the front of Jove himself, / An eye like Mars" (56–57)—is not more a son's sentimental reconstruction of an adored parent than a portrait from life, either of the man himself or of the counterfeit image of him to which he calls his mother's attention.

Yet his chief accusation against his mother is that her own perceptions are distorted, a point he belabors:

> Sense sure you have,
> Else could you not have motion, but sure that sense
> Is apoplex'd, for madness would not err
> Nor sense to ecstasy was ne'er so thrall'd
> But it reserv'd some quantity of choice
> To serve in such a difference. (71–76)

And indeed, whatever the pictures of her two husbands or her prior judgment tell Gertrude, Hamlet's visual evocations are so powerful that her vision is turned inward, to "such black and grained spots / As will not leave their tinct" (90–91). This is only one of the several instances in which Hamlet seems able to make others see and believe what he wishes them to. Perhaps Polonius, discerning in the clouds the shapes of camels, weasels and whales at Hamlet's direction, is only humoring a madman, and Osric, hot and cold by turns at the prince's suggestion, merely playing the sycophantic courtier. But our attention is nevertheless directed at these moments to the role which an observer's own disposition and perspective plays in determining what he sees, hears, and feels. The point is made explicit in the Gentleman's description of Ophelia's rambling discourse and the court's attempts to interpret it:

> Her speech is nothing,
> Yet the unshaped use of it doth move
> The hearers to collection; they yawn at it,
> And botch the words up fit to their own thoughts. . . .
>   (4.5.7–10)

Each listener must supply for himself whatever meaning is to be found in Ophelia's speech; it is not simply a matter of construing the content of what she says, but of manufacturing it. "Meaning" may thus be located exclusively within the perceiving consciousness, with no reference whatever to the object being perceived in the external world; like Galileo's Secondary Qualities, meanings "hold their residence solely in the sensitive body." The next logical step would be to question whether, in this world-picture, there need be posited any such entity as the object being perceived, or, indeed, any such place as the external world, if that is taken to mean an objective location shared and experienced in the same way by all of us. Hamlet denies that this is the case:

> *Ham.* Denmark's a prison.
> *Ros.* Then is the world one.
> *Ham.* A goodly one, in which there are many confines,
>   wards, and dungeons, Denmark being one o' th' worst.
> *Ros.* We think not so, my lord.
> *Ham.* Why then 'tis none to you; for there is nothing
>   either good or bad, but thinking makes it so. To me it
>   is a prison. (2.2.243–51)

Hamlet's statement has usually been taken as an expression of moral relativism, part of what Soellner calls "the age's increasing disillusion with norms" (141). In somewhat more detail, Harry Levin charts a progression from Montaigne's notion "That the taste of good or evils doth greatly depend on the opinion we have of them" to Donne's affirmation that "There's nothing simply good, nor ill alone, / Of every quality comparison / The only measure is" ("Metempsychosis" 517–20) to Hamlet's view that "there is nothing either good or bad, but thinking makes it so"—which Levin calls "the boldest of the three formulations" (75). And it is, though perhaps not in just the way Levin means. Hamlet is proclaiming a good deal more here than merely "that there are no ethical absolutes, that good and evil are value-judgments determined by relative standards," as Levin paraphrases him (75). The "good" and "bad" to which Hamlet refers are part of but are not limited to a moral context; they embrace states of feeling as well. More important, though, is the question of what these qualities are presumably relative to. Donne suggests that the comparison is one of good and ill as they are embodied in a variety of external forms; according to this view, one baker's bread is better than another's, not simply good in and of itself. But for Hamlet, though he compares Denmark to other dungeons in the prison of the world and pronounces it "one o' th' worst," the world itself is a prison not because it is relatively more restrictive than some other place but simply because he experiences it as one.

This is not relativism, then, but absolutism. Hamlet's subjectivity is independent of the world of external reality altogether: "0 God, I could be bounded in a nutshell, and count myself a king of infinite space—were it not that I have bad dreams" (254–56). Everything and everyplace is within; both the world Hamlet's body inhabits and the world of his dreams are self-created, like the meaning of Ophelia's meaningless words. It matters to Hamlet little or not at all what external objects stimulate his sense-perceptions; what matters to him is that the mechanism of that perception itself is "apopolexed," like his mother's. The only aspect of all this that could be called relativistic is his comparison of current sense-data with past; he can remember when the sky seemed a "most excellent canopy," a "brave o'erhanging firmament," a "majestical roof fretted with golden fire," and it may yet be so in fact, but that is beside the point, since now "it appeareth nothing to [him] but a foul and pestilential congregation of vapors" (299–303), in the same way that it is beside the point that the nightmares which may wake in the sleep of death are "merely" dreams. Appearance is everything; reality is not worth debating.

Subjectivity that shuts out any external standard is the ultimate form of absolutism. So too are Hamlet's moral judgments absolute. The evil of Claudius is never measured against any other evil, but is stated in the most extreme and definitive terms: he is a "Bloody, bawdy villain! / Remorseless, treacherous, lecherous, kindless villain!" (580–81). But the *existence* of Claudius's evil, and indeed of Claudius himself as a being on equal footing with Hamlet—of that, Hamlet is less positive. He experiences Claudius's sin as a stench in the nostrils, an overwhelming sensation of melancholy, a conviction that man is nothing more than a "quintessence of dust" (308). His focus, however, is not upon the supposed cause of these disturbing sensations, but upon the sensations themselves. The evil of Claudius has become disembodied, more real than Claudius; it has become, in fact, not Claudius's evil but Hamlet's disease. As Lawrence Danson has pointed out, Hamlet is "driven back to the only place where indubitable truth can reside, to the self: 'But I have that within which passeth show'" (*Tragic* 32). And if his mission is to rid the world of the evil that Claudius has loosed on it, given Hamlet's subjective conception of the world as a state of his own consciousness, his task might be accomplished by altering his perception of that evil, or by destroying the seat of consciousness that perceives it, as well as by killing Claudius.

Thus, both alternatives of the dilemma posed in the fourth soliloquy might be said to be equally effective, though in different ways: whether Hamlet turns his dagger against Claudius or against himself, the stench of Claudius's crime will be expunged from his nostrils. So Hamlet must decide whether to be or not to be, and if we translate this choice into theatrical terms, it might be put as follows: finding himself profoundly disturbed by the spectacle to which he is audience, shall Hamlet leave the theater? Or shall he enter the play?

Besides the possibility of an afterlife composed of incessant nightmare, there is another aspect of suicide that gives Hamlet pause. Though the act would indeed purge the rank odor of Claudius from his nostrils, it would leave the stench of his own decomposing corpse in Denmark's. "Not to be" expresses an impossible yearning—not for death, with its attendant putre-faction, but for that state of antiseptic non-being described in his first soliloquy: "0 that this too too solid[10] flesh would melt, / Thaw, and resolve itself into a dew!" (1.2.129–30). It may justly be asked why, if Denmark exists essentially in Hamlet's mind, he should care what (if anything) might remain behind after that mind ceased to exist. In fact, the distinction between melting, evaporating, and disappearing, on one hand, and "self-slaughter" (132) on the other, is itself an earlier version of the "To be or not to be" dilemma, an opposition of the subjective and objective conceptions of reality, and by implica-tion, of stage life and real life. "Real" people die, rot, and stink; "actors" are simply "melted into air, into thin air," as Prospero puts it (*The Tempest* 4.1.150).

So Hamlet, whose view of acting when the play begins is so jaundiced that he bridles when he believes that Gertrude is accusing him of playing his grief, must, in order to resolve his dilemma, get himself "a fellowship in a cry of players" (3.2.277–78). Acting is the way out of thought and into action, as he comes to realize. What sets actors apart from the rest of us, and particularly from Hamlet, is that they need not choose between alternatives, or weigh the consequences of what they act; they have only to play the parts written for them. By choosing not to withdraw from the theater but to enter the performance instead, Hamlet ultimately overcomes the obsta-cles that social decorum, psychological inhibition and dramatic convention have erected between him and the fate that "cries out" (1.4.81) for its fulfillment.

It is almost inevitable that Hamlet should choose theatrical means—*The Murder of Gonzago,* of which he is in part producer, playwright, and, as Ophelia calls him, chorus—to accomplish what is, finally, a dramatic purpose. Whether as spectator, dramatist or actor, he is throughout the play fascinated by the actor's craft. His prophetic soul tells him that it is his destiny to act, and the acting metaphor quite simply disposes of the problem of his "inaction": it is the necessary period of rehearsal that precedes all successful performances, during which the actor becomes secure enough in his role that his playing can take on the quality of spontaneity that Hamlet calls "rashness." When Hamlet has reached that point, he begins to speak of acting not as something he wills into being but as something that simply happens, without thought or conscious effort, as in his account to Horatio of his shipboard behavior: "Being thus benetted round with villainies, / Or I could make a prologue to my brains, / They had begun the play" (5.2.29–31).

In order to act, Hamlet must abandon the contempt for "seeming" that he displays at the beginning of the play in his passionate assertion that he has "that within which passes show"—as if all acting were necessarily hollow, a matter of technical imitation with neither substance nor feeling beneath it. Claudius appears to share this prejudice against surfaces when he asks Laertes, who has returned from France seeking vengeance, " . . . was your father dear to you? / Or are you like the painting of a sorrow, / A face without a heart?" (4.7.106–08). The difficult question of just how appearance— "show"—is related to inner substance—"that which passeth show"—is the subject of the third soliloquy. Hamlet has just performed[11] the first part of the Pyrrhus speech, and he has done it creditably, if we may believe Polonius. The player finishes the speech that Hamlet had begun, the stage empties save for Hamlet, and he makes the incident, as he so often does, an occasion for self-reproach:

> O, what a rogue and peasant slave am I!
> Is it not monstrous that this player here,
> But in a fiction, in a dream of passion,
> Could force his soul so to his own conceit
> That from her working all the visage wann'd,
> Tears in his eyes, distraction in his aspect,
> A broken voice, an' his whole function suiting
> With forms to his conceit? (2.2.550–57)

It is a difficult speech, full of abstract and archaic locutions, and it is not easy to recover the precise meanings of "conceit," "function," and "forms," or to sort out their relationship to each other in this particular context. But it would seem that the triumph of the player's performance, in Hamlet's view, lies in his ability to summon, through an act of will, an emotion that he has no cause in reality to experience, to the point where he can weep with Hecuba as he limns her grief. This represents a contrast to Hamlet's performance of the Pyrrhus speech, which must have come more easily to him since, as has often been noted, there are many similarities between Pyrrhus and himself.[12]

But what Hamlet finds "monstrous," he explains, is not the player's technical manipulation of feeling as a means to action, but his own inaction; already in possession of "the motive and the cue for passion" (561), he nevertheless cannot suit forms to his conceit—cannot, as Roy W. Battenhouse paraphrases it, "suit his action of body and voice . . . to his imagining of how he ought to behave" ("Significance" 11). Acting, then, should be an outward expression of what is inside; if there is nothing inside, or if the form belies the conceit (as in the case of Claudius, who smiles and is a villain), it is corrupt indeed—hence Hamlet's indignation at his mother's innocent question, "Why seems it so particular with thee?" (1.2.75). Hamlet's is the opposite problem: the conceit is in place but the form is missing.

The player, though, has successfully aligned what is inside and what is outside in a fashion that Hamlet envies. And he works out, during the course of this soliloquy, the proposition that there are two legitimate ways of fashioning this unity. One may begin with one's conceit, and discover a proper form in which to embody it; this Hamlet has been attempting to do without success. Or one may, like the player, do the reverse: begin with the form—the role in which one is cast—and "force his soul" to it. Eliot complained that Hamlet "is dominated by an emotion which is inexpressible, because it is in *excess* of the facts as they appear" (125), but it is really the *player's* emotion that is in excess of the facts; Hecuba may be a fiction, but the actor's tears are real, and quite expressive.

From the strictly theatrical point of view that the world/stage metaphor allows us to take toward what Hamlet sees as his own inaction, then, we may give the following description of it: the role in which he has been cast by fate is one that does not correspond to the promptings of his soul. Where an avenger is conventionally angry, hot-headed and hot-blooded, Hamlet is melancholy, introspective and passive; though the role seems to demand of him that his father's commandment "all alone shall live / Within the book and volume of [his] brain,/ Unmix'd with baser matter" (1.5.102–04), it is his mother's falling-off that continues to preoccupy him, together with the very fact of his continuing inaction, which, as I have argued at length, he experiences as a kind of psychic exile to a point outside the boundaries of the play. What the player's performance suggests to him is the possibility of willing a change in his inner self in order to bring it into conformity with the role which he must play.

Such a change he contemplated earlier, when he spoke of wiping from the table of his memory all the impressions, knowledge and other data that his youth had stored there—in effect, eradicating his original character and refashioning himself into a personification of revenge, a monomaniac whose only thought and purpose was the destruction of Claudius. But such a change is as difficult to achieve as it is horrible to contemplate; it is not simply a matter of speaking in a voice appropriate to such a figure, as he discovers when he attempts it:

Bloody, bawdy villain!
Remorseless, treacherous, lecherous, kindless villain![13]
Why, what an ass am I! This is most brave,
That I, the son of a dear father murthered,
Prompted to my revenge by heaven and hell,
Must like a whore unpack my heart with words
And fall a-cursing like a very drab,
A stallion! (2.2.580–87)

Battenhouse has suggested, in his interesting article on Hamlet's advice to the players, that the words with which he attempts to inspire in himself a will to vengeance that he does not at the moment possess "escalate into noisy bellow" (9); the speech to which he is "prompted" becomes so nakedly, emptily fustian that delivering it makes him feel like that most dishonest of all actors, the whore who counterfeits a passion she does not feel. Perhaps the reason that Hamlet is so consistently rude to everyone in the play is that social pleasantries call for just this sort of pretense on a lesser scale. The Hamlet of the past, "the glass of fashion and the mould of form" (3.1.153) as Ophelia called him, may have had a talent for courtesy, but he has lost it now; when he attempts to receive Rosencrantz and Guildenstern as friends and gentlemen, even those dull fellows notice that he can do so only "with much forcing of his disposition" (3.1.12).

If a role is to be well acted, then, it must be rehearsed until it penetrates down through the layers of pretense and reaches "the heart's core." Suiting forms to one's conceit involves a movement from within to without; getting up a part reverses the direction. Hamlet's instructions to his mother on ridding herself of her attachment to Claudius illustrate the workings of the mechanism:

Assume a virtue, if you have it not.
That monster custom, who all sense doth eat,
Of habits devil, is angel yet in this,
That to the use of actions fair and good
He likewise gives a frock or livery
That aptly is put on. Refrain to-night,

> And that shall lend a kind of easiness
> To the next abstinence, the next more easy;
> For use almost can change the stamp of nature. . . .
>   (3.4.160–68)

"Easiness," "ease"—just the quality he is to recommend to the player, that "smoothness" with which a good actor's "temperance" mollifies the expression of his passion without tearing it to tatters (3.2.7–10). Hamlet's speech to his mother is echoed by Horatio's explanation of how a man may sing as he digs up skulls: "Custom hath made it in him a property of easiness" (5.1.67). Thus reiteration itself may, if carried out for a sufficient length of time, make a role fit more "easily"; conceit may be modified to accord more nearly with form. Hamlet, of course, feels positively miscast, but as any professional actor knows, the part given him may also be modified; by changes of tone and emphasis, by the introduction of gesture and business, by rewriting and improvisation, the actor may gain some control over material that at first seemed intractable. Hamlet has been presented with a role that embarrasses him, calling as it seems to for rhetorical flourishes and gestures that saw the air. It is a part that better suits Pyrrhus or Laertes, the latter already something of a stock figure, who has no difficulty delivering the sort of speech associated with hotblooded young avengers:

> How came he dead? I'll not be juggled with.
> To hell allegiance! vows, to the blackest devil!
> Conscience and grace, to the profoundest pit!
> I dare damnation. To this point I stand,
> That both the worlds I give to negligence,
> Let come what comes, only I'll be reveng'd
> Most throughly for my father. (4.5.131–37)

Laertes even manages to surpass the hyperbole of this speech in a later one, delivered at Ophelia's funeral:

> O, treble woe
> Fall ten times treble on that cursed head
> Whose wicked deed thy most ingenious
>   sense

Depriv'd thee of! Hold off the earth a while,
Till I have caught her once more in mine
  arms.
          [*Leaps in the grave.*]
Now pile your dust upon the quick and
  dead,
Till of this flat a mountain you have made
T' o'ertop old Pelion, or the skyish head
Of blue Olympus. (5.1.246–54)

The fulsome overstatement of "ten times treble," the pedantry of the classical allusions, the self-dramatizing leap itself—these so offend Hamlet, the proponent of acting that must "o'erstep not the modesty of nature" (3.2.19), that he himself leaps after Laertes, moved not by Laertes's declaration of hatred for him, nor by Ophelia's death, but by his impatience with overblown and egotistical ranting; " . . . the bravery of his grief did put me / Into a tow'ring passion" (5.2.79–80), he later explains to Horatio. Hamlet's distaste for immodest speech and gesture (the flourishes and salvos that accompany Claudius's drinking are another example) is manifest throughout the play, and, just as he is to parody the courtly flatteries and obfuscations of Osric in the next scene, Hamlet parodies Laertes's overstatement here:

     . . . And if thou prate of mountains, *let them throw*
     Millions of acres on us, till our ground,
     Singeing his pate against the burning zone,
     Make Ossa like a wart! Nay, and thou'lt mouth,
     I'll rant as well as thou. (5.1.280–84; emphasis
       added)

   Hamlet finds Laertes's ornamented rhetoric objectionable on both moral and esthetic grounds. Not only is it, from a strictly theatrical point of view, bad dialogue, but it corrupts the communicative function of language itself, the only vehicle for exchanging and disseminating truth that people have at their disposal, as Danson points out (*Tragic* 25). And it is here, at Ophelia's funeral, that Hamlet finds at last a voice in which he can play the role of avenger without feeling like a usurper—a voice quieter and more meditative than that of Pyrrhus or Laertes, full of silky menace, couching its threats not in ear-splitting hyperbole but in the opposite figure, litotes or understatement:

> I prithee take thy fingers from my throat.
> For though I am not splenitive and rash,
> Yet have I in me something dangerous,
> Which let thy wisdom fear. (260–63)

Virtually all of the purple passages, the bloody expostulations, exaggerations and epithets that awaken Hamlet's contempt (whether in his own or someone else's mouth) occur in soliloquies or in lines addressed to no one in particular. These are speeches that do not advance the course of the action, but comment on it. Soliloquies fit most actors less "easily" than dialogue; Hamlet, who is always listening for "cues," is therefore in need of the cooperation actors get from each other in ensemble scenes, where lines spoken by one character to another provide the stimulus, the "motive and the cue," for an unhesitating response, which in turn provokes a response of its own, and so carries the scene along. Hamlet requires just this sort of incentive in the first two acts of the play, before he tricks Claudius into betraying his guilt; his third soliloquy expresses what is in effect a wish for a stimulus that will move him to violent response:

> Am I a coward?
> Who calls me villain, breaks my pate across,
> Plucks off my beard and blows it in my face,
> Tweaks me by the nose, gives me the lie i' th' throat
> As deep as to the lungs? Who does me this?
> Hah, 'swounds, I should take it; for it cannot be
> But I am pigeon-liver'd, and lack gall
> To make oppression bitter. . . . (2.2.571–78)

His conclusion is false, of course; whenever in the play he is confronted by the sort of goad or spur to action that he invokes

rhetorically here—as when Polonius calls out from behind the
arras, when Laertes expostulates from Ophelia's grave, when
his ship is boarded by pirates, or when, at the end, Claudius
quails before his already bloody sword—Hamlet acts unhesita-
tingly. What the above speech catalogues is the ways in which
men move other men to violence. Hamlet is describing a scene
he needs to play with Claudius, one in which the king leaves
off smiling and offers instead some form of insolent provoca-
tion. Hamlet's knowledge of his uncle's crime is intellectual
(what the ghost told him), emotional (what he feels toward
Claudius), and even olfactory, but it is not audible or visible. It
comes from within himself or from the ghost, when what he
requires is a cue from Claudius that will trigger in him action
that is not reasoned but "rash"—reckless, reflexive, automatic,
and instantaneous—"as swift / As meditation or the thoughts
of love." This is the more important function of *The Murder of
Gonzago*: not merely to validate the ghost's report, but to
compel Claudius to discard the appearance of amiability that
Hamlet knows to be false but that nonetheless, since it belies
Claudius's true role, prevents Hamlet from playing his own.

The play-within-a-play succeeds, if not in providing
"grounds," then in providing a cue to action; whether or not
Claudius's behavior objectively constitutes incontrovertible
proof of his guilt is a moot question, but Hamlet is ready after
the King's interruption of the play to "drink hot blood, / And
do such bitter business as the day / Would quake to look on"
(3.2.390–92). Earlier he had called for the most sweeping
alteration in himself—not that he should simply kill Claudius
but that he should become nothing more nor less than a killer.
At this he has almost succeeded, for he now finds himself
struggling with the inclination to kill Gertrude, and before he
leaves her closet, he will have remorselessly killed Polonius. To
be an avenger is to be a kind of machine for slaughter, and
Hamlet, before he dies, will have sent Rosencrantz and Guildenstern to their deaths and slain Laertes along with Claudius
in the final scene. No wonder passion seems to him bestial, at

the opposite extreme from both human feeling and rational calculation.

Claudius's behavior at the play assists Hamlet in another way as well. It gives him a precedent for his own behavior, for it shows him that a spectator may indeed interfere with, even put an end to, a show. Of course, there are reasons why Claudius should not be presumed to be governed by the restraints that inhibit most spectators. First, where the rest of us are in some sense guests of the actors, to whose "house" we have come, these actors are in Claudius's house—and more as servants than as guests. Second, *The Murder of Gonzago* is not designed merely to inspire the emotions we all might experience when watching a tragedy, but instead speaks directly to Claudius, isolating him in terror unmitigated by pity, a "guilty creature" (2.2.589) among, as Hamlet puts it, "we that have free souls" (3.2.241–42).

Still, it is significant that the king is so "struck to the soul" by what he sees—not merely by the image of his crime that is contained in the dumb-show, to which he may or may not be attending, but by the threat to his life implicit in the fact that the player-king is killed by his nephew—as to acknowledge, by his actions, that he is more a performer in a regicidal drama than a mere spectator to one. In effect, he here assumes his proper role in *Hamlet*, at last suiting forms to his own carefully-hidden conceit. And Hamlet, himself a member of the audience at *The Murder of Gonzago* as well as its presenter, watches the player-king of *Hamlet* begin the play in earnest, and is moved to play himself.

This movement from audience to stage is the pattern of the second half of *Hamlet*; the interruption of the play-within-a-play is followed by several other instances in which spectators fail to keep the place assigned them by custom and inhibition. The first is the closet scene, in which Polonius, ensconced behind the arras "To hear the process" (3.3.29) between Gertrude and Hamlet, cries out in alarm at the unexpected course that the action is taking, and pays with his life for that breach of decorum. Following that, as we have noted, both

Hamlet and Laertes interrupt Ophelia's funeral ("rites" already "maimed" [5.1.219], as Hamlet notes) in an extreme and startling manner. By so doing, Hamlet earns the disapproval of his mother, one of the ceremony's legitimate participants, who has played her own part with decorous solemnity and who calls her son's intrusion "mere madness" (284), even as Hamlet himself is outraged by what he regards as the impropriety of Laertes's upstaging him: "Dost thou come here . . . / To outface me with leaping in her grave?" (277–78), he demands.

This scene offers us a useful glimpse of the process by which, as Hamlet explained earlier to his mother, "use almost can change the stamp of nature" (3.4.168). Just as the Clown can sing while digging graves, having been habituated to his task, so Hamlet, now deeply occupied with plot and counter-plot, is for the moment so self-absorbed that he cannot remember how he has offended Laertes: "What is the reason that you use me thus? / I lov'd you ever" (5.1.289), he asks the son of the man he has recently butchered. The psychological restraints that kept him among the spectators are gone now, along with certain moral restraints as well.

Indeed, the casual way in which he kills Polonius, the lack of remorse he displays afterwards, the jokes he makes about the old man being at supper "Not where he eats, but where 'a is eaten" (4.3.19) have shocked certain of the play's most eminent commentators; Bradley used the word "callous" (90) to describe both Hamlet's usage of Polonius and his treatment of Rosencrantz and Guildenstern as well. Yet what else should we expect? If Hamlet as a spectator to the action of *Hamlet* was, as is typical of spectators, inwardly sensitive but outwardly quiescent, Hamlet as an actor illustrates Holland's principle that activity in one sphere precludes activity in the other. The player can weep for Hecuba because of, not in spite of, the fact that in reality she is nothing to him; into the emotional vacuum an esthetic conceit is introduced that suits the pre-existing form, as Hamlet tells his mother, and that comes to feel at home there. The Hamlet whom we most admire, and with whom we comfortably identify, is the introspective and humane man whose links to us are dramatized by the metaphor that presents his *in*action to us in dramatic terms: he is a spectator, one of us. But the Hamlet who exterminates Claudius at the end of the play calls to a darker side of the audience. He must be ready to drink hot blood—Claudius's or anybody else's. It is natural that this new quality should strike us as callous, as something that, in its purest form, is like the indiscriminate bloodthirstiness of a wild beast. But in terms of the theatrical metaphor, it is simply the absorption of an actor in his role, regarding his actions not in moral but in esthetic terms, as is appropriate for a man about to engage in a form of play.

That Hamlet has become such a man is clear at the end of the closet scene, when he says of Claudius's plot, "Let it work, / For 'tis the sport to have the enginer / Hoist with his own petar . . ." (3.4.205–07), and when he comes to think of the approaching confrontation as "most sweet" (209). Their joining of battle is in every sense a co-operative endeavor, uncle and nephew attuned at last "when in one line two crafts directly meet" (210). Hamlet is now more a member of Claudius's company than of ours, a fellow-player in both senses of the word. His new resemblances to Claudius are apparent in his treatment of Polonius: Hamlet, who wept for the foul and unnatural murder of his own father, finds the death of Laertes's father an irresistible occasion for comic banter. Even if we grant that King Hamlet was the paragon his son thinks him, and Polonius nothing more than an officious dotard, the difference in character hardly justifies killing the latter in the process of avenging the former—particularly if we look at his death, as we are soon obliged to do, from Laertes's and Ophelia's perspective. This "tedious old fool" was as much a paragon to his children as King Hamlet was to his son, and what can Hamlet seem to Laertes but precisely what Claudius seems to Hamlet: one who smiles, and smiles, and is a villain? The mirroring is complicated but precise, as Hamlet later admits: " . . . by the image of my cause I see / The portraiture of his [Laertes's]" (5.2.77–78).

It is not enough to say that as Hamlet attains the state of

mind in which he can kill, he comes more and more to resemble the smiling killer Claudius, for Claudius is more than that. At first, perhaps, we are willing to accept Hamlet's picture of a "remorseless, treacherous, lecherous, kindless, villain," but in the chapel scene we find a man more complex, more sensitive and altogether more human than the one-dimensional figure Hamlet takes Claudius to be—a man by no means remorseless, and one whose guilt makes him resemble the self-reproachful Hamlet, even as Hamlet is coming to resemble him in other respects. In fact, Claudius is caught in a dilemma of his own, as we discover in the chapel:

> Pray can I not,
> Though inclination be as sharp as will.
> My stronger guilt defeats my strong intent,
> And like a man to double business bound
> I stand in pause where I shall first begin,
> And both neglect. (3.3.38–43)

The "absolutist Hamlet," as Danson calls him (*Tragic* 31), is not aware of Claudius's tortured state; his view of the King's psyche is an oversimplified one, as is his approach to most of the ethical questions that bear on his relationships to the other characters. Neither his fortuitous killing of Polonius nor his purposeful but unnecessary killing of Rosencrantz and Guildenstern seem to him to be morally questionable; he is the heaven-appointed "scourge" (3.4.175) of those whom he takes to be Claudius's accomplices, and even his two old friends, he tells Horatio, "are not near my conscience" (5.2.58).

Yet it is inappropriate for us to reproach Hamlet in these instances for his "callousness" unless we are certain that we do not share it. Referring to the jokes that Hamlet makes while playing his grisly game of hide-and-seek with Polonius's corpse, Wilson Knight uses the term "horrible" (*Wheel* 27), and Bradley suggests that "it pains us, for Hamlet's sake, to hear them" (89–90). Whether Bradley was giving an accurate account of his contemporaries' responses or merely expressing an idealistic wish, we cannot know, but modern audiences, like

Elizabethan ones, are perhaps more tough-minded about such gallows humor than Victorians were likely to be, and Eleanor Prosser's modification of Wilson Knight's epithet seems appropriate: not horrible but "horribly comic," she calls Hamlet's gibes and sallies (202).

But if we find Hamlet's jokes funny—if we laugh at his claim to have taught Polonius at last the stillness and gravity that become a statesman, or at the line that particularly offended Bradley, "I'll lug the guts into the neighbor room" (3.4.212)— we share with Hamlet whatever inhumanity he is displaying by making those jokes. Kenneth Burke wrote that the tragic poet, in imagining the "crime" of which he treats, "symbolically commits it. Similarly, in so far as the audience participates in the happenings, it also participates in the offense" (48).14 It is in just this way that we experience the ease with which one's humanity slips away when one's judgment passes from the control of moral standards to that of esthetic ones. Not until Laertes's reappearance and Ophelia's death are we reminded that Polonius was something more than the foolish *senex* of Plautine farce, and that our laughter is precisely as "horrible" as the jokes themselves.

Hamlet's first words to Horatio in the play are, "Horatio—or I do forget myself" (1.2.161). Forgetting himself is what Hamlet attempts to do throughout the rest of the action. From the moment when he records his intention to wipe from the table of his memory all that makes him who he is to his final assertion of a new identity as "Hamlet the Dane!" (5.1.258), the play chronicles the tragic course of a man who is forced to become something that he despises in order to accomplish what he must. One of the most significant features of the change that Hamlet wills in himself as he struggles to suit forms to his conceit is his gradual surrender to and embrace of irresponsibility as an animating principle. His admiration for Horatio, "Whose blood and judgment are so well co-med-dled, / That they are not a pipe for Fortune's finger / To sound what stop she please" (3.2.69–71), is testimony to his earlier conviction that men inhabit a morally ordered universe, one in which the passions must and can be held in check by the restraints of reason. But the consequences of this belief are what Maynard Mack calls his "egocentricity" (62), his insistence not merely upon killing Claudius but upon reconciling his revenge with that moral order. Both Mack and Levin see in Hamlet's self-image and behavior a desire to emulate God— both in that he feels bound not only to decide whether or not Claudius shall die but also to determine the disposition of his soul as well (Mack 62), and also in that God may be conceived of as "the Ultimate Playwright," the function that Hamlet assumes when he inserts his dozen or sixteen lines into *The Murder of Gonzago* (Levin 84).

And of course, the man who could count himself king of infinite space, the sole occupant of his own universe, would necessarily feel in himself to some degree the sensations of godhead. But the responsibility of acting both efficaciously and rationally is paralyzing until he finds a way of avoiding the crushing burden of weighing alternatives and predicting consequences. His penetration of Rosencrantz's and Guildenstern's part in the king's plot, he tells Horatio, was accomplished not as the result of calculation but "Rashly" (5.2.6)— and from this experience Hamlet derives a principle of great importance:

> Our indiscretion sometimes serves us well
> When our deep plots do pall, and that should learn us
> There's a divinity that shapes our ends,
> Rough-hew them how we will. . . . (8–11)

Hamlet's dilemma is now not resolved but transcended; he is not God but God's minister, a role in which choice and decision are unnecessary. The important thing, at last, is only to act— the conceit is nothing, the form everything. Hamlet the actor puts himself at the disposal of Providence, who is a better "jig-maker" than he. The prince is responsible only for the accumulation of momentum; God will determine the direction of his motion, shape his ends. Having assimilated this principle, Hamlet can even afford to return to what looks like his earlier state of passive watchfulness, but what is really a kind of fatalism: "If it be now, 'tis not to come; if it be not to come, it will be now; if it be not now, yet it will come—the readiness is all" (220–22).

Another way of understanding the profound change in Hamlet without recourse either to theology or to theatrical metaphor is to see it as the gradual process by which he makes his father's cause his own. At the beginning of the play, when Claudius's evil is capable of being smelled but cannot be seen, Hamlet is continually perplexed by dilemmas of ontology, of being and seeming, of his own relationship to the rest of the world. By the end of the play, he has ceased to wonder whether his participation in the affairs of Denmark has any meaning or validity; he can act recklessly, thoughtlessly, "rashly." He has assimilated his duty and transformed it into desire. Foreign to his earlier character, it is part of him now, the "something dangerous" of which he warns Laertes, which has appeared in a nature not "splenitive and rash." The new element in his character is not, of course, under rational control, and Levin is correct in pointing out that when he does kill Claudius, he is not acting upon his duty to revenge but reacting to the stimulus of the moment, in "spontaneous retaliation for several other deaths—including, in a minute or two, his own" (35).

So Hamlet is able to turn his passive subjectivity into a kind of thoughtless self-assertiveness, not unlike the "flight or fight" mechanism by which animals reflexively respond to a noise or a movement without pausing to ascertain its meaning or cause. Men, too, possess this mechanism, and though the necessity of descending atavistically to the point where he allows it to govern his life appalls Hamlet, it leads him where the nobility of reason cannot.

The measure of Hamlet's tragedy is the distance he has been removed from us by the end of the play. The Hamlet "who is us," trapped in a maze of ambiguities, wandering among opposed but equally tenable points of view, is gone, and the wild man who forces poison down his uncle's throat, though he provides the play with a fitting conclusion, does not induce many people to say, "I have a smack of Hamlet myself."

The distance is once again illustrated by means of the world/stage metaphor. The direction of the predominant movement of *Hamlet* is out of the audience-world and into the play-world, as we have seen. When Hamlet has killed Claudius and Laertes, and taken his leave of Horatio and his dead mother, he turns—presumably to the "wonder-wounded" members of the Danish court, transfixed by what they have seen and heard—and addresses them for the last time:

> You that look pale, and tremble at this chance,
> That are but mutes or audience to this act,
> Had I but time—as this fell sergeant, Death,
> Is strict in his arrest—0, I could tell you—
> But let it be. (5.2.334–38)

The frame is broken one last time; the speech is aimed not only at the audience onstage but at those who mirror it, the larger offstage audience as well. J. V. Cunningham tells us that the pale, trembling survivors of Claudius's court are now our mediators or representatives, whose function it is "to express the proper emotional attitude and so convey that attitude directly to the larger audience" (15), and this is true. But it is a function previously fulfilled by Hamlet himself, who is now so deeply a participant in the play, so completely a resident of Denmark (even, for the moment between Claudius's death and his own, the *de facto* ruler and embodiment of the state itself) that other genuine characters in *Hamlet* can seem to him at best "mutes"—actors without lines.

I have suggested that Hamlet's abortive journey toward England may be understood as an attempt to escape the play-world for our own. In any case, whether this interpretation will work for Hamlet, nothing Hamlet does or says after his return to Denmark can be construed as equivocal; matters are pretty much settled by his startling reappearance. When Hamlet does address us from across the space between stage and audience, moreover, he has nothing to say to us, and resigns the task of reporting his cause aright to Horatio. In the last few moments of his life, only Denmark exists for him; he no longer lives bounded in the nutshell of self, but in the ancestral land of which he is, for the briefest of tenures, king. The instant of his reign is long enough for him to proclaim his successor and restore legitimacy to the throne. Then Hamlet dies, taking the final journey in a series that removed him by stages from the original and inappropriate position in which we first encountered him, vainly asserting his existence in what Righter terms our "more permanent" realm (73).

The play is full of journeys among various rungs of what Forker has called the "Platonic ladder": Hamlet moves from our world to the play-world to the world of "ultimate reality" (216n) to which all the major characters are consigned before the conclusion. When the stasis in which Hamlet's dilemma holds him prior to the closet scene is broken, he is no longer poised between being and non-being, subject and object, humanity and (as he conceives of it) bestiality. He is free to move toward his revenge and then past it to the fulfillment of his earliest wish: oblivion. That is the rest to which flights of angels sing him, and it is all we have to mitigate for us the tragedy of his agonizing transformations from spectator to player and from prince to king.

Notes

[1] Desperate to introduce some shred of spontaneity into his performance, Richard Burton is said on at least one occasion to have delivered the speech in German.

[2] Among the debts *Hamlet* owes to Kyd's *The Spanish Tragedy* is the resemblance of this speech to Balthazar's ambiguous description of his "yielding" to both Lorenzo and Horatio (discussed in Chapter 1), in which it is all but impossible to assign pronouns in such a way as to discover who is being named at any given point: "He spoke me fair, this other gave me strokes; / He promised life, this other threatened death," etc.

[3] Stephen Booth, to whose exegesis of the speech I am greatly indebted here, notes that in it (as in the play as a whole), "any identity can be indistinguishable from its opposite," resulting in "an impossible coherence of truths that are both undeniably incompatible and undeniably coexistent" ("On the Value of *Hamlet*" 116, 171).

⁴ Or those three other player-kings, Hamlet included, whom Anne Righter has discovered in the play (161).

⁵ The word "play" occurs four times in less than a hundred lines in 5.2.

⁶ The obsolete meaning of *distracted* is an architectural one—a distracted building has been demolished or pulled apart.

⁷ In Francis Fergusson's view, when Hamlet refers directly to the parallels between Denmark and the England of Shakespeare's audience," he "steps out of the narrative course of the play, out of the world of Denmark" (124–25). Here again, as at so many points, Shakespeare seems in Kyd's debt; *The Spanish Tragedy* similarly juxtaposes the world of the play with the world of the play's audience, in that case Spain/Portugal and England. See my article "The Settings of *The Spanish Tragedy*" for elaboration of this point.

⁸ Hamlet's subliminal awareness of his simultaneous existence in two opposed worlds is suggested by his habit of referring to himself at times as if he were inhabited by two opposed selves at once, as, for example, in his apology to Laertes: "If Hamlet from himself be ta'en away, / And when he's not himself does wrong Laertes, / Then Hamlet does it not, Hamlet denies it" (5.2.234–36).

⁹ Charles R. Forker is one critic who has addressed this issue: "The spectator knows that *Hamlet* is just a play. But Hamlet, the character, is not so sure, for the action in which he takes part is real from his point of view and unreal from the other" (219). I maintain, of course, precisely the opposite position: that if the action were "real" from Hamlet's point of view, he would have little difficulty in being engaged by it. Recently, Terry Eagleton has argued that any conclusions about "reality" in *Hamlet* must rest upon the ontological status of the Prince himself. In Eagleton's view, Hamlet has no "essence," but is "pure deferral and diffusion, a hollow void which offers nothing determinate to be known. His 'self' consists simply in the range of gestures with which he resists available definitions . . ." (72). Perhaps the most suggestive and illuminating discussion of the consequences and implications of Shakespeare's breaking of the dramatic frame is still Robert M. Adams's chapter "Trompe l'oueil in Shakespeare and Keats" in *Strains of Discord*.

¹⁰ I depart from Evans's text, which emends the F1 "solid" to "sallied"; obviously, my reading requires the original word, which is preserved by a number of other modern editors, such as Willard Farnham in the Pelican edition.

¹¹ "Performed" is, I admit, inexact, the speech consisting of third-person narration rather than dialogue. But certainly, delivering it requires that Hamlet assume Pyrrhus's character to an extent, and that he project, dramatically, Pyrrhus's state of mind.

¹² Note Pyrrhus's momentary paralysis, which prefigures Hamlet's own: "So as a painted tyrant Pyrrhus stood / And, like a neutral to his will and

matter, / Did nothing" (2.2.480–82). And, as Booth and others have pointed out, Pyrrhus and Hamlet are but two of four sons in the play who have fathers' deaths to avenge.

[13] Alone among modern editors, Evans omits "O vengeance" at what would be 2.2.581.

[14] Stephen Booth points out that both the audience and Polonius "overestimate the degree of safety that they have as innocent bystanders" (159); it is this misplaced sense of security that costs Polonius his life and (in my view) the audience its innocence.

5

"Welcome and Unwelcome Things at Once": Macbeth and The Dilemmas of The Psyche

Though Hamlet dwells at length on the rottenness of Denmark, on the relationship between the *malaise* of the state and his own infirmity, it is not clear that the connection is a causal one or that it exists outside his own perception of it. Certain features of his melancholy may be rooted in the play's setting, but others seem not to be; Denmark may be, as Hamlet claims it is, "an unweeded garden," or a particularly obnoxious dungeon in the prison of the world, but such settings, however unpleasant, do not necessarily induce in their inhabitants Hamlet's peculiar penchant for seeing all alternatives as antitheses, for converting all decisions into dilemmas. His dilemmas, if not his melancholy, are more the product of his intensely subjective vision of the world than they are the result of his interaction with that world as we see it in the play.

Macbeth's Scotland, however, is a different matter. It complements almost perfectly the landscape of Macbeth's mind, nourishing and reinforcing the dualism that is the most obvious and significant feature of both. It is doubleness that informs the nightmarish world of the play—doubleness primarily in the form of a central and continuous paradox first announced by the witches when they intone, "Fair is foul, and foul is fair" (1.1.11), and immediately echoed by Macbeth when he remarks to Banquo, "So foul and fair a day I have not seen" (1.3.38). The play's "multitudinous antitheses,"[1] as Kenneth Muir calls them (Arden xiii), are a feature of perception and expression shared by most of the other characters as well, one that threatens them with a series of stalemates brought about by the conflict of equally powerful oppositions. It is, indeed, almost impossible to overestimate the degree with which the play is saturated with antithesis. It is woven into the fabric of everyday speech, as when Macbeth describes the night as being "Almost at odds with morning, which is which" (3.4.126), or when a captain, reporting the battle in which Macbeth distinguishes himself at the beginning of the play, compares the warring armies to "two spent swimmers that do cling together / And choke their art" (1.2.8–9), or when the Porter discourses on the manner in which drink both "provokes, and unprovokes" lechery (2.3.29). Our attention is in this manner constantly drawn to all that is paralyzing and self-defeating in human experience, and to the ultimate state of entropy toward which events and people ever seem to drift. The Porter continues:

> Therefore much drink may be said to be an equivocator
> with lechery: it makes him, and it mars him; it sets him
> on, and it takes him off; it persuades him, and disheart-
> ens him; makes him stand to, and not stand to. . . .
> (30–34)

The function of these mirror-like dualities is to provide a context for Macbeth, who is himself, as the play opens, a mirror of the treacherous Thane of Cawdor, whom he has sup-planted—"Bellona's bridegroom, lapp'd in proof, / Confronted him with self-comparisons, / Point against point, rebellious arm 'gainst arm" (1.2.54–56), Rosse tells us. But Macbeth is also a mirror of himself. His peculiar nemesis is a state of psychic dissociation that divides his character into two antithetical halves. We see the effect of this opposition when, at the play's opening, Macbeth describes the effects of Duncan's murder in the following terms:

> My thought, whose murther yet is but fantastical,
> Shakes so my single state of man that function
> Is smother'd in surmise, and nothing is
> But what is not. (1.3.139–42)

Herbert Grierson suggests that *single*, in the vague but crucial phrase "my single state of man," means *indivisible* (qtd. in Muir

21n), and most of the play's recent commentators have joined
him in conceiving of Macbeth's life after his murder of Duncan
and his usurpation of the Scottish throne as a quest for
indivisibility—as a search for "wholeness" (Terence Eagleton
13), as an exorcism of the psychological "discontinuity" that
plagues him throughout the play (Traversi 155), as an attempt
to heal "that dichotomy between intellect and action which is to
sunder his nature into two warring entities" (Parker 476–77).

What is difficult to credit, though, is Macbeth's implicit claim
that he (or for that matter, anybody else in Scotland) possesses,
or could possess, the homogeneity of spirit, the psychic consistency, that the phrase "my single state of man" suggests. He
himself argues that major discontinuities are foreign to his, or
anyone's nature: "Who can be wise, amaz'd, temp'rate, and
furious, / Loyal, and neutral, in a moment? No man"
(2.3.108–09) he insists, in order to justify having killed the
grooms outside Duncan's chamber on what he tries to pass off
as an unconsidered impulse. But by this point in the play, we
have become aware that any man may be composed of just
such contradictions, and that Macbeth, of all men, is most
susceptible to them. The consistency that Macbeth claims for
himself and others is, in Scotland as Shakespeare has conceived
it as a setting for the play, merely wishful—a desire to regain
that "single state" that is both an ideal condition of mental
equilibrium and the primary symbol of the lost order associated
with an earlier, less troubled age in Scottish history.

It is Macbeth's preoccupation—one might call it his obsession—with making his character homogeneous that provides
Lady Macbeth with the means of tempting him to the assassination. She takes full advantage of his intense absorption with
his "single state" by accusing him, figuratively, of lacking it—
of being two different men at once:

> Was the hope drunk
> Wherein you dress'd yourself? Hath it slept since?
> And wakes it now to look so green and pale
> At what it did so freely? (1.7.35–38)

188   *Welcome and Unwelcome Things at Once*

And she sometimes greets him by several different names—
"Great Glamis! worthy Cawdor!" (1.5.54) she calls him—as do
the hallucinatory voices that Macbeth hears after Duncan's
murder, crying, "'Glamis hath murther'd sleep, and therefore
Cawdor / Shall sleep no more—Macbeth shall sleep no more'"
(2.2.39–40).

It is not surprising, then, that she is able to tempt him to
murder by promising him that actually committing the crime
will restore to him just the unified sensibility that his fantasies
of the murder seem to have destroyed:

> Art thou afeard
> To be the same in thine own act and valor
> As thou art in desire? Wouldst thou have that
> Which thou esteem'st the ornament of life,
> And live a coward in thine own esteem,
> Letting "I dare not" wait upon "I would,"
> Like the poor cat i' th' adage?[2] (1.7.39–45)

Lady Macbeth is correct in discerning, in the dualism of
Macbeth's character, the potential for a similar dilemma:

> Thou wouldst be great,
> Art not without ambition, but without
> The illness should attend it. What thou wouldst highly,
> That wouldst thou holily; wouldst not play false,
> And yet wouldst wrongly win. (1.5.18–22)

Macbeth regards the witches' prophesy as a "suggestion"
that he kill Duncan in order to become king (1.3.134), but in fact
they say nothing of the means by which their prophesy will be
realized, as Macbeth immediately recognizes: "If chance will
have me king, why, chance may crown me / Without my stir"
(143–44) he tells himself almost wistfully, though the logic of
this passive course of action is powerless against his "black and
deep desires" (1.4.51). His impulse to kill—to gain the throne
through a particularly horrible act of bloodshed—comes from
within himself, as do both his revulsion against the act and the
concomitant weakening of his resolve not to perform it. His

reasons for letting Duncan live are many and compelling: Duncan is his kinsman, his liege and his guest, and besides, has been "So clear in his great office, that his virtues / Will plead like angels, trumpet-tongu'd against / The deep damnation of his taking-off" (1.7.18–20). Against these motives are arrayed his wife's imputation of cowardice—"When you durst do it, then you were a man" (49), she chides him—and his own fascination with killing: though thoughts of murdering Duncan produce in him the physical symptoms of horror, the standing hair and knocking heart of which he complains (1.3.135–37), Macbeth is "bent to know / By the worst means the worst" (3.4.133–34). He insists that they "proceed no further in this business" (1.7.31), protesting to his wife, "I dare do all that may become a man; / Who dares do more is none" (46–47), but only a moment later, he is won over again to her cause, not by any logical persuasions on her part but by a self-presentation as ghastly as any imagining of Duncan's murder:

> *Lady M.*   I have given suck, and know
> How tender 'tis to love the babe that milks me;
> I would, while it was smiling in my face,
> Have pluck'd the nipple from his boneless gums,
> And dash'd the brains out, had I so sworn as you
> Have done to this. (54–59)

His scruples apparently overwhelmed by this paradoxical vision of nurturing womanliness and destroying manliness wedded together into a single monstrous parent, Macbeth offers no further resistance to the project.

Predictably, since he looks at the murder from two antithetical points of view at once, he cannot resolve his dilemma by choosing one or the other of the alternatives and living with the consequences of his choice. Instead, he yields to external "suggestion" (1.3.134), to "soliciting" (130), and the result is that the act, instead of unifying him, exacerbates the original condition of dissociation. In order to kill Duncan, he must further alienate his faculties from each other, no matter how such an action threatens his quest for his single state of man: "The eye wink at the hand; yet let that be / Which the eye fears, when it is done, to see" (1.4.52–53). Kenneth Muir has observed that Macbeth regards his hand as having "an independent existence of its own" (Arden xxxi); actually, Macbeth goes even farther than this, willfully polarizing his being, setting his hand and his eye in opposition to each other. These organs represent, respectively, the outer and the inner man—the active, logical, worldly component of his character and the ethical and emotional consciousness that is now directly in conflict with it. Nor is he alone in this regard. Lady Macbeth, too, despite her claim that she possesses the brutality and strength of purpose her husband lacks, calls for the concealing blanket of darkness, "That my keen knife see not the wound it makes" (1.5.52). For her, the sheer horror of the deed has, by the end of the play, overwhelmed all rational considerations of its beneficial consequences: "What need we fear who knows it, when none can call our pow'r to accompt? Yet who would have thought the old man to have had so much blood in him?" (5.1.37–40). Unlike Macbeth, she never succeeds in blunting the tortured sensibility that at last deprives her of her wits and her life.

A radical disjunction is thus introduced into the very course of Macbeth's life. Once Duncan is dead, his past and his present have little in common with each other. To have been a paragon of loyalty and service, and to metamorphose, with terrifying suddenness, into an arch-traitor, is to render one's personal history incoherent and therefore incomprehensible. In a speech that is both a public expression of mourning and a telling piece of self-analysis, Macbeth muses, with the wistfulness that is becoming characteristic of his meditations,

> Had I but died an hour before this chance,
> I had liv'd a blessed time; for from this instant
> There's nothing serious in mortality:
> All is but toys. . . . (2.3.91–94)

"Nothing serious in mortality" is a way station between Macbeth's earlier presentiment that the murder would make reality and illusion indistinguishable from one another ("Whatever is, is not") and his ultimate conception of life as "a tale / Told by an idiot, full of sound and fury, / Signifying nothing" (5.5.26–28). Seriousness, significance, reality itself—all are defined for Macbeth by the single quality of coherence, and he is increasingly hard put to function in the play's world as it becomes, largely due to his own actions, a place of anarchy.

Macbeth's failure to resolve the dilemma with which he confronts himself when he makes the witches' prophesies a pretext for contemplating Duncan's murder has a predictable result: instead of disappearing, the dilemma merely changes form. Having killed Duncan, Macbeth finds that he must kill Banquo and Fleance; Banquo's blood begets more guilt, and more blood is required to obscure from Macbeth the sight of what he has done, until, as he puts it, "I am in blood / Stepp'd in so far that, should I wade no more, / Returning were as tedious as go o'er" (3.4.135–37). Again he is, like "the poor cat i' th' adage," poised immobile between two alternatives. Traversi finds in this speech evidence of a penitent Macbeth, one who discovers, after Banquo's death, "that his real wish is to retrace his steps, to recover an original state of innocence, but that . . . he cannot do so" (174). But a closer look at the metaphor reveals that, far from yearning for repentance, Macbeth finds the prospect "tedious"—no less tedious, and no more, than the prospect of further bloodshed.

The trouble with examining Macbeth's conscience in the light of doctrinaire Christian ethics, as Traversi does, is that Macbeth experiences his guilt more as a psychic and even a physical phenomenon than a moral one; the absolutes of his personality are therefore more concretely presented than the necessarily abstract discourse of conventional morality would permit. What Macbeth desires is not his "original state of innocence" but his "single state of man," and he believes (not without some justification) that he can as readily attain that state by continuing to shed blood as by ceasing to do so. To restore unity to his character, Macbeth requires simply to be one thing or the other—either a man covered with blood or one washed clean. What is intolerable is to remain a motley combination of both.

Unity of character, then, is not a moral attribute. Monsters may possess it as readily as saints; men, in this play, cannot possess it at all. We cannot ignore the moral implications of Macbeth's choice, but we obscure his character if we insist upon seeing him as a moralist, or alternatively, with Stephen Booth, as "morally shallow" (*Indefinition* 106), rather than as a man searching for psychic relief in whatever form it is available. How far he is from craving "innocence" we may discern from the fact that he resolves this dilemma as impulsively as he attempted to resolve his earlier one: "Strange things I have in head, that will to hand, / Which must be acted ere they may be scann'd" (138–39), he announces, and wades further into blood by sending the murderers to slaughter Macduff's wife and children. If the memory of Duncan's blood tortures him, he believes that it may be blotted out and submerged by the blood of countless new victims; if he feels himself torn in two, perhaps one more piece of killing will dispense with the unwanted half for good. This he suggests when, upon learning that Fleance has escaped his plot, he exclaims, "Then comes my fit again. I had else been perfect, / Whole as the marble . . ." (20–21).

To whatever extent we wish to see Macbeth's behavior in ethical terms, it is important that we recognize him for the moral absolutist he is, a man for whom no compromises, no accommodations, no half-measures are possible. This is not a new idea; B. L. Reid wrote some time ago that the play "deals with absolutes, the fullest moral absolutes available in the kingdom of this world" (19). So it does, but we should be aware that such absolutism entails as well the sort of moral rigidity that is almost invariably fatal in tragedy, however awe-inspiring the spectacle of the ensuing catastrophe may be. In Euripides's *Hippolytus*, for example, the tragic hero is destroyed because, in conformity with his principles, he ignores the worldly and practical advice of the Chorus that he should make obeisances to Aphrodite whether he reveres her or not. Theirs is typical, even conventional, counsel; choruses usually espouse the virtues of moderation, conciliation, and flexibility. But these are qualities foreign to the protagonists of Greek and Shakespearean tragedy, particularly to the absolutist Macbeth, who insists upon being "perfect," and who, his wife recognizes, will settle for no less than all: a man who, in her words, "wouldst not play false, / And yet wouldst wrongly win" (1.5.21–22).

It is Macbeth's absolutism, logically enough, that makes the riddles of the Weird Sisters more assimilible than his own dilemmas. Riddles have a kind of appeal for his absolutist temperament because, as we have discovered in examining the "problem comedies," they are themselves whole and self-contained; they offer "perfect" answers, neat and total solutions. As Phyllis Gorfain has said, "Macbeth himself becomes suicidal until the riddling prophesies are fulfilled. Only then are deeds done and understood, and he accordingly attains a resolute view of his self-delusion" (202). Macbeth may complain that the witches are "imperfect speakers" (1.3.70), but as each prophesy comes true, his satisfaction becomes more evident— even at the conclusion of the play and of his life, when Birnam Wood advances on Dunsinane, and he discerns the message implicit in "th' equivocation of the fiend / That lies like truth" (5.5.42–43).

Macbeth's absolutist quest for perfection and psychic coherence accounts for an important irregularity in the play's structure. It is customary in those of Shakespeare's plays that deal with questions of sovereignty for the various political, moral and thematic conflicts to find their dramatic representation in the personal and/or political struggle between two men: one thinks immediately of Richard II and Bolingbroke, Hal and Hotspur, and Richard III and Richmond. In *Antony and Cleopatra*, in fact, one function of Lepidus is to emphasize, through his temporary and distracting presence, the inevitability of the ultimate confrontation between the world's "pair of chaps"

(3.5.13), Antony and Octavius Caesar. And in *Hamlet*, the moral learned by all of the prince's lesser antagonists was, as he put it, "'Tis dangerous when the baser nature comes / Between the pass and fell incensed points / Of mighty opposites" (5.2.660–62). To be sure, such distinct polarization is not invariable; the assassination of Julius Caesar and the usurpation of Prospero's dukedom were both accomplished by groups of conspirators rather than by single antagonists. Still, the traditional agon or contest between two opponents is so central to the development of Western dramatic tragedy that it is worth noting those occasions on which Shakespeare departs from the dramatic structure associated with it, and worth inquiring into the function of those departures as well.

Macbeth is such as occasion, for the forces that oppose Macbeth are under dual leadership. It is Malcolm who represents royal legitimacy in Scotland, but it is Macduff who defends it by confronting and killing Macbeth. Both have seen their families destroyed by Macbeth's treachery, both are loyal to the line that traces itself from Duncan, and both are falsely suspected of perfidy; if their roles are not actually redundant, they overlap a good deal, and, purely for the sake of dramatic expediency, there seems no compelling reason why Malcolm should not have assumed both functions, with Macduff absenting himself from the play altogether—particularly if one finds in Macduff, as Stephen Booth does, "a role in which no actor has a chance of capturing our attention . . . until IV.iii,— where Shakespeare entirely undoes him by making his presence painful to his moral allies, the audience" (*Indefinition* 107).

Part of the reason why Macduff figures prominently in the play may be that the historical figure on whom Shakespeare modeled him was perhaps too well-known to have been left out of the play entirely. Since the events treated in *Macbeth* had a good deal of bearing on the establishment of the royal family that occupied the English throne at the time the play was written, moreover, following Holinshed with some fidelity may have been the playwright's most politic course. But the play offers us another critique of Macduff's function, one that is more satisfying for our purposes because it demonstrates its necessity in terms of Macbeth's quest for his "single state of man."

Macduff's nature is revealed to us most tellingly in the strange scene to which Booth referred, in which Malcolm confesses to a series of increasingly monstrous crimes in order to determine, by Macduff's responses, what sort of man he is and where his loyalties lie. Macduff listens to Malcolm's accounts of his "lust" and "avarice" with growing disapproval, but is willing, for the sake of Scotland, to overlook them: "All these are portable, / With other graces weigh'd" (4.3.89–90), he explains. But when Malcolm asserts that he would "confound / All unity on earth" (99–100), Macduff can temporize no longer, and pronounces Malcolm unfit either to govern or to live. This is, surprisingly, the response for which Malcolm has been waiting. He now retrieves his confessions, announcing that they are part of an elaborate test designed to affirm not Macduff's personal loyalty to him but rather its opposite: because Macduff gives his allegiance to causes, not to individuals, Malcolm pronounces him a man of principle, and he praises Macduff's indignation, pronouncing it a "noble passion, / Child of integrity" (114–15).

The key term here is the ambiguous word *integrity*. If by it we understand Malcolm to mean devotion to a moral principle rather than to personalities or private ends, it would then appear that Macduff's role in the play is to exemplify a disinterested concern for justice (news of the slaughter of his family by Macbeth has not yet reached him), in contrast to Malcolm, whose reasons for hating Macbeth are, of course, intensely personal. However, this view of Macduff's character makes more problems for us than it solves, for there are grounds on which it has been argued that his integrity is seriously open to question. Robert Ornstein states the case against him concisely: "Macduff . . . displays a curious worldliness in his interview with Malcolm. Of course he finally passes the test which Malcolm offers, he is finally revolted by Malcolm's self-portrait of vice; yet how much, how very much of vice will Macduff accept before his stomach turns" (*Moral* 233).

Yet Malcolm is not wrong to call attention to Macduff's "integrity," for in another and more literal sense, "integrity" means just that wholeness, completeness, or coherence that has been Macbeth's chief preoccupation from the start. The function of Macduff as the focus of opposition to Macbeth is rooted in this form of integrity, which Macbeth lacks and which Macduff, more than any other character in the play, possesses. It manifests itself primarily in the flexibility, the willingness to settle for halves, that permits Macduff to overlook Malcolm's lesser sins because they are "portable." It is a human quality that will make him not a tragic hero but a survivor, in a country whose survival is at issue throughout the play, and it is precisely because of his willingness to accommodate his principles to the exigencies of a hostile universe, for which Ornstein and Booth take him to task, that he is Scotland's best hope. Ornstein is correct in asserting that Macduff's tolerance for vice is high, but in this play, tolerance for vice is not a fault for which Macduff is to be condemned. Had Macbeth been better able to tolerate the vicious impulses he discovered within himself, he might have been better able to contain them.

This is not to argue that Macduff's willingness to compromise, to accept human imperfection in himself and others, is an admirable quality *per se*; Ornstein may be justified in reproaching him (as Macduff reproaches himself) with failing to assure the safety of his family in Scotland before departing for England (*Moral* 233). But the alternative to Macduff's imperfections is far more dangerous. Macbeth's compulsion to make himself "perfect"—perfection representing, in psychological terms, a concept of himself as whole and complete; in moral terms, a devotion to an absolute ideal of ethical conduct—is such that, as we have seen, if he cannot be a saint, he must transform himself into a devil. Men like Macduff, by contrast, represent a human alternative to a morality and a psychology that deal in inhuman and abstract absolutes. If we look at the passage in which Macduff receives the news of his family's destruction, we perceive an essential difference between his character and that of Malcolm, who shares many of Macbeth's absolutist traits: when Malcolm insists upon a unilateral response—"Dispute it like a man"—Macduff explains that manhood is not the simple, single thing that Malcolm thinks it: "I shall do so; / But I must also feel it as a man" (220–21).

The play has been to this point, and continues to be, an extended debate on the definition of manhood. Lady Macbeth's extreme position, that manliness consists in daring to murder sleeping old men in their beds, or to dash out the brains of one's own nursing children, is echoed late in the play by Old Siward, whose sole concern, when he loses his son in battle, is that the boy died "like a man," his wounds "on the front." Even Malcolm finds this view callous: "He's worth more sorrow, / And that I'll spend for him," says the prince, to which the unmoved father replies, "He's worth no more" (5.9.8–17). Macbeth's original conception of manhood, which contrasted with that of his wife, was similar to Macduff's in its moderation: "I dare do all that may become a man; / Who dares do more is none"—but by the fifth act, this has changed; what is humanly responsive in him, capable of discriminating between what becomes a man and what does not, is no longer discernible. Indeed, the entire affective component of his nature has all but disappeared, and he cannot even rouse himself to respond when the cries of women announce his wife's death.

Macduff, by contrast, is a complete man. He is both a soldier and a father; he can weep and revenge, can play "the woman with mine eyes, / And braggart with my tongue!" (4.3.230–31); he is a man "of no woman born" (5.8.31) but altogether the most human character in the play. For all his contradictory parts, he is not afflicted, as Macbeth is, with sensations of psychic conflict, or turned into a moral schizophrenic; composed of disparate elements, he is able to synthesize them, accepting his weakness along with his strength, vice and error along with virtue and truth. He alone possesses something that might be described as the "single state of man"—a personality that is single because it is integrated, the most meaningful form integrity can assume in this play. Macduff's integrity is not, as might be supposed, set in opposition to the flexibility of his character; on the contrary, these two seemingly antithetical qualities are united and reconciled in him. He retains his "single state of man" because he is in all respects a man, and does not demand more of himself than that he should be one.

Malcolm, however, though he is Scotland's only political alternative to Macbeth, bears a remarkable resemblance to his enemy in temperament—far more than to his ally Macduff. The crimes that Malcolm confesses to, L. C. Knights points out, are Macbeth's own, particularly his readiness to "confound / All unity on earth" (*Explorations* 28); indeed, the disunity of Malcolm's own character is evident throughout the testing scene, and lends to it a quality of incoherence, even of paradox. Robert Grudin claims that the resemblance is misleading, that Macbeth's character is in fact antithetical to that of Malcolm, who borrows his enemy's evil disposition "briefly and harmlessly" (163). But we should note that when Malcolm disavows his crimes and boasts of his truthfulness, he does so in the course of confessing to a lie; as a consequence, his claim to "innocence," with which he means to allay Macduff's anxieties, has much the opposite effect—perhaps because such innocence, as Malcolm describes and illustrates it, sounds more like freedom from experience and knowledge than freedom from guilt:

> I am yet
> Unknown to woman, never was forsworn,
> Scarcely have coveted what was mine own,
> At no time broke my faith, would not betray
> The devil to his fellow, and delight
> No less in truth than life. My first false
>   speaking
> Was this upon myself. (4.3.125–31)

Traversi feels that Malcolm "reveals himself as a truly dedicated man" in this passage (176), but in a play filled with terrible self-discoveries made through bitter experience, Malcolm's insistence upon his virginity, sexual and otherwise, is not as reassuring as it is intended to be. His scornful dismissal of Macbeth and Lady Macbeth in the final speeches of the play should not surprise us, for if he regards those dark impulses to which Macbeth surrenders as "strangers to [his] nature" (125), how can he know what it is to struggle against them? B. L. Reid, who admires Malcolm, is nonetheless compelled to admit that "it is not easy to forgive his contemptuous reference to 'this dead butcher and his fiend-like queen.' For that is only literal truth, not complex enough to be wholly true" (41). The fact that Malcolm seems incapable of comprehending complex or paradoxical truths does not augur well for the prospects of renewed harmony and order in Scotland.

Malcolm's recantation leaves Macduff momentarily in a dilemma—speechless, though hardly with admiration:

> *Mal.*   Why are you silent?
> *Macd.* Such welcome and unwelcome things at once
>   'Tis hard to reconcile. (137–39)

Macduff is understandably happy to discover that Malcolm is not the lecherous, covetous, anarchic tyrant he confessed to being, but he seems at the same time understandably offended by the machinations of his future king's devious test. Indeed, Roy Walker claims that for Macduff, "the opposites are not merely hard but impossible to reconcile" (163). But the ending of the play refutes this argument. Macduff's talent for compromise has allowed him to shrug off his dismay; he has followed Malcolm against Macbeth because Malcolm is clearly the lesser of two evils, and in Act 5, his enthusiasm for the new regime seems unalloyed. The important question is not whether Macduff can reconcile the opposites in Malcolm's character, but whether Malcolm can.

For Malcolm may be seen, potentially at least, as a Macbeth in embryo—a man who, boasting of perfection in himself though he lives in an imperfect world, may fall as Macbeth did.

Reid praises Malcolm for "the simplicity with which he describes his own young chastity and innocence," a simplicity that "creates another lovely absolute, the polar opposite of Macbeth's weary and ramified criminality" (41). But in this play, polar opposites have a way of turning into one another, and a man who has never lied, never coveted, never lusted is less a man than a figure of allegory³—a conventional "man of snow," like Angelo in *Measure for Measure* or Malheureux in John Marston's *The Dutch Courtesan*. When temptation seeks such a figure out, as it invariably does, his fall from grace and from innocence is violent and complete, like that of Macbeth. Whatever else absolutes are in this play, they are not "lovely."

Shortly before his death, Macbeth succeeds in purging himself of his internal conflicts and contradictions, but he does so by achieving a state of single-mindedness that has little to do with being a man. He rids his nature of its last vestiges of moral sensitivity, and consequently of its capacity to experience horror:

> I have almost forgot the taste of fears.
> The time has been, my senses would have cool'd
> To hear a night-shriek, and my fell of hair
> Would at a dismal treatise rouse and stir
> As life were in't. I have supp'd full with horrors;
> Direness, familiar to my slaughterous thoughts,
> Cannot once start me. (5.5.9–15)

The earlier dilemmas are past; no longer poised between heaven and hell, pity and terror, he has waded into blood until it has covered him completely, and his momentum has carried him past any danger of physical or moral paralysis. Though there is no reason whatever to do so, though his resolution has begun to fail him at the approach of Birnam Wood and Macduff's elucidation of the witches' riddles, though he believes at last the prophesy of his imminent doom, he continues mechanically upon his present course: "I'll fight, till from my bones my flesh be hack'd" (5.3.32), he vows, and does—

indeed, until, in a final ironic image of dissociation, his head is severed from his body.

The effect of his personal fate on the dramatic structure of the play, and our response to its ending, is problematic. Traversi sees Malcolm as "a king . . . to whom the loyalty of free men is properly due, and from whom royal bounty may again be expected to flow" (181), but this is to look beyond the ending of the play to an indeterminate future; moreover, if the "bounty" consists of titles and honors parcelled out to the victorious, it recalls the beginning of the play, when the dispensing of royal bounty brought assassination and usurpation to Duncan.

Unlike Walker, Stephen Booth does not depend upon conjecture about events that occur after the play's conclusion for his understanding of that conclusion; he argues that, unlike *King Lear*, *Macbeth* does have a definitive and final ending, that "in the last speech of the play, Malcolm ties off all the loose threads of Scottish politics" (*Indefinition* 91). But anyone familiar with the broad outlines of Scottish political history, as Shakespeare's audience must have been, knew that the witches' prophesy concerning the disposition of the throne would eventually prove accurate: Banquo's issue, the Stuart line, would sooner or later prevail. Booth himself, commenting on the chorus of "Hails" with which Malcolm is greeted at the ending, is reminded of the witches' earlier greeting to Macbeth, and confesses to a "vague, free-floating sense that the old cycle is starting all over again in the new" (*Indefinition* 92–93).[4]

Many scholars have proposed the view that the play was written as a compliment to King James I, the reigning Stuart monarch. If that is so, the apparently celebrative quality of the last speeches must be severely undercut by the inherent suggestion that one more convulsion is to occur in Scotland before "The time is free" (5.59.21); as Booth suggested, with the inauguration of Malcolm, it may all begin again,[5] in a recurrent pattern that is of a piece with the abstract symmetry of Macbeth's absolutist imagination. It is a movement not to likely to be arrested by Malcolm, who stands in opposition to Macbeth and at the same time resembles him both morally and psychologically. The hope of Scotland is embodied in the sympathetic and humane Macduff, whose manhood is not in question because the polarities, symmetries, and antitheses that lie at the farthest remove from the vagaries of human nature are foreign to him.

Notes

[1] For other interesting discussions of the subject, see G. J. Guthrie's article "Antithesis in *Macbeth*," *Shakespeare Survey* 19 (1966) and Robert Grudin's *Mighty Opposites: Studies in Renaissance Contrariety*, discussed in Chapter 1.

[2] The "poor cat i' th' adage" is an animal caught in a proverbial dilemma: it wants to catch fish in the river, but it also wants to keep its paws dry (Wright and Lamar, Folger *Macbeth*, 1.7.45n).

[3] It has become a commonplace of Shakespeare criticism that, in Maurice Charney's words, "It is sometimes necessary to assume an absolute degree of good or evil in a Shakespearean character . . . and to allow for abrupt shifts in character that violate logical progression" (*How to Read Shakespeare* 75). But this convention, which undeniably attaches to an Iago or a Desdemona, does not apply to Malcolm, since another character within the frame has violated it—Macduff does so when he calls our attention to the inconsistency of Malcolm's character by announcing his inability to accommodate it.

[4] Indeed, a central point of his discussion throughout his book is that "Finality is regularly unattainable throughout *Macbeth*" (93).

[5] Certainly that inference has been drawn by some of the play's modern adaptors and directors. Eugene Ionesco's *Macbett*, for example, ends with Macol delivering *verbatim* the long speech in which Shakespeare's Malcolm confesses his desire to "confound / All unity on earth" (4.3.99)—but without any subsequent retraction, so that the audience is left with the conviction of Macol's intent to continue Macbett's reign of terror. And Roman Polanski inserted at the conclusion of his 1972 film of Shakespeare's play a wordless scene in which Donalbain seeks out the witches, presumably to discover whether he, like Macbeth before him, is destined to wrest the throne from its present occupant.

6

Conclusion

We have examined, during the course of this study, almost a score of dilemmas—serious and trivial ones, tragic dilemmas that lead to murder or madness and comic dilemmas that provoke only laughter, dilemmas that prove nonexistent or turn out to be riddles in disguise and dilemmas that remain with the audience when the characters have left the stage. Some reflect a predisposition on the part of characters who are afflicted with them toward abstract or dualistic modes of thought; others are evidence of a propensity built into the worlds in which the plays are set to generate problems that take the form of symmetrical antitheses. Certain of these dilemmas are choices between alternatives that are precisely equal in the degree of advantage or disadvantage that they offer; others are true *dialyses*, paradoxes in which the very act of choosing renders the chosen alternative inaccessible.

The earliest of the plays discussed (excepting *Richard III*) is *The Merchant of Venice*, which was written in 1596 or 1597; the latest, *Antony and Cleopatra*, was composed in 1606 or 1607. Earlier in the present century, it might have been assumed by biographically-oriented critics that Shakespeare must during this decade have been preoccupied with dilemmas of his own, which inevitably found their way into his plays in a variety of guises—just as it was often assumed that the various genres of his plays pointed to the existence of a corresponding set of moods, or even a corresponding set of events, in the life of the playwright at the time of their conception. These days, things seem less simple. With new information as to the dates of composition at our disposal, together with more sophisticated techniques of inference, we no longer speak of the periods of

203

Shakespeare's career as being devoted to a particular genre; the ironic, the tragic, the comic and the romantic visions seem to overlap and intertwine in such a way as to preclude such simplistic assumptions as, for example, that the writer's own mid-life crisis turned his thoughts to the sufferings of old age and subsequently produced the tragedy of *King Lear*. My own ascription of Shakespeare's interest in dilemmas to the second trimester of his career is not meant to obscure the fact that during this period he wrote at least as many plays that have not found their way into this study as those that have (though a place might have been found, with a certain amount of pushing and pulling, for two more plays of the middle years, *Henry IV, Part One* and *Troilus and Cressida*). And it is unnecessary to remind the reader of the likelihood that, in plays written earlier or later, there exist significant dilemmas that would have found a place in this study had they not escaped my notice.

Still, though it is by now a commonplace assumption that many of Shakespeare's themes, plots, and traits of character tend to appear, successively transformed, at intervals throughout his dramatic works, dilemmas seem not to be among them. *The Winter's Tale* gives us, as did *Othello*, a husband obsessively and groundlessly jealous of a virtuous wife as the central motif of its plot. But where, in the earlier play, the process by which doubt becomes suspicion, progresses to certainty and emerges as blind conviction occupies most of the middle section of the play, during which time Othello experiences the growing torment of his dilemma, Leontes's jealousy is not presented as the result of any extended process, but springs into spontaneous life at the start of the play and is as quickly extinguished by the unequivocal oracle that exonerates Hermione a short time later. Where Othello's sufferings are the result of his inability to endure the exquisite torments of a dilemma, a compulsion to act coupled with an inability to decide what action is called for, Leontes's more passive and more muted pain takes the form of sixteen years' guilt and mourning for what he believes to be an act already past and therefore irrecoverable.

Similarly, *The Tempest* presents us with another version of the characters and events of *Measure for Measure*, but again without its dilemmas. Prospero, like Vincentio, is a duke with the vision and temperament of a dramatist, who assumes control over the action and the lives of the other characters in order to bring about a resolution that conforms to his own sense of what is just and fitting—a resolution that is in both cases theatrical in the extreme. But where the Duke of Vienna's manipulations leave intact the original and serious problems of his city—of which the two most obvious are the licentiousness of most of its inhabitants and Isabella's ambivalence toward her brother—the Duke of Milan, exhibiting a much surer dramatic instinct, secures through his magical illusions a general agreement at the end that his is a viable and admirable solution to the problems of both public and private life, thus sparing all concerned the dilemmas that remain at the close of the earlier play.

At the risk of ignoring my own caveat concerning the folly of turning Shakespeare's career into a series of generic periods, I will point out that the plays we have been examining are particularly rich in ironies of all kinds. Perhaps this is to be expected. Dilemmas are, after all, ironic predicaments; the parallel perspectives of the ironic view, which superimpose what is upon what might be or what should have been, are just the means by which we identify the alternatives that a dilemma offers us. What is to a certain extent true of most of Shakespeare's plays is particularly obvious in these: they are arenas in which alternative points of view compete, setting in opposition to each other the world and the stage, the disorderly flux of experience and the decorum of art, subjectivity that may amount almost to solipsism and objectivity that calls itself science, fair and foul, skepticism and faith.

It is also to be expected that dilemmas should take on much of the emotional climate associated with the ironic vision: its wintriness, its sere intellectuality, its lack of affect. To be in a dilemma is to wander a universe devoid of color, texture, warmth, human instinct and human feeling. Dilemmas are sterile, abstract, geometrically symmetrical. Characters beset by dilemmas are often of a notably logical and calculative turn of mind, more attuned to the categories of experience than to experience itself; they are those who, in Hamlet's phrase, are given to "thinking too precisely on th' event." The cast of mind that is most likely to produce dilemmas is associated in several of the plays with modern scientific materialism and with the rise, in the economic sphere, of capitalism, hence the critique of those phenomena—indeed of all rational calculation—found in *The Merchant of Venice, All's Well That Ends Well, Othello, Hamlet* and *Macbeth*.

The conviction that all action must be the product of reasoned judgment is likely either to create or to worsen a dilemma; anyone who has tried to reach a difficult decision by listing pros and cons on opposite sides of a ruled sheet knows that the product of such activity is not a satisfactory answer but merely a tidy visual simulacrum of one's own irresoluteness. There exist "reasons," after all, why Bassanio should give up Portia's ring and why he should keep it, why Isabella should assent to Angelo's conditions and why she should scorn them, why Othello should believe both that Desdemona loves him and that she loves Cassio, why Hamlet should kill Claudius and why he should kill himself, why Antony should leave Cleopatra and why he should remain with her. Only impulse is of any use in making such choices, as Hamlet explains in his encomium to "rashness"—the impulse of a true son, a true friend, a true lover. He or she who languishes in a dilemma, in these plays, is to be pitied, but at the same time it must be acknowledged that the dilemma itself may be evidence of an aberration of personality or a defective character—an unwillingness to trust one's deepest motives, perhaps, or at least a susceptibility to being led by the seductive appearance of a beguiling but illusory rationality in others.

Of course, the impulses that enable one to transcend dilemmas are not necessarily virtuous ones; Macbeth's impulses led him to homicide and madness, though ultimately his indiscriminate slaughter of innocents did unbalance the static tension between his fair and foul selves. We refer to a problem as a dilemma only because it is cast in a distinctive form; the content of the problem, and the degree of its gravity, is determined not by the fact that it is a dilemma but by the genre of the play in which it appears, together with the particular conception of character and setting employed by Shakespeare on the given occasion. At the opposite extreme from the bloody impulses of Macbeth, which are perfectly suited to the militaristic orientation of the feudal Scotland that he inhabits, are the loving and magnanimous impulses of Bassanio, and it is only because in his generosity he fails to peruse Portia's betrothal speech that he is vulnerable to the dilemma imposed upon him from without, in the most comic of the plays we have analyzed.

Thus, a dilemma is a trap into which anyone may fall—both those who are psychologically maimed and those who are merely unlucky or unwary. Though the dilemma-play is a uniquely Shakespearean accomplishment, and may therefore be thought to express a personal preoccupation with this particular psychic bind, it is a predicament that seems to me, and I believe must have seemed to the original audiences of many of Shakespeare's plays, evocative of the age in which they lived. I have tried to suggest, in my introductory chapter, what intellectual and scientific preoccupations came together at the close of the sixteenth century to produce the sensibility associated with dilemmas—a frame of mind receptive to, and appreciative of, the *yin* and *yang* of this particular snare. I have likewise tried, in successive chapters, to demonstrate the extent to which the greatest playwright of the English Renaissance shaped them into a powerful device for the exposition and exploration of character in both moral and emotional contexts.

The popularity of dilemma-plots during the late Tudor and early Stuart periods was not, in fact, as great as it was to become in the succeeding age. Where Shakespeare is virtually the only dramatist of his time to make extensive use of them— a fact that will not, I hope, invalidate my claim that they are apt expressions of his age's peculiar anxieties—the English theater after the Restoration elevated the dilemma to a central and paramount position: theater-goers of the later seventeenth and early eighteenth centuries witnessed the dilemmas of Antony in Dryden's *All for Love*, of Jaffeir in Otway's *Venice Preserv'd*, of Margery Pinchwife in Wycherley's *The Country Wife*, of George Barnwell in Lillo's *The London Merchant*, and indeed, of all those characters like them who are torn between "mighty opposites" as great as love and honor or as trivial as town and country.

But dilemmas had become, in even the best of these later plays, a familiar and therefore largely unexamined convention of plotting—a given, rather than an outgrowth of character and circumstance. This is never the case with Shakespeare's plays. Even where Shakespeare took over the dilemma from his source (Isabella's, for instance, is preserved intact from George Whetstone's *Promos and Cassandra*), there is always in his manner of presenting it a freshness and an immediacy that permits us to relish the sheer ingenuity with which Portia fashions for Bassanio, or fate fashions for Antony, or Macbeth fashions for himself, a predicament whose design and dimensions are perfectly tailored to their own individual deserts and vulnerabilities, as well as to those of the audience for whom they were created.

Works Cited

Adams, Joseph Quincy, ed. *Chief Pre-Shakespearean Dramas: A Selection of Plays Illustrating the History of English Drama from Its Origin Down to Shakespeare.* Cambridge: The Riverside Press, 1924.

Adams, Robert M. *Strains of Discord: Studies in Literary Openness.* Ithaca: Cornell Univ. Press, 1956.

Adelman, Janet. *The Common Liar: An Essay on* Antony and Cleopatra. New Haven: Yale Univ. Press, 1973.

Arthos, John. "The Comedy of Generation." *Essays in Criticism* 5 (1955): 97–117.

Bacon, Francis. *Sir Francis Bacon: A Selection of his Works.* Ed. Sidney Warhaft. New York: Odyssey, 1965.

Barber, C. L. *Shakespeare's Festive Comedy: A Study of Dramatic Form and its Relation to Social Custom.* Princeton: Princeton Univ. Press, 1959.

Barish, Jonas A. *Ben Jonson and the Language of Prose Comedy.* Cambridge: Harvard Univ. Press, 1960.

——————. "*The Spanish Tragedy*, or the Perils and Pleasures of Rhetoric." *Elizabethan Theatre*, Stratford-upon-Avon Studies 9. London: Edwin Arnold, 1966.

Barnet, Sylvan. "Prodigality and Time in *The Merchant of Venice.*" *PMLA* 87 (1972): 26–30.

Barth, John. *End of the Road.* New York: Avon Books, 1960.

Battenhouse, Roy W. "*Measure for Measure* and the Christian Doctrine of Atonement." *PMLA* 61 (1946): 1029–51.

——————. "The Significance of Hamlet's Advice to the Players." *The Drama of the Renaissance: Essays for Leicester Bradner.* Ed. Elmer M. Blistein. Providence: Brown Univ. Press, 1966.

Bennett, Josephine Waters. Measure for Measure *as Royal Entertainment.* New York: Columbia Univ. Press, 1966.

Berger, Milton M., ed. *Beyond the Double Bind.* New York: Brunner/Mazel, 1978.

Bethell, S. L. *Shakespeare and the Popular Dramatic Tradition.* London: Staples Press, 1940.

Bevington, David, ed. *Twentieth-Century Interpretations of* Hamlet: *A Collection of Critical Essays.* Englewood Cliffs: Prentice-Hall, 1968.

Boccaccio, Giovanni. *Il Filocolo: The Most Pleasant and Delectable Questions of Love*. Trans. "H.G." 1566. New York: Hartsdale House, 1931.

Booth, Stephen. *King Lear, Macbeth, Indefinition and Tragedy*. New Haven: Yale Univ. Press, 1983.

—————. "On the Value of *Hamlet*." *Reinterpretations of Elizabethan Drama*. Ed. Norman Rabkin. New York: Columbia Univ. Press, 1969.

Bowers, Fredson. *Elizabethan Revenge Tragedy: 1587–1642*. Princeton: Princeton Univ. Press, 1940.

Bradley, A.C. *Shakespearean Tragedy*. 1904. Cleveland: World Press, 1962.

Bronowski, Jacob. *The Identity of Man*. Rev. ed. Garden City: Natural History Press, 1965.

Brower, Reuben A. *Hero and Saint: Shakespeare and the Graeco-Roman Heroic Tradition*. New York: Oxford Univ. Press, 1971.

Brown, John Russell. *Shakespeare and his Comedies*. London: Methuen, 1957.

Brown, Norman O. *Life Against Death: The Psychoanalytical Meaning of History*. Middletown: Wesleyan Univ. Press, 1959.

Burckhardt, Sigurd. *Shakespearean Meanings*. Princeton: Princeton Univ. Press, 1968.

Burke, Kenneth. *The Philosophy of Literary Form*. Baton Rouge: Louisiana State Univ. Press, 1941.

Burtt, E. A. *The Metaphysical Foundations of Modern Physical Science*. 1924. New York: Anchor Books, 1954.

Cantor, Paul A. *Shakespeare's Rome: Republic and Empire*. Ithaca: Cornell Univ. Press, 1976.

Caputi, Antony. "Scenic Design in *Measure for Measure*." *Twentieth-Century Interpretations of* Measure for Measure: *A Collection of Critical Essays*. Ed. George L. Geckle. Englewood Cliffs: Prentice-Hall, 1970.

Carson, Neil. "Hazarding and Coveting in *The Merchant of Venice*." *English Language Notes* 9 (1972): 168–77.

Carter, Albert Howard. "In Defense of Bertram." *Shakespeare Quarterly* 17 (1956): 21–31.

Chambers, R. W. *Man's Unconquerable Mind*. London: Jonathan Cape, 1939.

Charney, Maurice. *How to Read Shakespeare*. New York: McGraw-Hill, 1971.

—————. *Shakespeare's Roman Plays: The Function of Imagery in the Drama*. Cambridge: Harvard Univ. Press, 1961.

Chaucer, Geoffrey. *The Canterbury Tales*. Ed. John Matthews Manly. New York: Henry Holt, 1928.

Coghill, Nevill. "*All's Well* Revalued." *Studies in English Language and Literature in Honor of Margaret Schlauch*. Ed. Miecyzlaw Brahmer. Warsaw: P. W. N., 1966.

Coleridge, Samuel Taylor. *Specimens of the Table-Talk of the Late Samuel Taylor Coleridge*. New York: Harper & Bros., 1835.

Colie, Rosalie. *Paradoxia Epidemica: The Renaissance Tradition of Paradox*. Princeton: Princeton Univ. Press, 1966.

Coryat, Thomas. *Coryat's Crudities; hastily gobbled up in five months' travels in France, Savoy, Italy, Rhetia (commonly called the Grisons country), Helvetia (alias Switzerland), some parts of high Germany and the Netherlands*. 1611. Glasgow: J. MacLehose & Sons, 1905.

Cunningham, J. V. *Woe or Wonder: The Emotional Effects of Shakespearean Tragedy*. Denver: Alan Swallow, 1960.

Danson, Lawrence. *The Harmonies of* The Merchant of Venice. New Haven: Yale Univ. Press, 1978.

————. *Tragic Alphabet: Shakespeare's Drama of Language*. New Haven: Yale Univ. Press, 1974.

Dean, Leonard, ed. *Renaissance Poetry*. 2nd ed. Englewood Cliffs: Prentice-Hall, 1961.

Dollimore, Jonathan. *Radical Tragedy: Religion, Ideology and Power in the Drama of Shakespeare and his Contemporaries*. Chicago: Univ. of Chicago Press, 1984.

Donne, John. *Complete Poetry of John Donne*. Ed. John T. Shawcross. New York: New York Univ. Press, 1968.

Dorius, R. J. "Antony and Cleopatra." *How to Read Shakespearean Tragedy*. Ed. Edward Quinn. New York: Harper & Row, 1978.

Driver, Tom F. *The Sense of History in Greek and Shakespearean Drama*. New York: Columbia Univ. Press, 1960.

Eagleton, Terence. *Shakespeare and Society*. New York: Schocken, 1967.

Eagleton, Terry. *William Shakespeare*. London: Basil Blackwell, 1986.

Ellis-Fermor, Una. *The Jacobean Drama: An Interpretation*. London: Methuen, 1953.

Eliot, T. S. "Hamlet and his Problems." *Selected Essays, 1917- 1932*. London: Faber & Faber, 1932.

Empson, William. *Seven Types of Ambiguity*. 1940. New York: Meridian, 1955.

————. *The Structure of Complex Words*. New York: New Directions, 1951.

Enright, D. J. *Shakespeare and the Students*. New York: Schocken Books, 1970.

Fergusson, Francis. *The Idea of a Theater: A Study of Ten Plays: The Art of Drama in a Changing Perspective*. Princeton: Princeton Univ. Press, 1949.

Fiedler, Leslie A. *The Stranger in Shakespeare*. New York: Stein and Day, 1972.

Forker, Charles R. "Shakespeare's Theatrical Symbolism." *Shakespeare Quarterly* 14 (1963): 215–19.

Frye, Northrop. *Anatomy of Criticism: Four Essays*. Princeton: Princeton Univ. Press, 1957.

————. *A Natural Perspective: The Development of Shakespearean Comedy and Romance*. New York: Harcourt, Brace & World, 1965.

————. *Fables of Identity: Studies in Poetic Mythology*. New York: Harcourt, Brace & World, 1963.

Geckle, George L., ed. *Twentieth-Century Interpretations of* Measure for Measure: *A Collection of Critical Essays.* Englewood Cliffs: Prentice-Hall, 1970.

Gelb, Hal. "Duke Vincentio and the Illusion of Comedy or All's Not Well That Ends Well." *Shakespeare Quarterly* 22 (1971): 25–34.

Georges, Robert A. and Alan Dundes. "Toward a Structural Definition of the Riddle." *Journal of American Folklore* 76 (1963): 111–18.

Gless, Daryl F. Measure for Measure, *the Law, and the Convent.* Princeton: Princeton Univ. Press, 1979.

Goddard, Harold. *The Meaning of Shakespeare.* Chicago: Univ. of Chicago Press, 1951.

Goldberg, Jonathan. *James I and the Politics of Literature: Jonson, Shakespeare, Donne and Their Contemporaries.* Baltimore: Johns Hopkins Univ. Press, 1983.

Gorfain, Phyllis. "Riddles and Tragic Structure in *Macbeth.*" *Mississippi Folklore Register* 10 (1976): 187–209.

Grudin, Robert. *Mighty Opposites: Shakespeare and Renaissance Contrariety.* Berkeley: Univ. of California Press, 1979.

Hamnett, Ian. "Ambiguity, Classification and Change: The Function of Riddles." *Man* 2 (1967): 377–92.

Hapgood, Robert. "Portia and *The Merchant of Venice*: The Gentle Bond." *Modern Language Quarterly* 28 (1967): 19- 32.

Hawkes, Terence. *Shakespeare and the Reason: A Study of the Tragedies and Problem Plays.* New York: Humanities Press, 1965.

Hawkins, Harriet. *Likenesses of Truth in Elizabethan and Restoration Drama.* Oxford: Clarendon, 1972.

Haydn, Hiram. *The Counter-Renaissance.* New York: Scribner's, 1950.

Hazlitt, William. "Characters in Shakespeare's Plays." *Collected Works.* Ed. A. R. Waller and Arnold Glover. 12 vols. London: J. M. Dent, 1902.

——————. *Shakespeare's Library.* London: Reeves and Turner, 1875.

Heilman, Robert B. *Magic in the Web: Action and Language in* Othello. Lexington: Univ. of Kentucky Press, 1956.

——————. *This Great Stage: Image and Structure in* King Lear. Baton Rouge: Louisiana State University Press, 1948.

——————. "'Twere Best Not Know Myself': Othello, Lear, Macbeth." *Shakespeare Quarterly* 15 (1964): 89–98.

Heisenberg, Werner. *Physics and Philosophy.* New York: Harper & Row, 1958.

Heller, Joseph. *Catch-22.* New York: Simon & Schuster, 1961.

Holland, Norman N. *The Dynamics of Literary Response.* New York: Oxford Univ. Press, 1968.

Holloway, John. "*Antony and Cleopatra.*" *Twentieth-Century Interpretations of* Antony and Cleopatra: *A Collection of Critical Essays.* Ed. Mark Rose. Englewood Cliffs: Prentice-Hall, 1977.

Homer. *The Iliad of Homer.* Trans. Richmond Lattimore. Chicago: Univ. of Chicago Press, 1951.

Horwich, Richard. "Integrity in *Macbeth*: The Search for the 'Single State of Man'." *Shakespeare Quarterly* 29 (1978): 365–73.

—————. "Riddles and Dilemmas in *The Merchant of Venice.*" *Studies in English Literature 1500–1900* 17 (1977): 191–200.

Howell, W. S. *Logic and Rhetoric in England, 1500–1700.* New York: Russell & Russell, 1961.

Huizinga, Johan. *Homo Ludens: A Study of the Play Element in Culture.* 1944. Boston: Beacon, 1955.

Hyman, Stanley Edgar. *Iago: Some Approaches to the Illusion of his Motivation.* New York: Atheneum, 1970.

Ionesco, Eugene. *Macbett.* Trans. Charles O. Marowitz. New York: Grove, 1973.

Joseph, Sr. Miriam. *Rhetoric in Shakespeare's Time: Literary Theory of Renaissance Europe.* New York: Harcourt, Brace & World, 1947.

Kermode, Frank. *The Sense of an Ending: Studies in the Theory of Fiction.* New York: Oxford Univ. Press, 1967.

King, Walter N. "Shakespeare's Mingled Yarn." *Modern Language Quarterly* 21 (1960): 33–44.

Knight, G. Wilson. "*Measure for Measure* and the Gospels." *Twentieth-Century Interpretations of* Measure for Measure. Ed. George L. Geckle. Englewood Cliffs: Prentice-Hall, 1970.

—————. *The Sovereign Flower: On Shakespeare as the Poet of Royalism Together with Related Essays and Indexes to Earlier Volumes.* New York: Barnes & Noble, 1958.

—————. *The Wheel of Fire: Interpretations of Shakespeare's Tragedies.* London: Methuen, 1949.

Knights, L.C. *Drama and Society in the Age of Jonson.* London: Chatto & Windus, 1937.

—————. *Explorations: Essays in Criticism, Mainly on the Literature of the Seventeenth Century.* London: Chatto & Windus, 1946.

—————. "The Ambiguity of *Measure for Measure.*" *Scrutiny* 10 (1942): 223–33.

Knox, Bernard. "Sophocles' Oedipus." *Tragic Themes in Western Literature.* Ed. Cleanth Brooks. New Haven: Yale Univ. Press, 1955.

Kott, Jan. *Shakespeare Our Contemporary.* Trans. Boleslaw Taborski. Garden City: Doubleday Anchor, 1964.

Kuhn, Thomas S. *The Copernican Revolution: Planetary Astronomy in the Development of Modern Thought.* Cambridge: Harvard Univ. Press, 1966.

Kyd, Thomas. *The Spanish Tragedy*, ed. J. R. Mulryne. New York: Hill & Wang, 1970.

Lawrence, W. W. *Shakespeare's Problem Comedies.* New York: Macmillan, 1931.

214 *Works Cited*

214 *Works Cited*

Leavis, F. R. "The Greatness of *Measure for Measure.*" *Scrutiny* 10 (1942): 234–47.

Levin, Harry. *The Question of Hamlet*. Oxford: Oxford Univ. Press, 1959.

Lovejoy, Arthur O. *The Great Chain of Being: A Study of the History of an Idea*. Cambridge: Cambridge Univ. Press, 1936.

Lyly, John. *Endimion. Minor Elizabethan Drama*. Ed. Ashley Thorndike. London: J. M. Dent, 1958.

Lyman, Stanford M. and Marvin Scott. *The Drama of Social Reality*. New York: Oxford Univ. Press, 1973.

Mack, Maynard. "The World of Hamlet." *Twentieth-Century Interpretations of Hamlet: A Collection of Critical Essays*. Ed. David Bevington. Englewood Cliffs: Prentice-Hall, 1968.

McAlindon, T. *Shakespeare and Decorum*. New York: Harper & Row, 1973.

McGuire, Philip C. "*Othello* as an 'Assay of Reason.'" *Shakespeare Quarterly* 24 (1973): 198–209.

Markels, Julian. *The Pillar of the World:* Antony and Cleopatra *in Shakespeare's Development*. Columbus: Ohio State Univ. Press, 1968.

Montaigne, Michel de. *Complete Essays*. Trans. Donald M. Frame. 4 vols. Garden City: Anchor, 1960.

Nochimson, Richard L. "The End Crowns All: Shakespeare's Deflation of Tragic Possibility in *Antony and Cleopatra*." *English* 26 (1977): 99–132.

Nuttall, A.D. "*Measure for Measure*: The Bed-Trick." *Shakespeare Survey* 28. Ed. Kenneth Muir. Cambridge: Cambridge Univ. Press, 1975.

Ornstein, Robert. "The Ethic of the Imagination: Love and Art in *Antony and Cleopatra*." *Later Shakespeare*, Stratford-upon-Avon Studies. Ed. J. R. Brown and Bernard Harris. London: Edward Arnold, 1966.

——————. *The Moral Vision of Jacobean Tragedy*. Madison: Univ. of Wisconsin Press, 1960.

Parker, Barbara. "*Macbeth*: The Great Illusion." *Sewanee Review* 78 (1970): 476–87.

Plutarch. *Shakespeare's Plutarch*. Ed. F. Tucker Brooke. 2 vols. New York: Duffield, 1909.

Popkin, Richard. *The History of Scepticism from Erasmus to Spinoza*. Berkeley: Univ. of California Press, 1979.

Price, Joseph. *The Unfortunate Comedy: A Study of* All's Well That Ends Well *and Its Critics*. Toronto: Univ. of Toronto Press, 1968.

Prosser, Eleanor. *Hamlet and Revenge*. Stanford: Stanford Univ Press, 1971.

Puttenham, George. *The Art of English Poesy*. 1589. London: Edmund Arber, 1869.

Rabkin, Norman. *Shakespeare and the Common Understanding*. New York: The Free Press, 1967.

Reid, B. L. "*Macbeth* and the Play of Absolutes." *Sewanee Review* 73 (1965): 18–46.

Righter, Anne. *Shakespeare and the Idea of the Play*. 1962. Harmondsworth: Penguin, 1967.

Rogers, Stephen. "*Othello* and the Ways of Thinking." *How to Read Shakespearean Tragedy*. Ed. Edward Quinn. New York: Harper & Row, 1978.

Rose, Mark, ed. *Twentieth-Century Interpretations of* Antony and Cleopatra: *A Collection of Critical Essays*. Englewood Cliffs: Prentice-Hall, 1977.

Rosen, William. *The Craft of Tragedy*. Cambridge: Harvard Univ. Press, 1967.

Ryle, Gilbert. *Dilemmas*. Cambridge: Cambridge Univ. Press, 1954.

Sale, Roger. "The Comic Mode of *Measure for Measure*." *Shakespeare Quarterly* 19 (1968): 55–61.

Salingar, Leo. *Shakespeare and the Traditions of Comedy*. Cambridge: Cambridge Univ. Press, 1974.

Schanzer, Ernst: *The Problem Plays of Shakespeare: A Study of* Julius Caesar, Measure for Measure, Antony and Cleopatra. New York: Schocken, 1963.

Schell, Edgar and J. D. Schuchter, eds. *English Morality Plays and Moral Interludes*. New York: Holt, Rinehart & Winston, 1969.

Shakespeare, William. *All's Well That Ends Well*. Ed. Jonas A. Barish. The Pelican Shakespeare. Baltimore: Penguin, 1964.

—————————. *All's Well That Ends Well*. Ed. G. K. Hunter. The Arden Shakespeare. Cambridge: Harvard Univ. Press, 1959.

—————————. *Hamlet, Prince of Denmark*. Ed. Willard Farnham. The Pelican Shakespeare. Baltimore: Penguin, 1970.

—————————. *Macbeth*. Ed. Kenneth Muir. The New Arden Shakespeare. Cambridge: Harvard Univ. Press, 1957.

—————————. *Macbeth*. Ed. Louis B. Wright and Virginia A. Lamar. The Folger Library Shakespeare. New York: Simon & Schuster, 1959.

—————————. *The Merchant of Venice*. Ed. John Russell Brown. The New Arden Shakespeare. Cambridge: Harvard Univ. Press, 1959.

—————————. *The Riverside Shakespeare*. Ed. G. Blakemore Evans. Boston: Houghton Mifflin, 1974.

—————————. *Sonnets*. Ed. Douglas Bush. The Pelican Shakespeare. Baltimore: Penguin, 1961.

Siemon, James Edward. "'The Strong Necessity of Time': Dilemma in *Antony and Cleopatra*." *English Studies* 54 (1973): 316–25.

—————————. "*The Merchant of Venice*: Act V as Ritual Reiteration." *Studies in Philology* 67 (1969): 201–09.

Sisk, John P. "Bondage and Release in *The Merchant of Venice*." *Shakespeare Quarterly* 20 (1969): 217–23.

Soellner, Rolf. *Shakespeare's Patterns of Self-Knowledge*. Columbus: Ohio State Univ. Press, 1972.

Spencer, Theodore. *Shakespeare and the Nature of Man*. New York: Macmillan, 1942.

Spivack, Bernard. *Shakespeare and the Allegory of Evil: The History of a Metaphor in Relation to His Major Villains.* New York: Columbia Univ. Press, 1958.

Stevenson, David Lloyd. *The Achievement of Shakespeare's* Measure for Measure. Ithaca: Cornell Univ. Press, 1966.

Stone, Lawrence. *The Family, Sex and Marriage in England 1500–1800.* New York: Harper & Row, 1977.

Sypher, Wylie. *Four Stages of Renaissance Style: Transformations in Art and Literature 1400–1700.* 1955. Garden City: Anchor, 1960.

——————. *The Ethic of Time: Structures of Experience in Shakespeare.* New York: Seabury Press, 1976.

Taylor, Archer. *English Riddles from Oral Tradition.* Berkeley: Univ. of California Press, 1951.

Thorndike, Ashley, ed. *Minor Elizabethan Drama.* 2 vols. London: J. M. Dent, 1958.

Tillyard, E. M. W. *Shakespeare's Problem Plays.* Toronto: Univ. of Toronto Press, 1949.

Traversi, Derek A. *An Approach to Shakespeare.* 2nd ed. 1956. Garden City: Doubleday Anchor, 1969.

Walker, Roy. *The Time is Free: A Study of* Macbeth. London: Andrew Dakers, 1949.

Weil, Herbert S. "On Expectation and Surprise: Shakespeare's Construction of Character. *Shakespeare Survey* 34 (1981): 39–50.

White, Hayden. *Metahistory: The Historical Imagination in Nineteenth-Century Europe.* Baltimore: Johns Hopkins Univ. Press, 1973.

Whitehead, Alfred North. *Science and the Modern World.* New York: Macmillan, 1926.

Williamson, Marilyn. "The Ring Episode of *The Merchant of Venice.*" South Atlantic Quarterly 71 (1972): 587–94.

Wilson, Thomas. *The Art of Rhetoric.* London: George Robinson, 1585.

INDEX

Absolutism vs. relativism, 15 ; in
  Othello, 116; in *Hamlet*, 163-164,
  177; in *Macbeth*, 191-193, 196-
  197, 200-201
Adelman, Janet, 118, 119, 124, 133
  passim, 145n, 146n
All's Well That Ends Well, 16-17, 32,
  47-63, 73 *passim*, 81-85, 145n,
  159, 206; ambivalence in, 49-53,
  61; science vs. magic in, 50-56;
  time in, 53-56, 58, 85-86n. *See
  also* Genre; Riddles; Setting;
  Supernatural
All for Love, 121, 127, 133, 208
Antithesis: in *Oedipus the King*, 7;
  in *The Spanish Tragedy*, 24-25; in
  Richard III, 28-29; in *Antony and
  Cleopatra*, 120-124; in *Macbeth*,
  185-186, 189, 190, 198, 202. *See
  also* Dualism; Euphuistic style;
  Settings
"Apology for Raymond Sebond,
  The," **14-15**. *See also* Montaigne,
  Michel de
Antony and Cleopatra, 32, 90, 92
  117-145, 149, 193, 203; perversity
  in, 118-122; decorum in, 136,
  143, 149; historiography in, 130,
  131-145, 149; varieties of love in,
  125-127, 130-131. *See also* Genre;
  Setting
Art of Courtly Love, The, 127
As You Like It, 92
Audiences, dilemmas of: in *Antony
  and Cleopatra*, 118; in *Measure for
  Measure*, 63, 82-83, 85

Bacon, Francis, 14, 17
Barber, C. L., 38, 40, 47, 85n
Barish, Jonas A., 22-23, 25, 47, 60,
  61
Barth, John. See *End of the Road*
Bateson, Gregory. *See* Double bind
Battenhouse, Roy W., 63, 75, 86n,
  167, 169
Bed-tricks: in *All's Well That Ends
  Well*, 55-56, 58; in *Measure for
  Measure*, 73-74, 77
Boccaccio, Giovanni. See *Il Filocolo*
  and *The Decameron*
Booth, Stephen, 33n, 156 *passim*,
  182n, 183n, 184n, 192, 194-196,
  201
Bradley, A. C., 175
Brown, Norman O., 17, 35, 86n
Burckhardt, Sigurd, 35, 36, 38
Burke, Kenneth, 178
Burtt, E. A., 16

Caesar and Cleopatra, 133
Calculation. See Rationalism
Castiglione, Baldassare, 9
Catch-22, 3
Charney, Maurice, 145n, 202n
Chaucer, Geoffrey. *See* "The
  Knight's Tale" *and* "The Wife of
  Bath's Tale"
City comedy, 95
Coleridge, Samuel Taylor, 156
Colie, Rosalie, 8-12
Comedy. *See* Genres
Complementarity, 12, 33n, 62

Copernicus, 17, 22. *See also* "New philosophy"
Country Wife, The, 208
Crashaw, Richard, 66, 99
Cymbeline, 76

Danson, Lawrence, 164, 177
Decameron, The, 10
Descartes, René, 13-15, 17. *See also* Rationalism; Skepticism
Dialysis, 1, 2, 203. *See also* Paradox
Dickens, Charles, 91
Donne, John, 1-2, 13, 21, **93-97**, 99, 107, 163. *See also* Metaphysical mode
Double bind, 34n
Dryden, John. See *All for Love*
Dualism, 13, 18, 203; in *Macbeth*, 185-186. *See also* Antithesis
Dubbio, 11, 19, 31, 48, 68, 96, 111. See also *Il Filocolo*
Dutch Courtesan, The, 200

Eliade, Mircea, 86n
Eliot, T. S., 168
Empiricism: in *All's Well That Ends Well*, 50ff; in *Othello*, 109-110. *See also* Rationalism
End of the Road, 3-4
Endimion, **23-24**, 27, 42
Epistemology, 15, 133; in *Othello*, 101-104, 115, 145n; in *Hamlet*, 159. *See also* Rationalism
Euphuistic style, 22; in *Endimion*, 22-24; in *The Spanish Tragedy*, 24-27; in *Richard III*, 28-29
Euripides. See *Hippolytus*

Forker, Charles R., 161, 182, 183n
Frye, Northrop, 47, 76, 81-82, 93, 135. *See also* Genres

Galileo, Galilei, 13, 16 ff.; doctrine of Primary and Secondary

Qualities, 16, 160-162. *See also* "New philosophy"
Genres, 19, 21, 27, 203-207; conflict between: in *The Merchant of Venice*, 39, 46-47, 85; in *All's Well That Ends Well*, 55, 57, 85; in *Measure for Measure*, 63, 73, 75-76, 79, 80-85; in Elizabethan poetry, 90, 95; in *Antony and Cleopatra*, 130, 135-136, 141-145
Grudin, Robert, 13, 198, 202n

Hamlet, 26, 27, 32, 141, **149-182**, 185, 194, 206. Hamlet on acting, 152, 156-157, 165-176, 178-179; role of spectators in, 153-157, 165-166, 174-177, 180-182; world/stage metaphor in, 150, 152-158, 165, 168, 181-182; plays-within-plays, 153, 156, 158, 166, 173, 174, 179, 181; Hamlet's resemblances to Claudius, 157, 174, 176-177; ontological problems in, 150-152, 156-166; 174-177, 180-182; "rashness" in, 161, 166, 172-173, 175, 179-180, 206. *See also* Absolutism; Epistemology; Rationalism; Setting; Skepticism; Subjectivity; Theatricality
Hazlitt, William, 156
Heilman, Robert, 104-105, 106, 108, 113
Heisenberg, Werner, 33n
Heller, Joseph. See *Catch-22*
Henry IV, Part 1, 193, 204
Holland, Norman N., 154
Homer. See *The Iliad*
Huizinga, Johan, 7
Hippolytus, 192-193

Il Filocolo, **9-11**, 18, 20, 31-32, 68, 151

Marina Tarlinskaja

SHAKESPEARE'S VERSE
Iambic Pentameter and the Poet's Idiosyncrasies

American University Studies: Series IV (English Language and Literature).
Vol. 41
ISBN 0-8204-0344-X   408 pages   hardcover about US $ 50.00*

*Recommended price - alterations reserved

This book presents a magisterial linguistic-metrical study of Shakespeare's verse in the context of the English poetic tradition. Marina Tarlinskaja concentrates on the correlation between phrasal stresses and the iambic metrical scheme and goes on to explore links between meter, grammar and semantics. Her exhaustive statistical analysis helps to define minute idiosyncrasies of Shakespeare's particular type of iambic pentameter, shedding new light on the problem of chronology and authorship. Tarlinskaja also studies Shakespeare's use of verse rhythm for expressive purposes, e.g., to oppose character types. The book will interest not only students of Shakespeare and literary theory, but also people such as theatre directors and actors interested in Shakespeare's own interpretation of his dramatis personae.

"... one of the best studies to have been written about English versification for many decades. ... no previous or present day metrists have succeeded in tracing the evolution of the English meter so precisely and in so much fine detail. ... Tarlinskaja's work should also represent an important new contribution to the textology and attribution of Shakespeare's plays or parts of them."

James Bailey
University of Wisconsin-Madison

PETER LANG PUBLISHING, INC.
62 West 45th Street
USA - New York, NY 10036